VENERABLE GESHE KELSANG
GYATSO RINPOCHE

How to Transform Your Life

A BLISSFUL JOURNEY

THARPA PUBLICATIONS
US UK CANADA
AUSTRALIA ASIA

Third edition revised and published as *How to Transform Your Life* 2017.
Second edition 2015.
First Edition 2007.

21 20 19 18 17   1 2 3 4 5 6 7 8 9

Tharpa Publications US   Tharpa Publications UK
47 Sweeney Road   Conishead Priory
Glen Spey, NY 12737   Ulverston, Cumbria
USA   LA12 9QQ, England

Tharpa Publications has offices around the world,
and our books are available in most major languages.
See page 365 for more information.

Cover image © scyther5/depositphotos

ISBN 978-1-61606-052-7 paperback
ISBN 978-1-61606-053-4 ePub
ISBN 978-1-61606-054-1 Kindle

Library of Congress Control Number: 2007901723

Printed in the United States of America on FSC certified paper.

Contents

PART ONE: *Foundation*

Introduction   3

Inner Peace   7

How to Develop and Maintain Peace of Mind   17

Rebirth   23

Death   31

Karma   45

Samsara   61

A Common Spiritual Practice for Everyone   81

Meaningful Objects   97

PART TWO: *Progress*

Learning to Cherish Others   111

How to Enhance Cherishing Love   133

Exchanging Self with Others   161

Great Compassion   195

Wishing Love   211

Taking and Giving   219

The Supreme Good Heart   243

Ultimate Bodhichitta   251

Dedication   309

Appendix I—*Liberating Prayer* &
   Prayers for Meditation   311
Appendix II—What is Meditation?   321
Appendix III—*The Kadampa Way of Life*   329

Glossary   343
Bibliography   359
Tharpa Publications Worldwide   365
Index   367

ABOUT THE ILLUSTRATIONS

The illustrations in this book depict the eight auspicious symbols, a peacock, the mirror of Dharma, the sun shining through clouds and hands in prayer.

The symbolism of the eight auspicious symbols reveals how to begin, make progress on and complete the Buddhist path to enlightenment. Just as peacocks are said to thrive on plants that are poisonous to other birds, sincere spiritual practitioners can make good use of whatever circumstances arise in their daily life. Through the mirror of Buddha's teachings, Dharma, we can see our own faults and have the opportunity to overcome them. Like the sun dispelling clouds, we can develop the wisdom that can remove all delusions from our mind; and the hands in prayer holding a wishfulfilling jewel symbolize that by following the spiritual path we will eventually experience the completely pure mind of enlightenment.

PART ONE

Foundation

Come under the great umbrella of Buddhism

Introduction

Through practicing the instructions presented in this book we can transform our life from a state of misery into one of pure and everlasting happiness. These instructions are scientific methods to improve our human nature. Everybody needs to be good-natured with a good heart, because in this way we can solve our own problems as well as those of others, and we can make our human life meaningful. Every living being has the same basic wish—to be happy and avoid suffering. Even newborn babies, animals and insects have this wish. It has been our main wish since beginningless time and it is with us all the time, even during our sleep. We spend our whole life working hard to fulfill this wish.

Since this world evolved, human beings have spent almost all their time and energy improving external conditions in their search for happiness and a solution to their problems. What has been the result? Instead of their wishes being fulfilled, human suffering and problems have continued to increase while the experience of happiness and peace is decreasing. This clearly shows that until now we have not found a correct method for reducing our problems and increasing happiness. The actual correct method for doing this is changing our attitude from negative to positive. We must understand this through our own experience. If we check carefully how we are experiencing problems and unhappiness, we can understand that they are all created by our uncontrolled desire, wishing ourself to be happy all the time. By stopping this wish and instead wishing for others to be happy all the time, we will not have any problems or unhappiness at all. If we sincerely practice every day stopping wishing for ourself to be happy all the time and instead wishing for others to be happy all the time, then we will understand from our own experience that through this practice, which prevents attachment to the fulfillment of our own wishes, we will have no experience of problems or unhappiness at all. Thus, if we really want pure and everlasting happiness and freedom from misery, we must learn to control our mind, principally our desire.

With wisdom we can understand how our human life is precious, rare and meaningful. Due to the limitations of their body and mind, those who have taken rebirth as animals, for example, have no opportunity to understand or practice spiritual teachings that are methods to control delusions such as uncontrolled desire, anger and ignorance. Only humans are free from such hindrances and have all the necessary conditions for engaging in spiritual paths, which alone lead to pure and everlasting happiness. This freedom and possession of necessary conditions are the special characteristics that make our human life so precious.

Although there are many humans in this world, each one of us has only one life. One person may own many cars and houses, but even the richest person in the world cannot possess more than one life; and, when that is drawing to an end, he or she cannot buy, borrow or manufacture another. When we lose this life, it will be very difficult to find another similarly qualified human life in the future. A human life is therefore very rare.

If we use our human life to accomplish spiritual realizations, it becomes immensely meaningful. By using it in this way, we actualize our full potential and progress from the state of an ordinary, ignorant being to that of a fully enlightened being, the highest of all beings; and when we have done this we will have the power to benefit all living beings without exception. Thus, by using our human life for gaining spiritual realizations we can solve all our human problems and fulfill all our own and others' wishes. What could be more meaningful than this?

Maintain harmony and joy all the time

Inner Peace

*I*nner peace, or mental peace, is the source of all our happiness. Although all living beings have the same basic wish to be happy all the time, very few people understand the real causes of happiness. We usually believe that external conditions such as food, friends, cars and money are the real causes of happiness, and as a result we devote nearly all our time and energy to acquiring them. Superficially it seems that these things can make us happy, but if we look more deeply we will see that they also bring us a lot of suffering and problems.

Happiness and suffering are opposites, so if something is a real cause of happiness it cannot give rise to suffering. If food, money and so forth really are causes of happiness, they can never be causes of suffering; yet we know from our own experience that they often do cause suffering. For example, one of our main interests is food, but the food we eat is also the principal cause of most of our ill health and sickness. In the process of producing the things we feel will make us happy, we have polluted our environment to such an extent that the very air we breathe and the water we drink now threaten our health and well-being. We love the freedom and independence a car can give us, but the cost in accidents and environmental destruction is enormous. We feel that money is essential for us to enjoy life, but the pursuit of money also causes immense problems and anxiety. Even our family and friends, whose company we enjoy, can also bring us a lot of worry and heartache.

In recent years our knowledge of modern technology has increased considerably, and as a result we have witnessed remarkable material progress, but there has not been a corresponding increase in human happiness. There is no less suffering in the world today and there are no fewer problems. Indeed, it might be said that there are now more problems and greater dangers than ever before. This shows that the cause of happiness and the solution to our problems do not lie in knowledge of material things. Happiness and suffering are states of mind, and so their main causes are not to be found outside the mind. If we want to be truly happy and free from suffering, we must learn how to control our mind.

The real source of happiness is inner peace. If our mind is peaceful, we will be happy all the time, regardless of external conditions, but if it is disturbed or troubled in any way, we will never be happy, no matter how good our external conditions may be. External conditions can only make us happy if our mind is peaceful. We can understand this through our own experience. For instance, even if we are in the most beautiful surroundings and have everything we need, the moment we get angry any happiness we may have disappears. This is because anger has destroyed our inner peace.

We can see from this that if we want true, lasting happiness we need to develop and maintain a special experience of inner peace. The only way to do this is to train our mind through spiritual practice—gradually reducing and eliminating our negative, disturbed states of mind and replacing them with positive, peaceful states. Eventually, through continuing to improve our inner peace we will experience supreme permanent peace of mind, or "nirvana." Once we have attained nirvana we will be happy throughout our life, and in life after life. We will have solved all our problems and accomplished the true meaning of our human life.

Since we all have within us our own source of peace and happiness, we may wonder why it is so hard to maintain a continually peaceful and joyful mind. This is because of the delusions that so often crowd our mind. Delusions are distorted ways of looking at ourself, other people and the world around us—like a distorted mirror they reflect a distorted world. The deluded mind of hatred, for example, views other people as intrinsically bad, but there is no such thing as an intrinsically bad person. Uncontrolled desire, also known as desirous attachment, on the other hand, sees its object of desire as intrinsically good and as a true source of happiness. If we have a strong craving to eat chocolate, chocolate appears to be intrinsically desirable. However, once we have eaten too much of it and start to feel sick, it no longer seems so desirable and may even appear repulsive. This shows that in itself chocolate is neither desirable nor repulsive. It is the deluded mind of attachment that projects all kinds of pleasurable qualities onto its objects of desire and then relates to them as if they really did possess those qualities.

All delusions function like this, projecting onto the world their own distorted version of reality and then relating to this projection as if it were true. When our mind is under the influence of delusions we are out of touch with reality and are not seeing things as they really are. Since our mind is under the control of at least subtle forms of delusion all the time, it is not surprising that our lives are so often filled with frustration. It is as if we are continually chasing mirages, only to be disappointed when they do not give us the satisfaction for which we had hoped.

When things go wrong in our life and we encounter difficult situations, we tend to regard the situation itself as our problem, but in reality whatever problems we experience come from the mind. If we were to respond to difficult situations with a positive or peaceful mind, they would not be problems for us; indeed, we may even come to regard them as challenges or opportunities for growth and development. Problems arise only if we respond to difficulties with a negative state of mind. Therefore, if we want to be happy all the time and to be free from problems, we must develop and maintain a peaceful mind. Sufferings, problems, worries, unhappiness and pain all exist within our mind; they are all unpleasant feelings, which are part of the mind. Through controlling and purifying our mind we can stop them once and for all.

To understand this fully, we need to understand the relationship between the mind and external objects. All objects, whether pleasant, unpleasant or neutral, are mere appearances to the mind, just like things experienced in a dream. This is not easy to understand at first, but we can gain some understanding by thinking about the following. When we are awake many different things exist, but when we fall asleep they cease. This is because the mind to which they appear ceases. When we dream, the only things that appear are dream objects. Later, when we wake up, these dream objects cease. This is because the dreaming mind to which they appear ceases. If we think deeply about this, we will understand how we can cause all the unpleasant things that we dislike to cease simply by abandoning impure, deluded states of mind; and we can cause all the pleasant things that we desire to arise simply by developing a pure mind. Purifying our mind of delusions through spiritual practice fulfills our deepest longing for true, lasting happiness. We should memorize and contemplate the meaning of the following words:

The things that I normally see in dreams do not exist.
This proves that the things that I normally see while
   awake do not exist,
Since both of these things are equally mistaken
   appearance.
I will never grasp at the things that I normally see,
But just be satisfied with their mere name.
By doing this I will liberate myself permanently
From the sufferings of this life and countless future
   lives.
In this way I will be able
To benefit each and every living being every day.

We should understand that although delusions are deeply
ingrained, they are not an intrinsic part of our mind and
so they can definitely be removed. Delusions are just bad
mental habits, and like all habits they can be broken. At the
moment our mind is like muddy water, murky and polluted
by delusions. However, just as it is possible to separate mud
from water, so it is possible to purify the mind of all delusions. With no delusions remaining in our mind, there is
nothing that can disturb our inner peace and joy.

Since time without beginning we have been under the
control of our mind, like a puppet on a string. We are like a
servant working for our mind; whenever our mind wants to do
something, we have to do it without any choice. Sometimes
our mind is like a crazy elephant, creating so many problems
and dangers for ourself and others. By sincerely engaging

in spiritual practice we can reverse this situation and gain mastery over our mind. Transforming our mind in this way, we will finally enjoy real freedom.

For our spiritual practice to be successful, we need the blessings and inspiration of those who have already gained deep inner realizations, but we also need to give ourself constant encouragement. If we cannot encourage ourself, how can we expect anyone else to? When we understand clearly that inner peace is the real source of happiness, and how, through spiritual practice, we can experience progressively deeper levels of inner peace, we will develop tremendous enthusiasm to practice. This is very important because to attain the supreme permanent inner peace of nirvana we need to engage in spiritual practice sincerely and diligently.

This does not mean that we should ignore external conditions. We need inner peace, but we also need good physical health, and for this we need certain external conditions such as food and a comfortable environment in which to live. There are many people who concentrate exclusively on developing the material side of their life, while completely ignoring spiritual practice. This is one extreme. However, there are other people who concentrate exclusively on spiritual practice, while ignoring the material conditions that are necessary for supporting a healthy human life. This is another extreme. We need to maintain a middle way that avoids both extremes of materialism and spirituality.

Some people believe that those who strive to attain nirvana are being selfish because they seem to be concentrating only on their own inner peace, but this belief is incorrect. Our real purpose in attaining the supreme permanent inner peace of nirvana is to help others do the same. Just as the only way to solve our own problems is to find inner peace, so the only way to help others to solve theirs is to encourage them to engage in spiritual practice and discover their own inner peace. This way of benefiting others is by far the best. If through training our mind we succeed in pacifying—or even completely eliminating—our own anger, for example, we can certainly help others to control theirs. Then our advice will not be mere words, but will have behind it the power of personal experience.

We can sometimes help others by providing them with money or better material conditions, but we should remember that the greatest benefit we can give is to help them overcome their delusions and find true, lasting happiness within. Through technological progress and by organizing society in fairer, more humane ways, we can certainly help to improve people's lives in some respects, but whatever we do will inevitably have some unwanted side effects. The best we can hope for is to provide people with conditions that bring some temporary respite from problems and difficulties, but we cannot give them true, lasting happiness. This is because the real cause of happiness is inner peace, which can be found only within the mind, not in external conditions.

Without inner peace, outer peace is impossible. We all wish for world peace, but world peace will never be achieved unless we first establish peace within our own minds. We can send so-called "peacekeeping forces" into areas of conflict, but peace cannot be imposed from the outside with guns. Only by creating peace within our own mind and helping others do the same can we hope to achieve peace in this world.

This book presents many profound methods of spiritual training, all of which are practical ways to purify and control our mind. If we put these methods into practice we will definitely gain a special experience of mental peace. By continuing to improve this experience, deluded states of mind will gradually diminish and our inner peace will grow. Eventually, by abandoning delusions altogether, we will attain the supreme permanent inner peace of nirvana. Having overcome our own delusions, such as anger, attachment and ignorance, and developed profound spiritual realizations of universal love, compassion, concentration and wisdom, our ability to help others will be far greater. In this way we can help others solve their problems not just for a few days or a few years, but forever. We can help them discover an inner peace and joy that nothing, not even death, can destroy. How wonderful!

Take the precious jewels of wisdom and compassion from the treasure vase of Kadam Dharma

How to Develop and Maintain a Peaceful Mind

*W*e can develop and maintain a peaceful mind by transforming our mind from negative states into positive states through engaging in the pure spiritual practices that are presented in this book. Through this we can transform our life from a miserable state into a state of pure and everlasting happiness.

Happiness and suffering are parts of the mind; the former is a joyful feeling and the latter an unpleasant feeling. Since happiness and suffering are parts of the mind, if we want to avoid suffering and find true happiness we need to understand the nature and functions of the mind. At first, this might seem to be quite straightforward since we all have minds, and we all know what state our mind is in—whether it is happy or sad, clear or confused and so forth. However, if someone were to ask us what the nature of our mind is and how it functions, we would probably not be able to give a precise answer.

This indicates that we do not have a clear understanding of the mind.

Some people think that the mind is the brain or some other part or function of the body, but this is incorrect. The brain is a physical object that can be seen with the eyes and that can be photographed or operated on in surgery. The mind, on the other hand, is not a physical object. It cannot be seen with the eyes, nor can it be photographed or repaired by surgery. The brain, therefore, is not the mind but simply part of the body.

There is nothing within the body that can be identified as being our mind because our body and mind are different entities. For example, sometimes when our body is relaxed and immobile, our mind can be very busy, darting from one object to another. This indicates that our body and mind are not the same entity. In Buddhist scriptures, our body is compared to a guest house and our mind to a guest dwelling within it. When we die, our mind leaves our body and goes to the next life, like a guest leaving a guest house and going somewhere else.

If the mind is not the brain, nor any other part of the body, what is it? It is a formless continuum that functions to perceive and understand objects. Because the mind is formless, or non-physical, by nature, it is not obstructed by physical objects. Thus, it is impossible for our body to go to the moon without traveling in a spaceship, but our mind can reach the moon in an instant just by thinking about it.

Knowing and perceiving objects is a function that is unique to the mind. Although we say, "I know such and such," in reality it is our mind that knows. We know things only by using our mind.

It is very important to be able to distinguish disturbed states of mind from peaceful states. As explained in the previous chapter, states of mind that disturb our inner peace, such as anger, jealousy and desirous attachment, are called "delusions," and these are the principal causes of all our suffering. We may think that our suffering is caused by other people, by poor material conditions or by society, but in reality it all comes from our own deluded states of mind. The essence of spiritual practice is to reduce and eventually completely eradicate our delusions, and replace them with permanent inner peace. This is the real meaning of our human life.

Normally we seek happiness outside ourself. We try to obtain better material conditions, a better job, higher social status and so forth; but no matter how successful we are in improving our external situation, we still experience many problems and much dissatisfaction. We never experience pure, lasting happiness. This shows us that we should not seek happiness outside ourself, but instead establish it within by purifying and controlling our mind through sincere spiritual practice. If we train in this way we can ensure that our mind remains calm and happy all the time. Then, no matter how difficult our external circumstances may be, we will always be happy and peaceful.

In our ordinary life, even though we work very hard to find happiness it remains elusive for us, whereas suffering and problems seem to come naturally, without any effort. Why is this? It is because the cause of happiness within our mind—inner peace—is very weak and can give rise to its effect only if we apply great effort, while the internal causes of suffering and problems—delusions—are very strong and can give rise to their effects with no effort on our part. This is the real reason why problems come naturally while happiness is so difficult to find.

From this we can see that the principal causes of both happiness and problems are in the mind, not in the external world. If we were able to maintain a calm and peaceful mind all day long we would never experience any problems or mental suffering. For example, if our mind remains peaceful all the time, then even if we are insulted, criticized or blamed or if we lose our job or our friends, we will not become unhappy. No matter how difficult our external circumstances may become, for as long as we maintain a calm and peaceful mind they will not be a problem for us. Therefore, if we wish to be free from problems there is only one thing to do—learn to maintain a peaceful state of mind by following the spiritual path.

The essential point of understanding the mind is that liberation from suffering cannot be found outside the mind. Permanent liberation can be found only by purifying the mind. Therefore, if we want to become free from problems and attain lasting peace and happiness we need to increase our knowledge and understanding of how our mind develops.

There are three different levels of mind: gross, subtle and very subtle. During our dreams, we have dream awareness through which the various kinds of dream things appear to us; this awareness is a subtle mind because it is difficult to recognize. During deep sleep we have only one mental awareness, which perceives emptiness alone. This awareness is called the "clear light of sleep," and is a very subtle mind because it is extremely difficult to recognize.

During the waking day we have waking awareness through which various kinds of waking things appear to us. This awareness is a gross mind because it is not difficult to recognize. When we fall asleep our gross mind, or waking awareness, dissolves into our subtle mind of sleep. At the same time, all our appearances of the waking world become non-existent; and when we experience deep sleep, our subtle mind of sleep dissolves into our very subtle mind of sleep, the clear light of sleep. At this stage, we have become like a person who has died. Then, because of our maintaining a karmic connection with this life, from our clear light of sleep our gross mind, or waking awareness, will arise again and various kinds of waking things appear to us again.

The process of sleeping is very similar to the process of dying. The difference between these two is that when we are dying our gross and subtle minds will dissolve into our very subtle mind of death, known as the "clear light of death." Then, because of our karmic connection with this life ceasing, our very subtle mind leaves this body, goes to the next life and enters a new body, and then all the various kinds of things of the next life will appear to us. Everything will be completely new.

Living beings experience countless thoughts or minds, all of which are included within two: primary minds and mental factors. A detailed explanation of these can be found in the book *How to Understand the Mind*.

If we understand clearly the nature of our mind, we will definitely realize that the continuum of our mind does not cease when we die, and there will be no basis for doubting the existence of our future lives. If we realize the existence of our future lives, we will naturally be concerned for our welfare and happiness in those lives, and we will use this present life to make the appropriate preparations. This will prevent us from wasting our precious human life on the preoccupations of this life alone. Therefore, a correct understanding of the mind is absolutely essential.

Rebirth

*W*e should know that our sleeping is like death, our dreaming is like the intermediate state between death and rebirth and our waking up is like rebirth. The cycle of these three shows the existence of future rebirth, through which we can understand the existence of our countless future lives.

Many people believe that when the body disintegrates at death, the continuum of the mind ceases and the mind becomes non-existent, like a candle flame going out when all the wax has burned. There are even some people who contemplate committing suicide in the hope that if they die their problems and sufferings will come to an end. These ideas, however, are completely wrong. As already explained, our body and mind are separate entities, and so even though the body disintegrates at death, the continuum of the mind remains unbroken. Instead of ceasing, the mind simply leaves the present body and goes to the next life. For ordinary beings, therefore, rather than releasing us from suffering, death only brings new sufferings. Not understanding this, many people destroy their precious human life by committing suicide.

There is a special spiritual practice called "transference of consciousness into another body," which was quite widespread in ancient times. There are many examples of past practitioners who could transfer their consciousness from their normal body into another body. If mind and body were the same entity, how would it be possible for these practitioners to transfer their consciousness in this way? Even now, it is not that unusual for the mind temporarily to leave the physical body before death. For example, many people who are not spiritual practitioners have had so-called "out of body" experiences.

We can also gain an understanding of past and future lives by examining the process of sleeping, dreaming and waking, because this closely resembles the process of death, intermediate state and rebirth. When we fall asleep, our gross inner winds gather and dissolve inward, and our mind becomes progressively more and more subtle until it transforms into the very subtle mind of the clear light of sleep. While the clear light of sleep is manifest, we experience deep sleep, and to others we resemble a dead person. When it ends, our mind becomes gradually more and more gross and we pass through the various levels of the dream state. Finally, our normal powers of memory and mental control are restored and we wake up. When this happens, our dream world disappears and we perceive the world of the waking state.

A very similar process occurs when we die. As we die, our inner winds dissolve inward and our mind becomes progressively more and more subtle until the very subtle mind of the clear light of death becomes manifest. The experience of the clear light of death is very similar to the experience of deep sleep. After the clear light of death has ceased, we experience the stages of the intermediate state, which is a dream-like state that occurs between death and rebirth. After a few days or weeks, the intermediate state ends and we take rebirth. Just as when we wake from sleep, the dream world disappears and we perceive the world of the waking state, so, when we take rebirth, the appearances of the intermediate state cease and we perceive the world of our next life.

The only significant difference between the process of sleeping, dreaming and waking and the process of death, intermediate state and rebirth is that after the clear light of sleep has ceased, the relationship between our mind and our present body remains intact, whereas after the clear light of death has ceased this relationship is broken. By contemplating this, we can gain a clear understanding of the existence of past and future lives.

We generally believe that the things we perceive in dreams are unreal whereas the things we perceive when we are awake are true; but in reality everything we perceive is like a dream in that it is mere appearance to mind. For those who can interpret them correctly, dreams have great significance. For example, if we dream that we visit a particular country to which we have not been in this life, our dream will indicate one of four things: that we have been to that country in a previous life, that we will visit it later in this life, that we will visit it in a future life, or that it has some personal significance for us, as it would, for example, if we had recently received a letter from that country or had seen a television program about it. Similarly, if we dream we are flying, it may mean that in a previous life we were a being who could fly, such as a bird or a meditator with miracle powers, or it may predict that we will become such a being in the future. A flying dream may also have a less literal meaning, symbolizing an improvement in our health or state of mind.

It was with the help of dreams that I was able to discover where my mother was reborn after she had died. Just before she died, my mother dozed off for a few minutes and when she woke she told my sister, who was caring for her, that she had dreamed of me and that in her dream I had offered her a traditional white scarf. I interpreted this dream to mean that I would be able to help my mother in her next life, and so after she died, I prayed every day for her to be reborn in England, where I was living, so that I would have the opportunity to meet and recognize her reincarnation. I made strong prayers to see clear signs of where my mother's reincarnation could be found.

Later, I had three dreams that seemed to be significant. In the first, I dreamed that I met my mother in a place that appeared to be England. I asked her how she had traveled from India to England, but she replied that she had come not from India, but from Switzerland. In the second dream, I dreamed that I saw my mother talking to a group of people. I approached her and spoke to her in Tibetan, but she did not seem to understand what I was saying. While she was alive, my mother spoke only Tibetan, but in this dream she spoke English fluently. I asked her why she had forgotten Tibetan, but she did not reply. Later in the same dream, I dreamed of a Western couple who were helping me with the development of my spiritual activities in England.

Both dreams seemed to give clues as to where my mother had been reborn. Two days after the second dream, the husband of the couple of whom I had dreamed visited me and told me that his wife was pregnant. I immediately remembered my dream and thought that her baby might be my mother's reincarnation. The fact that in the dream my mother had forgotten Tibetan and spoke only English suggested that she would be reborn in an English-speaking country, and the presence of this couple in the dream might have been an indication that they were her parents. I then performed a traditional divination together with ritual prayers, and this indicated that their child was my mother's reincarnation. I was very happy but did not say anything to anyone.

One night I dreamed about my mother again and again. The next morning I considered the matter carefully and reached a decision. If the baby had been born that night, then it was definitely my mother's reincarnation, but if it had not, I would need to make further examinations. Having made this decision, I phoned the husband, who gave me the good news that his wife had given birth to a baby girl the previous night. I was delighted and performed a special offering ceremony.

A few days later, the father phoned and told me that if he recited the mantra of Buddha Avalokiteshvara, OM MANI PÄME HUM, when the baby cried, she would immediately stop crying and appear to be listening to the mantra. He asked me why this was and I replied that it was because of her tendencies from her previous life. I knew that my mother had recited this mantra with strong faith throughout her life.

The child was named Amaravajra. Later, when my mother's brother, Kuten Lama, visited England and saw Amaravajra for the first time, he was astonished by how affectionate she was toward him. He said that it was as if she recognized him. I also had the same experience. Although I was able to visit the young child only very occasionally, she was always extremely happy to see me.

When Amaravajra started to talk, one day she pointed to a dog and said, "kyi, kyi." After this she used to say "kyi" many times whenever she saw a dog. Her father asked me if "kyi" meant anything, and I told him that in the dialect of western Tibet, which is where my mother lived, "kyi" means "dog." This was not the only Tibetan word the little girl uttered spontaneously.

I later heard through my sister's husband that after my mother's death, a Tibetan astrologer had predicted that my mother would be born as a female in a country with a language other than Tibetan. This story comes from my own personal experience, but if we investigate we can find many other true stories about how people have been able to recognize the reincarnations of their husband, wife, Teachers, parents, friends and others.

In western Tibet, near my first monastery, there lived a man who had a reputation for being very bad tempered. He collected many silver coins and put them into a teapot, which he kept a secret even from his wife. Later, as he lay dying, out of attachment for the coins he became obsessed with the thought that they might be stolen. He tried to tell his wife about the coins, but because he was very weak he could only repeat the one word "tib," which means "teapot." Hearing this, his wife assumed that he wanted some tea, but when she offered him some he had no interest in it. Shortly afterward he died.

Sometime later, the wife found the hidden teapot. Wondering why it was so heavy, she opened the lid and discovered the coins. Coiled around these was a small snake. Terrified of the snake, she called for her family, who together tried to remove it from the teapot. Yet however hard they tried they could not part the snake from the coins. They were surprised and confused about this, and wondered where the snake had come from.

The wife then remembered her husband's last words, and realized that at the time of his death he had been trying to tell her about the coins. But what about the snake? Why was it so attached to the coins? She decided to visit a clairvoyant Yogi living nearby, who told her that the snake was the reincarnation of her husband. Due to the actions he had created out of anger, and due to his attachment to the coins when he was about to die, he had taken rebirth as a snake and had gone inside the teapot to be close to the coins. With tears falling from her eyes, she beseeched the Yogi, "Please tell me what I can do to help my husband." He suggested that she offer the coins to the nearby community of ordained Sangha, requesting them to pray for her husband to be released from his animal rebirth.

By contemplating such stories with a positive mind, and reflecting on the nature of the mind and the analogy of sleeping, dreaming and waking, we will definitely gain a deep understanding of the existence of our future lives. This knowledge is very precious and helps us to gain great wisdom. We will understand that the happiness of future lives is more important than the happiness of this life for the simple reason that countless future lives are far longer than this one short human life. This will motivate us to prepare for the happiness of our countless future lives, or to apply effort to attaining permanent liberation from suffering by abandoning our delusions.

Death

*N*o one wants to suffer. Day and night, even in our dreams, we instinctively try to avoid even the slightest suffering. This indicates that, although we are not fully aware of it, deep down what we are really seeking is permanent liberation from suffering.

There are times when we are free from physical suffering and mental pain, but these times never last. It is not long before our body again becomes uncomfortable or sick, and our mind is disturbed by worries and unhappiness. Whatever problem we overcome, it is only a matter of time before another arises to take its place. This shows that despite our wish for permanent liberation from suffering we have never managed to attain it. For as long as delusions remain in our mind, we will never be completely free from suffering. We may enjoy moments of respite, but before long our problems will return. The only way finally to end our suffering is by following the spiritual path. Since, in the depths of their hearts, everyone wants complete liberation from suffering, we can see that in reality everyone needs to follow the spiritual path.

However, because our desire for worldly enjoyment is so strong, we have little or no interest in spiritual practice. From a spiritual point of view, this lack of interest in spiritual practice is a type of laziness called "the laziness of attachment." For as long as we have this laziness, the door to liberation will be closed to us, and consequently we will continue to experience misery in this life and endless suffering in life after life. The way to overcome this laziness is to meditate on death.

We need to contemplate and meditate on our death again and again until we gain a deep realization of death. Although on an intellectual level we all know that eventually we are going to die, our awareness of death remains superficial. Since our intellectual knowledge of death does not touch our hearts, each and every day we continue to think, "I will not die today, I will not die today." Even on the day of our death we are still thinking about what we will do tomorrow or next week. This mind that thinks every day "I will not die today" is deceptive—it leads us in the wrong direction and causes our human life to become empty. On the other hand, through meditating on death we will gradually replace the deceptive thought "I will not die today" with the non-deceptive thought "I may die today." The mind that spontaneously thinks each and every day "I may die today" is the realization of death. It is this realization that directly eliminates our laziness of attachment and opens the door to the spiritual path.

In general, we may die today or we may not die today—we do not know. However, if we think each day, "I may not die today," this thought will deceive us because it comes from our ignorance; whereas if instead we think each day, "I may die today," this thought will not deceive us because it comes from our wisdom. This beneficial thought will prevent our laziness of attachment, and will encourage us to prepare for the welfare of our countless future lives or to put great effort into entering the path to liberation. In this way, we will make our human life meaningful.

To meditate on death, we contemplate that our death is certain and that the time of our death is uncertain. We then need to understand that at the time of death and after death only spiritual practice can help us.

DEATH IS CERTAIN

Death will definitely come and there is nothing that can prevent it. We contemplate:

No matter where I am born, whether it is in fortunate or unfortunate states of existence, I will definitely have to die. Whether I am born in the happiest condition of higher rebirth or in the deepest hell, I will have to experience death. However far and wide I travel, I will never find a place where I can hide from death, even if I voyage far into space or tunnel deep underground.

No one alive at the time of the first century remains alive today, and no one alive at the time of the second

*century and so forth remains alive today. Only their
names survive. All those who were alive two hundred
years ago have passed away, and all those alive today will
be gone in two hundred years' time.*

Contemplating these points we should ask ourself, "Could
I alone outlive death?"

When our karma to experience this life comes to an end,
no one and nothing can prevent our death. When the time
of our death arrives, there is no escape. If it were possible
to prevent death by using clairvoyance or miracle powers,
those who have possessed such powers would have become
immortal; but even clairvoyants die. The most powerful
leaders who have ruled in this world have been helpless
before the power of death. The king of beasts, the lion,
who can kill an elephant, is immediately destroyed when
he encounters the Lord of Death. Even billionaires have no
way of avoiding death. They cannot distract death with a
bribe or buy time, saying, "If you postpone my death, I will
give you wealth beyond your wildest dreams."

Death is relentless and will not be compromised. It is like
the collapse of an immense mountain in all four directions;
there is no way to hold back its devastation. This is also
true of aging and sickness. Aging progresses surreptitiously
and undermines our youth, our strength and our beauty.
Although we are hardly aware of the process, it is already
underway and cannot be reversed. Sickness destroys the
comfort, power and strength of our body. If doctors help

us to overcome our first illness, others take its place until, eventually, our sickness cannot be cured and we die. We cannot escape from sickness and death by running away from them. We cannot placate them with riches nor use miracle powers to make them vanish. Every single being in this world must suffer aging, sickness and death.

Our life span cannot be increased, and in fact it is decreasing continuously. From the moment of our conception we head inexorably toward death, just like a racehorse galloping toward the finish line. Even racehorses occasionally relax their pace, but in our race toward death we never stop, not even for a second. While we are sleeping and while we are awake, our life slips away. Every vehicle stops and breaks its journey from time to time, but our life span never stops running out. One moment after our birth, part of our life span has perished. We live in the very embrace of death. After our birth we have no freedom to remain even for a minute. We head toward the embrace of the Lord of Death like an athlete running. We may think that we are among the living, but our life is the very highway of death.

Suppose our doctor were to break the news to us that we were suffering from an incurable disease and that we had only one week left to live. If our friend were then to offer us a fantastic gift such as a diamond, a new car or a free vacation, we would not get very excited about it. Yet in reality, this is our very predicament, for we are all suffering from a mortal disease. How foolish it is to become overly interested in the passing pleasures of this brief life!

If we find it difficult to meditate on death, we can listen to a clock ticking and be aware that every tick marks the end of a moment of our life and draws us closer to death. We can imagine that the Lord of Death lives some distance from us. Then, as we listen to the clock ticking, we can imagine ourself taking steps in death's direction moment by moment. In this way we will understand that we are traveling toward death without a moment's rest.

Our world is as impermanent as autumn clouds, with our birth and death being like the entrance and exit of an actor on the stage. Actors frequently change their costumes and their roles, making their entrance in many different disguises. In the same way, living beings take different forms continually and enter new worlds. Sometimes they are human beings, sometimes they are animals and sometimes they enter hell. We should understand that the life span of a living being passes like lightning in the sky, and perishes quickly like water falling from a high mountain.

Death will come regardless of whether or not we have made the time for spiritual practice. Although life is short, it would not be so bad if we had plenty of time for spiritual practice, but most of our time is taken up with sleeping, working, eating, shopping, talking and so on, leaving very little time for pure spiritual practice. Our time is easily consumed by other pursuits until, suddenly, we die.

We keep thinking that we have plenty of time for spiritual practice, but if we closely examine our way of life we will see that the days slip by without our getting down to serious practice. If we do not make the time to engage in spiritual practice purely, we will look back on our life at the time of death and see that it has been of very little benefit. However, if we meditate on death, we will develop such a sincere wish to practice purely that we will naturally begin to modify our daily routine so that it includes at least a little time for practice. Eventually we will find more time for practice than for other things.

If we meditate on death again and again we may feel afraid; but it is not enough just to feel fear. Once we have generated an appropriate fear of dying unprepared, we should search for something that will offer real protection. The paths of future lives are very long and unfamiliar. We have to experience one life after another, and we cannot be sure where we will take rebirth—whether we will have to follow the paths to unhappy states of existence or the paths to happier realms. We have no freedom or independence but must go wherever our karma takes us. Therefore, we need to find something that will show us a safe way to future lives, something that will direct us along correct paths and away from wrong paths. The possessions and enjoyments of this life cannot protect us. Since only spiritual teachings reveal a flawless path that will help and protect us in the future, we must make effort with our body, speech and mind to put spiritual teachings, such as those presented in this book, into practice. The Yogi Milarepa said:

> There are more fears in future lives than in this one. Have you prepared anything that will help you? If you have not prepared for your future lives, do so now. The only protection against those fears is the practice of holy spiritual teachings.

If we think about our own life, we will see that we have spent many years with no interest in spiritual practice, and that now, even if we have the wish to practice, still, due to laziness, we do not practice purely. A great scholar called Gungtang said:

> I spent twenty years not wanting to practice spiritual teachings. I spent the next twenty years thinking that I could practice later on. I spent another twenty years engrossed in other activities and regretting the fact that I had not engaged in spiritual practice. This is the story of my empty human life.

This could be our own life story, but if we meditate on death we will avoid wasting our precious human life and we will strive to make it meaningful.

Through contemplating these points, we should deeply think, "I will certainly die." Considering that at the time of death only our spiritual practice will be of any real assistance to us, we make a firm resolution, "I must put spiritual teachings, known as Dharma, into practice." When this thought arises strongly and clearly in our mind, we hold it single-pointedly without distraction to become more and more familiar with it, until we never lose it.

THE TIME OF OUR DEATH IS UNCERTAIN

Sometimes we fool ourself by thinking, "I am young and so I will not die soon," but we can see how misguided this thought is merely by observing how many young people die before their parents. Sometimes we think, "I am healthy and so I will not die soon," but we can see that people who are healthy and looking after the sick sometimes die before their patients. People who go to visit their friends in the hospital may die sooner in a car crash, for death does not confine itself to those who are old and unwell. Someone who is alive and well in the morning could be dead by the afternoon, and someone who is well when he falls asleep may die before he wakes up. Some people die while they are eating, and some people die in the middle of a conversation. Some people die as soon as they are born.

Death may not give any warning. This enemy can come at any time and often he strikes quickly, when we least expect it. He may come as we are driving to a party, or switching on our television, or as we are thinking to ourself "I will not die today" and making plans for our summer vacation or our retirement. The Lord of Death can creep up on us as dark clouds creep across the sky. Sometimes when we go indoors the sky is bright and clear, but when we step outside again the sky is overcast. In the same way, death can quickly cast its shadow over our life.

There are many more conditions conducive to death than to survival. Although our death is certain and our life span is indefinite, it would not be so bad if the conditions that lead to death were rare; but there are innumerable external and internal conditions that can bring about our death. The external environment causes deaths by famine, floods, fires, earthquakes, pollution and so on. In a similar way, the four internal bodily elements of earth, water, fire and wind cause death when their harmony is lost and one of them develops in excess. When these internal elements are in harmony they are said to be like four snakes of the same species and strength abiding together peacefully; but when they lose their harmony it is like one snake becoming stronger than the others and consuming them, until finally it dies of hunger itself.

Besides these inanimate causes of death, other living beings such as thieves, hostile soldiers and wild animals can also bring about our death. Even things that we do not consider to be threatening, things that we think of as supporting and protecting our life, such as our house, our car or our best friend, can turn out to be causes of our death. People are sometimes crushed to death by their own house or they fall to their death from their own staircase, and each day many people are killed in their cars. Some people die on vacation, and some are killed by their hobbies and entertainments, such as horseback riders who are thrown to their death. The very food we eat to nourish and sustain our life can be a cause of death. Even our friends and lovers can become causes of our death, by mistake or by intention. We read in the news how lovers sometimes kill one another, and how parents sometimes kill their own children. If we investigate carefully, we will not be able to find any worldly enjoyment that is not a potential cause of death and that is solely a cause of remaining alive. The great scholar Nagarjuna said:

> We maintain our life in the midst of thousands of
> conditions that threaten death. Our life force is like a
> candle flame in a breeze, which is easily extinguished
> by the winds of death that blow from all directions.

Each person has created the karma to remain in this life for a certain period, but since we cannot remember what karma we have created we cannot know the exact duration of our present life. It is possible for us to die an untimely death before completing our life span because we can exhaust our merit, the cause of good fortune, sooner than we exhaust the karma that determines our life span. If this happens we become so ill that doctors cannot help us, or we find that we are unable to obtain food and other necessities to support our life. However, even when we become seriously ill, if our life span has not ended and we still have merit we can find all the conditions necessary for recovery.

The human body is very fragile. Although there are many causes of death it would not be so bad if our body were strong like steel, but it is delicate. It does not take guns and bombs to destroy our body; it can be destroyed by a small needle. As Nagarjuna said:

There are many destroyers of our life force.
Our human body is like a water bubble.

Just as a water bubble bursts as soon as it is touched, so a single drop of water in the heart or the slightest scratch from a poisonous thorn can cause our death. Nagarjuna said that at the end of this eon the entire world system will be consumed by fire and not even its ashes will remain. Since the entire universe will become empty, there is no need to say that this delicate human body will decay most swiftly.

We can contemplate the process of our breathing and how it continues without interruption between inhalation and exhalation. If it were to stop, we would die. Yet even when we are asleep and our mindfulness is no longer functioning, our breathing continues, although in many other respects we resemble a corpse. Nagarjuna said, "This is a most wonderful thing!" When we wake up in the morning we should rejoice, thinking, "How amazing it is that my breathing has sustained my life throughout sleep. If it had ceased during the night I would now be dead!"

Contemplating that the time of our death is completely uncertain, and understanding that there is no guarantee that we will not die today, we should think deeply, day and night, "I may die today, I may die today." Meditating on this feeling, we will then come to a strong determination:

Since I will soon have to depart from this life, there is no sense in my becoming attached to the things of this life. Instead I will take to heart the real essence of my human life by sincerely engaging in pure spiritual practice.

What does "engaging in pure spiritual practice" mean? When we are practicing spiritual teachings that are methods to control our delusions, such as uncontrolled desire, anger and ignorance, we are engaging in pure spiritual practice. This, in turn, means we are following correct spiritual paths. This pure spiritual practice has three levels: (1) the practice of a person of initial scope, (2) the practice of a person of middling scope, and (3) the practice of a person of great scope. A detailed explanation of these three levels can be found in the books *Joyful Path of Good Fortune* and *Modern Buddhism*.

Enjoy the purity of your mind and actions

Karma

*K*arma means actions: the actions of our body, speech and mind. This subject is very meaningful. Throughout our life we have to experience various kinds of suffering and problems without choice. This is because we do not understand what actions we need to abandon and what actions we need to practice. If we had this knowledge and put it into practice there would be no basis for experiencing suffering and problems.

The law of karma is a special instance of the law of cause and effect, according to which all our actions of body, speech and mind are causes and all our experiences are their effects. The law of karma explains why each individual has a unique mental disposition, a unique physical appearance and unique experiences. These are the various effects of the countless actions that each individual has performed in the past. We cannot find any two people who have created exactly the same history of actions throughout their past lives, and so we cannot find two people with identical states of mind, identical experiences or identical physical appearances. Each person has a different individual karma. Some people enjoy good health while others are constantly ill. Some people are seen as very beautiful while others are seen as very ugly. Some people have a happy disposition that is easily pleased while others have a sour disposition and are rarely delighted by anything. Some people easily understand the meaning of spiritual teachings while others find them difficult and obscure.

Every action we perform leaves an imprint, or potentiality, on our very subtle mind, and each imprint eventually gives rise to its own effect. Our mind is like a field, and performing actions is like sowing seeds in that field. Virtuous actions sow seeds of future happiness and non-virtuous actions sow seeds of future suffering. These seeds remain dormant in our mind until the conditions for them to ripen occur, and then they produce their effect. In some cases, this can happen many lifetimes after the original action was performed.

It is because of our karma or actions that we are born in this impure, contaminated world and experience so many difficulties and problems. Our actions are impure because our mind is contaminated by the inner poison of self-grasping. This is the fundamental reason why we experience suffering. Suffering is created by our own actions or karma—it is not given to us as a punishment. We suffer because we have accumulated many non-virtuous actions in our previous lives. The source of these non-virtuous actions is our own delusions such as anger, attachment and self-grasping ignorance.

Once we have purified our mind of self-grasping and all other delusions, all our actions will naturally be pure. As a result of our pure actions or pure karma, everything we experience will be pure. We will abide in a pure world, with a pure body, enjoying pure enjoyments and surrounded by pure beings. There will no longer be the slightest trace of suffering, impurity or problems. This is how to find true happiness from within our mind.

THE GENERAL CHARACTERISTICS OF KARMA

For every action we perform, we experience a similar result. If a gardener sows a seed of a medicinal plant, a medicinal plant and not a poisonous one will grow; and if he or she does not sow any seeds, then nothing will grow. In a similar way, if we perform positive actions we will experience happy results and not unhappiness, if we perform negative actions we will experience only unhappy results, and if we perform neutral actions we will experience neutral results.

For example, if we now experience any mental disturbance it is because at some time in the past we disturbed the minds of others. If we experience a painful physical illness it is because in the past we caused pain to others, such as by beating or shooting them, intentionally administering wrong medicines or serving them poisonous food. If we have not created the karmic cause to become ill it is impossible for us to experience the suffering of physical illness, even if we find ourself in the midst of an epidemic where everyone else around us is dying. Those who have attained nirvana, the supreme permanent inner peace, for example, never experience any physical or mental pain because they have abandoned engaging in harmful actions and purified all the non-virtuous potentialities that are the main causes of pain.

The main cause of the sufferings of poverty is an action of stealing. The main causes of being oppressed are looking down on, beating or demanding work from people of inferior position, or despising others instead of showing them loving kindness. The main causes of the sufferings of being separated from friends and family are actions such as seducing other people's partners or purposefully alienating their friends and the people who work for them.

Usually we assume that bad experiences arise only in dependence upon the conditions of this present life. Since we cannot account for many of them in these terms, we often feel that they are inexplicable and undeserved, and that there is no justice in the world. In reality, however, most of our experiences in this life are caused by actions we committed in past lives.

Through the following example given in Buddhist scriptures, we can begin to understand how our experiences in this life arise from actions in previous lives, as well as how the results of actions increase over time, just as a small seed can grow into a large tree. There was once a nun called Upala, who before her ordination experienced extraordinary misfortune. Of the two children she had by her first husband, one drowned and the other was savaged and eaten by a jackal. Her husband was later killed by a poisonous snake. After losing her family Upala returned to her parents' home, but soon after she arrived the house caught fire and burnt to the ground. She married again and had a child by her second husband, but he was an alcoholic and one night he got so drunk that he killed his child and forced Upala to eat its flesh. She fled from this crazy man and escaped to another country, where she was captured by a gang of thieves and forced to marry their leader. A few years later her third husband was caught and, in accordance with the custom of that country, she was buried alive with her husband. However, the thieves desired Upala so much they dug her up and forced her to live with them. Having experienced all these terrible miseries and misfortunes, Upala developed a very strong wish to find freedom from every kind of suffering existence, and went in search of Buddha to tell him her story. Buddha explained that in her previous life she had been one of the wives of a king and that she had been very jealous of the other wives. Her jealousy alone was enough to cause the terrible sufferings of her present life. Buddha then explained how she could purify her mind, and by sincerely practicing these teachings she attained nirvana in that life.

By contemplating how the results of our actions are definite and how they increase, we will develop a strong determination to avoid even the slightest non-virtue and to nurture even the smallest positive thoughts and constructive deeds. We then meditate on this determination to make it constant and stable. If we can keep our determination all the time and put it into practice, our actions of body, speech and mind will become increasingly more pure until there is no longer any basis for suffering.

If we do not perform an action, we cannot experience its effect. In a battle, some soldiers are killed while others survive. The survivors are not saved because they are braver than the others, but because they did not create any action that would cause them to die at that time. We can find many other such examples in the daily news. When a terrorist plants a bomb in a large building, some people are killed while others escape despite being at the center of the blast. When there is an airplane crash or a volcanic eruption, some people are killed while others, as if by a miracle, escape. In many accidents the survivors themselves are astonished to be alive when others right next to them were killed.

The actions of living beings are never wasted, even though a long time may pass before their effects are experienced. Actions cannot simply vanish, and we cannot give them away to someone else and thus avoid our responsibility. Although the momentary mental intentions that initiated our past actions have ceased, the potentialities they have created in our mind do not cease until their results have ripened. The only way to destroy negative potentialities before they ripen as suffering is to purify them.

Unfortunately, it is easier to destroy our positive potentialities, for if we fail to dedicate our virtuous actions they can be made completely powerless by just one moment of anger. Our mind is like a treasure chest and our virtuous actions are like jewels. If we do not safeguard them through dedication, whenever we become angry it is as if we had put a thief among our treasures.

THE SIX REALMS OF REBIRTH

The seeds of our actions that ripen when we die are very important because they determine what kind of rebirth we will take in our next life. Which particular seed ripens at death depends upon the state of mind in which we die. If we die with a peaceful mind, this will stimulate a virtuous seed and we will experience a fortunate rebirth. However, if we die with an unpeaceful mind, such as in a state of anger, this will stimulate a non-virtuous seed and we will experience an unfortunate rebirth. This is similar to the way in which nightmares are triggered by our being in an agitated state of mind just before falling asleep.

The example of sleeping, dreaming and waking is not accidental, for, as explained in the chapter on rebirth, the process of sleeping, dreaming and waking closely resembles the process of death, intermediate state and rebirth. While we are in the intermediate state, we experience different visions that arise from the karmic seeds that were activated immediately before death. If negative seeds were activated, these visions will be nightmarish, but if positive seeds were activated they will be predominantly pleasant. In either case, when the karmic seeds have fully ripened, they impel us to take rebirth in one or other of the six realms of samsara.

The six realms are actual places in which we can be reborn. They are brought into existence through the power of our actions, or karma. There are three types of action: bodily actions, verbal actions and mental actions. Since our bodily and verbal actions are always initiated by our mental actions, or intentions, ultimately the six realms are created by our mind. For example, a hell realm is a place that arises as a result of the worst actions, such as murder or extreme mental or physical cruelty, which depend upon the most deluded states of mind.

To form a mental image of the six realms, we can compare them to the floors of a large, old house. In this analogy the house represents samsara, the cycle of contaminated rebirth. The house has three floors above ground and three below. Deluded sentient beings are like the inhabitants of this house. They are continually moving up and down the house, sometimes living above ground, sometimes below.

The ground floor represents the human realm. Above this, on the second floor, is the realm of the demi-gods—non-human beings who are continually at war with the gods. In terms of power and prosperity they are superior to humans, but they are so obsessed with jealousy and violence that their lives have little spiritual value.

On the top floor live the gods. The lower classes of gods, the desire realm gods, live a life of ease and luxury, devoting their time to enjoyment and the satisfaction of their desires. Though their world is a paradise and their life span is very long, they are not immortal and they eventually fall to lower states. Since their lives are filled with distractions, it is difficult for them to find the motivation to engage in spiritual practice. From a spiritual point of view, a human life is much more meaningful than a god's life.

Higher than the desire realm gods are the gods of the form and formless realms. Having passed beyond sensual desire, the form realm gods experience the refined bliss of meditative absorption and possess bodies made of light. Transcending even these subtle forms, the gods of the formless realm abide without form in a subtle consciousness that resembles infinite space. Though their minds are the purest and most exalted within samsara, they have not overcome the ignorance of self-grasping, which is the root of samsara, and so, after experiencing bliss for many eons, eventually their lives end and they are once again reborn in the lower states of samsara. Like the other gods, they consume the merit they have created in the past and make little or no spiritual progress.

The three floors above ground are called "fortunate realms" because the beings who inhabit them have relatively pleasant experiences, which are caused by the practice of virtue. Below ground are the three lower realms, which are the result of negative bodily, verbal and mental actions. The least painful of these is the animal realm, which in this analogy is the first floor beneath the ground. Included in this realm are all mammals apart from humans, as well as birds, fish, insects, worms—the whole animal kingdom. Their minds are characterized by a complete lack of spiritual awareness, and their lives mainly by fear and brutality.

On the next floor down live the hungry ghosts, or hungry spirits. The principal causes of rebirth here are greed and negative actions motivated by miserliness. The consequence of these actions is extreme poverty. Hungry ghosts suffer continuous hunger and thirst, which they are unable to bear. Their world is a vast desert. If by chance they come across a drop of water or a scrap of food, it disappears like a mirage or transforms into something repulsive, such as pus or urine. These appearances are due to their negative karma and lack of merit.

The lowest floor is hell. The beings here experience unrelenting torment. Some hells are a mass of fire; others are desolate regions of ice and darkness. Monsters conjured up by the minds of the hell beings inflict terrible tortures on them. This suffering continues unremittingly for what seems an eternity, but eventually the karma that caused the beings to be born in hell is exhausted and the hell beings die and are reborn elsewhere in samsara. Hell is simply what appears to the most negative and distorted type of mind. It is not an external place that we can normally see, but is like a nightmare from which we do not wake up for a very long time. For those living in hell, the sufferings of the hell realm are as real as our present experience of the human realm.

This is a general picture of samsara. We have been trapped in samsara since beginningless time, wandering meaninglessly, without any freedom or control, from the highest heaven to the deepest hell. Sometimes we dwell on the upper floors as gods, sometimes we find ourself on the ground floor with a human rebirth, but most of the time we are trapped on the underground floors as animals, hungry ghosts or hell beings, experiencing terrible physical and mental suffering for very long periods of time.

Although samsara resembles a prison, there is one door through which we can escape. That door is emptiness, the ultimate nature of phenomena. By realizing emptiness we can escape from samsara. By training in the spiritual paths described in this book, we will eventually find our way to this door and, stepping through, discover that the house was simply an illusion, the creation of our impure mind. Samsara is not an external prison; it is a prison made by our own mind. It will never end by itself, but by diligently practicing a pure spiritual path, and thereby eliminating our self-grasping and other delusions, we can bring our samsara to an end. Once we attain liberation, or nirvana, ourself, we will then be in a position to show others how to destroy their mental prison by eradicating their delusions.

TYPES OF ACTION

Although there are countless different actions of body, speech and mind, all are included within three types: virtuous actions, non-virtuous actions and neutral actions. The practices of giving, moral discipline, patience, effort in spiritual training, meditative concentration and wisdom are examples of virtuous actions. Killing, stealing and sexual misconduct are bodily non-virtuous actions; lying, divisive speech, hurtful speech and idle chatter are verbal non-virtuous actions; and covetousness, malice and holding wrong views are mental non-virtuous actions. In addition to these ten non-virtuous actions, there are many other kinds of non-virtuous action, such as beating or torturing others, or otherwise deliberately causing them to suffer. Every day we also perform many neutral actions. Whenever we engage in daily actions such as shopping, cooking, eating, sleeping or relaxing without a specific good or bad motivation, we are performing neutral actions.

All non-virtuous actions are contaminated because they are motivated by delusions, particularly the delusion of self-grasping ignorance. Most of our virtuous and neutral actions are also based on self-grasping and are thus also contaminated. At the moment, even when we are observing moral discipline, for example, we still grasp at an inherently existent I or self who is acting in a moral way, and so our practice of moral discipline is a contaminated virtuous action, which causes higher rebirth in samsara.

We grasp at an inherently existent I and mine all the time, day and night. This mind is the delusion of self-grasping ignorance. Whenever we are embarrassed, afraid, angry, indignant or puffed up with pride, we have a very strong sense of self or I. The I that we are grasping on these occasions is the inherently existent I. Even when we are re-laxed and relatively peaceful we still grasp our I as inherently existent, though in a less pronounced way. This mind of self-grasping is the basis of all our delusions and the source of all our problems. To free ourself from delusions and the problems they cause, we need to understand that the inher-ently existent I we grasp so firmly and continuously does not exist at all. It never has existed and never will. It is merely the fabrication of our self-grasping ignorance.

To fulfill the wishes of this I—the inherently existent I that we believe actually exists—we normally perform in-numerable positive and negative actions. These actions are known as "throwing actions," which means actions that are motivated by strong self-grasping and that are the main cause of samsaric rebirth. Contaminated virtuous actions throw us into higher samsaric rebirths as a human, demi-god or god, whereas non-virtuous actions throw us into lower rebirths in the animal, hungry ghost or hell realms. When we are about to die, if we develop a negative state of mind such as anger, this causes the potential of a non-virtuous throwing action to ripen so that after death we will take a lower rebirth. Alternatively, if at the time of death we develop a virtuous state of mind—for example by remembering our daily spiritual practice—this causes the potential of a virtuous throwing action to ripen, so that after death we will be reborn as a human being or one of the other two types of higher samsaric being, and will have to experience the sufferings of these beings.

There is another type of contaminated action, which is called a "completing action." This is a contaminated action that is the main cause of the happiness or suffering we experience once we have taken a particular rebirth. All human beings are thrown into the human world by virtuous throwing actions, but the experiences they have as human beings vary considerably depending upon their different completing actions. Some experience a life of suffering, whereas others experience a life of ease. Similarly, animals have all been thrown into the animal world by non-virtuous throwing actions, but their experiences as animals vary considerably depending upon their different completing actions. Some animals, such as some domestic pets, can experience a life of luxury, receiving more care and attention than many human beings. Hell beings and hungry ghosts experience only the results of non-virtuous throwing actions and non-virtuous completing actions. From the day they are born to the day they die, they experience nothing but suffering.

One throwing action may throw us into many future lives. In Buddhist scriptures an example is given of a man who became very angry with an ordained monk and told him he looked like a frog. As a result, this unfortunate man was reborn many times as a frog. However, just one rebirth is sometimes sufficient to exhaust the power of our throwing action.

Some of our actions ripen in the same life in which they are performed, and these are necessarily completing actions; some ripen in the next life, some ripen in lives after that, and these can be either throwing or completing actions.

In conclusion, we can see that first we develop strong self-grasping, from which arise all the other delusions. These delusions impel us to create throwing karma, which causes us to take another samsaric rebirth in which we experience fear, suffering and problems. Throughout this rebirth we continuously develop self-grasping and other delusions, impelling us to create more throwing actions, and leading to yet further contaminated rebirths. This process of samsara is an endless cycle, unless we attain nirvana.

Listen to the precious sound of the conch of Dharma and contemplate and meditate on its meaning

Samsara

The word samsara is Sanskrit, and means cycle of contaminated rebirth, or cycle of impure life. The cycle of contaminated rebirth refers to repeatedly taking a contaminated body and mind, which are also called "contaminated aggregates." Normally, whenever our body is sick we think "I am sick," and whenever our mind is unhappy we think "I am unhappy." This clearly indicates that we believe our body and mind are our self. This belief is ignorance because our body and mind are not our self; they are the possessions of our self, as indicated by our saying "My body, my mind." Because of this ignorance believing that our body and mind are our self we develop various kinds of mistaken appearance through which we experience various kinds of suffering and problems as hallucinations, throughout this life and in life after life without end. From this we can understand that since beginningless time until now our way of identifying our self has been mistaken. To reduce and finally completely cease our experience of suffering and problems as hallucinations we need to identify our self correctly through training in the spiritual paths that I will explain in the chapter *Ultimate Bodhichitta*. Through the instructions presented in that chapter we will understand the way things really are.

We should know that our human life is precious and of real value only when we use it to train in spiritual paths. In itself it is a true suffering. We experience various types of suffering because we have taken a rebirth that is contaminated by the inner poison of delusions. This experience has no beginning, because we have taken contaminated rebirths since beginningless time, and it will have no end unless we attain the supreme inner peace of nirvana. If we contemplate and meditate on how we experience sufferings and difficulties throughout our life, and in life after life, we will come to the strong conclusion that every single one of our sufferings and problems arises because we took contaminated rebirth. We will then develop a strong wish to abandon the cycle of contaminated rebirth, samsara. This wish is called "renunciation," and it is through developing this wish that we actually enter the path to liberation, or nirvana. From this point of view, contemplating and meditating on suffering has great meaning. The main purpose of this meditation is to avoid having to go through all of these experiences again in the future.

While we remain in this cycle of contaminated rebirth, sufferings and problems will never end—we will have to experience them over and over again every time we take rebirth. Although we cannot remember our experience while we were in our mother's womb or during our very early childhood, the sufferings of human life began from the time of our conception. Everyone can observe that a newborn baby experiences anguish and pain. The first thing a baby does when it is born is scream. Rarely has a baby ever been born in complete serenity, with a peaceful, smiling expression on its face.

BIRTH

When our consciousness first enters the union of our father's sperm and our mother's ovum, our body is a very hot, watery substance like white yogurt tinted red. In the first moments after conception, we have no gross feelings, but as soon as these develop we begin to experience pain. Our body gradually becomes harder and harder, and as our limbs grow it feels as if our body were being stretched out on a rack. Inside our mother's womb it is hot and dark. Our home for nine months is this small, tightly compressed space full of unclean substances. It is like being squashed inside a small water tank full of filthy liquid with the lid tightly shut so that no air or light can come through.

While we are in our mother's womb, we experience much pain and fear all on our own. We are extremely sensitive to everything our mother does. When she walks quickly it feels as if we were falling from a high mountain and we are terrified. If she has sexual intercourse it feels as if we were being crushed and suffocated between two huge weights and we panic. If our mother makes just a small jump it feels as if we were being dashed against the ground from a great height. If she drinks anything hot it feels like boiling water scalding our skin, and if she drinks anything cold it feels like an ice-cold shower in midwinter.

When we are emerging from our mother's womb, it feels as if we were being forced through a narrow crevice between two hard rocks, and when we are newly born our body is so delicate that any kind of contact is painful. Even if someone holds us very tenderly, his or her hands feel like thorn bushes piercing our flesh, and the most delicate fabrics feel rough and abrasive. By comparison with the softness and smoothness of our mother's womb, every tactile sensation is harsh and painful. If someone picks us up it feels as if we were being swung over a huge precipice, and we feel frightened and insecure. We have forgotten all that we knew in our past life; we bring only pain and confusion from our mother's womb. Whatever we hear is as meaningless as the sound of wind, and we cannot comprehend anything we perceive. In the first few weeks we are like someone who is blind, deaf and dumb, and suffering from profound amnesia. When we are hungry we cannot say "I need food," and when we are in pain we cannot say "This is hurting me." The only signs we can make are hot tears and furious gestures. Our mother often has no idea what pains and discomforts we are experiencing. We are completely helpless and have to be taught everything—how to eat, how to sit, how to walk, how to talk.

Although we are most vulnerable in the first few weeks of our life, our pains do not cease as we grow up. We continue to experience various kinds of suffering throughout our life. Just as when we light a fire in a large house, the heat from the fire pervades the whole house and all the heat in the house comes from the fire, so when we are born in samsara, suffering pervades our whole life, and all the miseries we experience arise because we took a contaminated rebirth.

Since we have been born as a human, we cherish our human body and mind and cling to them as our own. In dependence upon observing our body and mind, we develop self-grasping, which is the root of all delusions. Our human rebirth is the basis of our human suffering; without this basis, there are no human problems. The pains of birth gradually turn into the pains of aging, sickness and death—they are one continuum.

SICKNESS

Our birth also gives rise to the sufferings of sickness. Just as the wind and snow of winter take away the glory of green meadows, trees, forests and flowers, so sickness takes away the youthful splendor of our body, destroying its strength and the power of our senses. If we are usually fit and well, when we become sick we are suddenly unable to engage in all our normal physical activities. Even a champion boxer who is usually able to knock out all his opponents becomes completely helpless when sickness strikes. Sickness makes all our experiences of daily enjoyments disappear and causes us to experience unpleasant feelings day and night.

When we fall ill, we are like a bird that has been soaring in the sky and is suddenly shot down. When a bird is shot, it falls straight to the ground like a lump of lead, and all its glory and power are immediately destroyed. In a similar way, when we become ill we are suddenly incapacitated. If we are seriously ill we may become completely dependent upon others and lose even the ability to control our bodily functions. This transformation is hard to bear, especially for those who pride themselves on their independence and physical well-being.

When we are ill, we feel frustrated as we cannot do our usual work or complete all the daily tasks we have set for ourself. We easily become impatient with our illness and depressed about all the things we cannot do. We cannot enjoy the things that usually give us pleasure, such as sports, dancing, drinking, eating rich foods or the company of our friends. All these limitations make us feel even more miserable; and, to add to our unhappiness, we have to endure all the physical pain the illness brings.

When we are sick, not only do we have to experience all the unwanted pain of the illness itself, but we also have to experience all sorts of other unwished for things. For example, we have to take whatever cure is prescribed, whether it be a foul-tasting medicine, a series of injections, a major operation or abstinence from something we like very much. If we need to have an operation, we have to go to the hospital and accept all the conditions there. We may have to eat food we do not like and stay in bed all day long with nothing to do, and we may feel anxiety about the operation. Our doctor may not explain to us exactly what the problem is and whether or not he or she expects us to survive.

If we learn that our sickness is incurable, and we have no spiritual experience, we will suffer anxiety, fear and regret. We may become depressed and give up hope, or we may become angry with our illness, feeling that it is an enemy that has maliciously deprived us of all our joy.

AGING

Our birth gives rise to the pains of aging. Aging steals our beauty, our health, our good figure, our fine complexion, our vitality and our comfort. Aging turns us into objects of contempt. It brings many unwanted pains and takes us swiftly to our death.

As we grow old we lose all the beauty of our youth, and our strong, healthy body becomes weak and burdened with illness. Our once firm and well-proportioned figure becomes bent and disfigured, and our muscles and flesh shrink so that our limbs become like thin sticks and our bones poke out. Our hair loses its color and shine, and our complexion loses its luster. Our face becomes wrinkled and our features grow distorted. Milarepa said:

How do old people get up? They get up as if they were heaving a stake out of the ground. How do old people walk about? Once they are on their feet, they have to walk gingerly, like bird-catchers. How do old people sit down? They crash down like heavy luggage whose harness has snapped.

We can contemplate the following poem on the sufferings of growing old, written by the great scholar Gungtang:

When we are old, our hair becomes white,
But not because we have washed it clean;
It is a sign we will soon encounter the Lord of
    Death.

We have wrinkles on our forehead,
But not because we have too much flesh;
It is a warning from the Lord of Death:
    "You are about to die."

Our teeth fall out,
But not to make room for new ones;
It is a sign we will soon lose the ability to eat human
    food.

Our faces are ugly and unpleasant,
But not because we are wearing masks;
It is a sign we have lost the mask of youth.

Our heads shake to and fro,
But not because we are in disagreement;
It is the Lord of Death striking our head with the
    stick he holds in his right hand.

We walk bent and gazing at the ground,
But not because we are searching for lost needles;
It is a sign we are searching for our lost beauty and
    memories.

We get up from the ground using all four limbs,
But not because we are imitating animals;
It is a sign our legs are too weak to support our
    body.

We sit down as if we had suddenly fallen,
But not because we are angry;
It is a sign our body has lost its strength.

Our body sways as we walk,
But not because we think we are important;
It is a sign our legs cannot carry our body.

Our hands shake,
But not because they are itching to steal;
It is a sign the Lord of Death's itchy fingers are
    stealing our possessions.

We eat very little,
But not because we are miserly;
It is a sign we cannot digest our food.

We wheeze frequently,
But not because we are whispering mantras to the
    sick;
It is a sign our breathing will soon disappear.

When we are young, we can travel around the whole world, but when we are old we can hardly make it to our own front door. We become too weak to engage in many worldly activities, and our spiritual activities are often curtailed. For example, we have little physical strength to perform virtuous actions, and little mental energy to memorize, contemplate and meditate. We cannot attend teachings that are given in places that are hard to reach or uncomfortable to inhabit. We cannot help others in ways that require physical strength and good health. Deprivations such as these often make old people very sad.

When we grow old, we become like someone who is blind and deaf. We cannot see clearly, and we need stronger and stronger glasses until we can no longer read. We cannot hear clearly, and so it becomes more and more difficult to listen to music or to the television, or to hear what others are saying. Our memory fades. All activities, worldly and spiritual, become more difficult. If we practice meditation, it becomes harder for us to gain realizations because our memory and concentration are too weak. We cannot apply ourself to study. Thus, if we have not learned and trained in spiritual practices when we were younger, the only thing to do when we grow old is to develop regret and wait for the Lord of Death to come.

When we are old we cannot derive the same enjoyment from the things we used to enjoy, such as food, drink and sex. We are too weak to play games and we are often too exhausted even for entertainment. As our life span runs out, we cannot join young people in their activities. When they travel around, we have to stay behind. No one wants to take us with them when we are old, and no one wants to visit us. Even our own grandchildren do not want to stay with us for very long. Old people often think to themselves, "How wonderful it would be if young people would stay with me; we could go out for walks and I could show them things," but young people do not want to be included in their plans. As their life draws to an end, old people experience the sorrow of abandonment and loneliness. They have many special sorrows.

DEATH

Our birth also gives rise to the sufferings of death. If during our life we have worked hard to acquire possessions, and if we have become very attached to them, we will experience great suffering at the time of death, thinking, "Now I have to leave all my precious possessions behind." Even now we find it difficult to lend one of our most treasured possessions to someone else, let alone to give it away. No wonder we become so miserable when we realize that in the hands of death we must abandon everything.

When we die, we have to part from even our closest friends. We have to leave our partner, even though we may have been together for years and never spent a day apart. If we are very attached to our friends we will experience great misery at the time of death, but all we will be able to do is hold their hands. We will not be able to halt the process of death, even if they plead with us not to die. Usually when we are very attached to someone we feel jealous if he or she leaves us on our own and spends time with someone else, but when we die we will have to leave our friends with others forever. We will have to leave everyone, including our family and all the people who have helped us in this life.

When we die, this body that we have cherished and cared for in so many ways will have to be left behind. It will become mindless like a stone, and will be buried in the ground or cremated. If we do not have the inner protection of spiritual experience, at the time of death we will experience fear and distress, as well as physical pain.

When our consciousness departs from our body at death, all the potentialities we have accumulated in our mind by performing virtuous and non-virtuous actions will go with it. Other than these we cannot take anything out of this world. All other things deceive us. Death ends all our activities—our conversation, our eating, our meeting with friends, our sleep. Everything draws to a close on the day of our death and we must leave all things behind, even the rings on our fingers. In Tibet beggars carry a stick to defend themselves against dogs. To understand the complete deprivation of death, we should remember that at the time of death beggars have to leave even this old stick, the most meager of human possessions. All over the world, we can see that names carved on stone are the only possessions of the dead.

OTHER TYPES OF SUFFERING

We also have to experience the sufferings of separation, having to encounter what we do not like and not fulfilling our wishes—which include the sufferings of poverty, and of being harmed by humans and non-humans, and by water, fire, wind and earth. Before the final separation at the time of death we often have to experience temporary separation from the people and things we like, which causes us mental pain. We may have to leave our country where all our friends and relatives live, or we may have to leave the job we like. We may lose our reputation. Many times in this life we have to experience the misery of departing from the people we like, or forsaking and losing the things we find pleasant and attractive; but when we die we have to part forever from all our companions and enjoyments, and from all the outer and inner conditions for our pure spiritual practice, or Dharma practice, of this life.

We often have to meet and live with people whom we do not like, or encounter situations that we find unpleasant. Sometimes we may find ourself in a very dangerous situation such as in a fire or a flood, or where there is violence such as in a riot or a battle. Our lives are full of less extreme situations that we find annoying. Sometimes we are prevented from doing the things we want to do. On a sunny day we may set off for the beach but find ourself stuck in a traffic jam. We continually experience interference from our inner demon of delusions, which disturbs our mind and our spiritual practices. There are countless conditions that frustrate our plans and prevent us from doing what we want. It is as if we are living in a thorn bush—whenever we try to move, we are wounded by circumstances. People and things are like thorns piercing our flesh and no situation ever feels entirely comfortable. The more desires and plans we have, the more frustrations we experience. The more we want certain situations, the more we find ourself stuck in situations we do not want. Every desire seems to invite its own obstacle. Undesired situations befall us without our looking for them. In fact, the only things that come effortlessly are the things we do not want. No one wants to die, but death comes effortlessly. No one wants to be sick, but sickness comes effortlessly. Because we have taken rebirth without freedom or control, we have an impure body and inhabit an impure environment, and so undesirable things pour in upon us. In samsara, this kind of experience is entirely natural.

We have countless desires, but no matter how much effort we make we never feel that we have satisfied them. Even when we get what we want, we do not get it in the way we want. We possess the object but we do not derive satisfaction from possessing it. For example, we may dream of becoming wealthy, but if we actually become wealthy our life is not the way we imagined it would be, and we do not feel that we have fulfilled our desire. This is because our desires do not decrease as our wealth increases. The more wealth we have, the more we desire. The wealth we seek is unfindable because we seek an amount that will satiate our desires, and no amount of wealth can do that. To make things worse, in obtaining the object of our desire we create new occasions for discontent. With every object we desire come other objects we do not want. For example, with wealth come taxes, insecurity and complicated financial affairs. These unwished for side effects prevent us from ever feeling fully satisfied. Similarly, we may dream of going on a tropical vacation, and we may actually go there on vacation, but the experience is never quite what we expect, and with our vacation come other things such as sunburn and great expense.

If we examine our desires we will see that they are excessive. We want all the best things in samsara—the best job, the best partner, the best reputation, the best house, the best car, the best vacation. Anything that is not the best leaves us with a feeling of disappointment—still searching for but not finding what we want. No worldly enjoyment, however, can give us the complete and perfect satisfaction we desire. Better things are always being produced. Everywhere, new advertisements announce that the very best thing has just arrived on the market, but a few days later another best thing arrives that is better than the best thing of a few days ago. There is no end of new things to captivate our desires.

Children in school can never satisfy their own or their parents' ambitions. Even if they become first in their class, they feel they cannot be content unless they do the same the following year. If they go on to be successful in their jobs, their ambitions will be as strong as ever. There is no point at which they can rest, feeling that they are completely satisfied with what they have done.

We may think that at least people who lead a simple life in the country must be content, but if we look at their situation we will find that even farmers search for but do not find what they want. Their lives are full of problems and anxieties, and they do not enjoy real peace and satisfaction. Their livelihoods depend upon many uncertain factors beyond their control, such as the weather. Farmers have no more freedom from discontent than businesspeople who live and work in the city. Businesspeople look well-dressed and efficient as they set off to work each morning carrying their briefcases but, although they look so smooth on the outside, in their hearts they carry many dissatisfactions. They are still searching for but not finding what they want.

If we reflect on this situation we may decide that we can find what we are searching for by abandoning all our possessions. We can see, however, that even poor people are looking for but not finding what they seek, and many poor people have difficulty in finding the most basic necessities of life; millions of people in the world experience the sufferings of extreme poverty.

We cannot avoid the suffering of dissatisfaction by frequently changing our situation. We may think that if we keep getting a new partner or a new job, or keep traveling around, we will eventually find what we want; but even if we were to travel to every place on the globe, and have a new lover in every town, we would still be seeking another place and another lover. In samsara, there is no real fulfillment of our desires.

Whenever we see anyone in a high or low position, male or female, they differ only in appearance, dress, behavior and status. In essence they are all equal—they all experience problems in their lives. Whenever we have a problem, it is easy to think that it is caused by our particular circumstances, and that if we were to change our circumstances our problem would disappear. We blame other people, our friends, our food, our government, our times, the weather, society, history and so forth. However, external circumstances such as these are not the main causes of our problems. We need to recognize that all the physical suffering and mental pain we experience are the consequences of our taking a rebirth that is contaminated by the inner poison of delusions. Human beings have to experience various kinds of human suffering because they have taken a contaminated human rebirth; animals have to experience animal suffering because they have taken a contaminated animal rebirth; and hungry ghosts and hell beings have to experience their own sufferings because they have taken contaminated rebirth as hungry ghosts and hell beings. Even gods are not free from suffering because they too have taken a contaminated rebirth. Just as a person trapped inside a raging fire develops intense fear, so we should develop intense fear of the unbearable sufferings of the endless cycle of impure life. This fear is also actual renunciation and arises from our wisdom.

In conclusion, having contemplated the above explanation we should think:

There is no benefit in denying the sufferings of future lives; when they actually descend upon me it will be too late to protect myself from them. Therefore I definitely need to prepare protection now, while I have this human life that gives me the opportunity to liberate myself permanently from the sufferings of my countless future lives. If I do not apply effort to accomplish this, but allow my human life to become empty of meaning, there is no greater deception and no greater foolishness. I must put effort now into liberating myself permanently from the sufferings of my countless future lives.

We hold this determination and we remain on it single-pointedly for as long as possible. We should practice this meditation continually until we develop the spontaneous wish to liberate ourself permanently from the sufferings of countless future lives. This is the actual realization of renunciation. The moment we develop this realization we enter the path to liberation. In this context, liberation refers to the supreme permanent peace of mind known as "nirvana," which gives us pure and everlasting happiness.

Once we have attained nirvana, we will never again experience contaminated environments, enjoyments, bodies or minds. We will experience everything as pure because our mind will have become pure, free from the inner poison of delusions. The first step toward the attainment of nirvana is gaining the realization of renunciation, the spontaneous wish to abandon samsara, or contaminated rebirth. We then abandon samsara and attain nirvana by gaining a direct realization of emptiness, the ultimate nature of phenomena, which will be explained in detail in the chapter on *Ultimate Bodhichitta*.

Apply great effort to attaining enlightenment

A Common Spiritual Practice for Everyone

In this practice we need to perform virtuous, or positive, actions because these are the root of our future happiness; we need to abandon non-virtuous or negative actions because these are the root of our future suffering; and we need to control our delusions because these are the root of our contaminated rebirths. In addition we need to develop faith, sense of shame, consideration for others, non-attachment, non-hatred, non-ignorance and effort.

FAITH

In the practice of faith we need to develop and maintain three types of faith: admiring faith, believing faith and wishing faith. Admiring faith is the nature of rejoicing—rejoicing in the complete purity of enlightened beings, in their teachings and in the realizations of their teachings. Believing faith is the nature of correct belief—believing that enlightened beings are actually present in front of us, even though we do not see them, and believing that their teachings and the realizations of their teachings are the actual refuge that directly protects living beings from suffering and fear. Wishing faith is the nature of wishing—wishing for ourself to become just like enlightened beings, wishing to put their teachings into practice and wishing to attain realizations of their teachings.

Since faith is the root of all pure spiritual attainments, it should be our main practice. While the famous Buddhist Master Atisha was in Tibet, a man once approached him asking for spiritual instructions. Atisha remained silent and so the man, thinking that he had not been heard, repeated his request very loudly. Atisha then replied, "I have good hearing, but you need to have faith."

Enlightened beings are called "Buddhas," their teachings are called "Dharma," and the practitioners who have gained realizations of these teachings are called "Sangha." These are known as the "Three Jewels"—Buddha Jewel, Dharma Jewel and Sangha Jewel—and are the objects of faith and refuge. They are called "Jewels" because they are very precious. In dependence upon seeing the fears and sufferings of samsara, and developing strong faith and conviction in the power of Buddha, Dharma and Sangha to protect us, we make the determination to rely upon the Three Jewels. This is the simple way of going for refuge to Buddha, Dharma and Sangha.

Without faith our mind is like a burnt seed, for just as a burnt seed cannot germinate, so knowledge without faith can never produce spiritual realizations. Faith in spiritual teachings or Dharma induces a strong intention to practice them, and this in turn induces effort. With effort we can accomplish anything.

Faith is essential. If we have no faith, even if we master profound teachings and become capable of skillful analysis, our mind will remain untamed because we will not be putting these teachings into practice. No matter how well we understand spiritual teachings on an intellectual level, if we have no faith this will never help us to reduce our problems of anger and other delusions. We may even become proud of our knowledge, thereby actually increasing our delusions. Spiritual knowledge without faith will not help us purify our negativity. We may even create heavy negative karma by using our spiritual position for money, reputation, power or political authority. Faith should therefore be cherished as extremely precious. Just as space pervades all places, so faith pervades all virtuous states of mind. With faith in enlightenment we will develop the intention to attain it, with this intention we will develop effort, and with effort we will accomplish it.

If practitioners have strong faith, then even if they make some mistake they will still receive benefits. Once in India there was a famine in which many people died. One old woman went to see her Spiritual Guide and said, "Please show me a way of saving my life." Her Spiritual Guide advised her to eat stones. The woman asked, "But how can I make stones edible?" and he replied, "If you recite the mantra of the goddess Tsunda, you will be able to cook the stones." He taught her the mantra, but he made a slight mistake. He taught OM BALE BULE BUNDE SÖHA, instead of OM TZALE TZULE TZUNDE SÖHA. However, the old woman placed great faith in this mantra and, reciting it with concentration, she cooked stones and ate them.

This old woman's son was a monk and he began to worry about his mother, and so he went home to see her. He was astonished to find her plump and well. He said, "Mother, how is it that you are so healthy when even young people are dying of starvation?" His mother explained that she had been eating stones. Her son asked, "How have you been able to cook stones?" and she told him the mantra that she had been given to recite. Her son quickly spotted the mistake and declared, "Your mantra is wrong! The mantra of the goddess Tsunda is OM TZALE TZULE TZUNDE SÖHA." When she heard this, the old woman was plunged into doubt. She tried reciting both the mantras, but now neither of them would work because her faith was destroyed.

To develop and increase our faith in spiritual teachings, we need a special way of listening and reading. For example, when we are reading a book that reveals pure spiritual practices we should think:

This book is a Dharma mirror that shows all the faults of my bodily, verbal and mental actions. By showing all my shortcomings, it provides me with a great opportunity to overcome them and thereby remove all faults from my mental continuum.

This book is supreme medicine. Through practicing the instructions contained within it I can cure myself of the diseases of the delusions, which are the real source of all my problems and suffering.

This book is the wisdom light that dispels the darkness of my ignorance, the divine eyes with which I can see the actual path to liberation and enlightenment, and the supreme Spiritual Guide from whom I can receive the most profound and liberating advice.

It does not matter whether the author is famous or not—if a book contains pure spiritual teachings it is like a Dharma mirror, supreme medicine, wisdom light and divine eyes, and it is a supreme Spiritual Guide. If we always read Dharma books and listen to teachings with this special recognition, our faith and wisdom will definitely increase. Contemplating in this way we can develop and maintain faith in spiritual teachings, in Teachers who show us spiritual paths and in our spiritual friends. This will make it easier for us to make progress in our spiritual practice.

SENSE OF SHAME AND CONSIDERATION FOR OTHERS

The difference between sense of shame and consideration for others is that with the former we avoid inappropriate actions for reasons that concern ourself, whereas with the latter we avoid inappropriate actions for reasons that concern others. Thus, sense of shame restrains us from committing inappropriate actions by reminding us that it is not suitable to engage in such actions because, for example, we are a spiritual practitioner, an ordained person, a spiritual Teacher, an adult and so on; or because we do not want to experience negative results from our actions. If we think, "It is not right for me to kill insects because this will cause me to experience suffering in the future," and then make a firm decision not to kill them, we are motivated by sense of shame. Our sense of shame guards us against committing negative actions by appealing to our conscience and to the standards of behavior that we feel to be appropriate. If we are unable to generate sense of shame, we will find it extremely difficult to practice moral discipline, the basis upon which spiritual realizations grow.

Examples of consideration for others are holding back from saying something unpleasant because it will upset another person, or giving up fishing because of the suffering it causes the fish. We need to practice consideration whenever we are with other people by being mindful of how our behavior might disturb or harm them. Our desires are endless, and many of them would cause other people much distress if we acted them out. Therefore, before we act on a wish we should consider whether it will disturb or harm others, and if we think that it will we should not do it. Consideration for others is being concerned with others' welfare.

Consideration for others is important for everyone. If we are considerate, others will like and respect us, and our relationships with our family and friends will be harmonious and long lasting. Without consideration for others, however, relationships quickly deteriorate. Consideration prevents others from losing faith in us, and is the basis for developing a mind of rejoicing.

Whether we are a good person or a bad person depends upon whether or not we have sense of shame and consideration for others. Without these two qualities our daily behavior will soon become negative and cause others to turn away from us. Sense of shame and consideration are like beautiful clothes that cause others to be attracted to us. Without them we are like a naked person whom everyone tries to avoid.

Both sense of shame and consideration for others are characterized by a determination to refrain from engaging in negative and inappropriate actions, and from breaking vows and commitments. This determination is the very essence of moral discipline. We generate and sustain this determination by contemplating the benefits of practicing moral discipline and the dangers of breaking it. In particular, we need to remember that without moral discipline we have no chance of taking any higher rebirth, let alone of attaining nirvana.

Sense of shame and consideration for others are the foundations of moral discipline, which is the basis for gaining spiritual realizations and the main cause of higher rebirth. Nagarjuna said that whereas enjoyments come from giving, the happiness of higher rebirth comes from moral discipline. The results of practicing giving can be experienced in a higher realm or a lower realm, depending upon whether or not we practice it in conjunction with moral discipline. If we do not practice moral discipline our action of giving will ripen in a lower realm. For example, as the result of actions of giving they accumulated in previous lives, some pet dogs have far better conditions than many humans—pampered by their owners, given special food and soft cushions and treated like a favorite child. Despite these comforts, these poor creatures have nevertheless taken rebirth in a lower life form with the body and mind of an animal. They have neither the bodily nor the mental basis to continue with their practice of giving or any other virtuous action. They cannot understand the meaning of spiritual teachings, nor transform their minds. Once their previous karma of giving is exhausted through enjoying such good conditions, because they have had no opportunity to create more virtuous actions their enjoyments come to an end, and in a future life they will experience poverty and starvation. This is because they did not practice giving in conjunction with moral discipline and so did not create the cause for a higher rebirth. Through practicing sense of shame and consideration for others, we can abandon non-virtuous or inappropriate actions, the root of our future sufferings.

What do "lower rebirth" and "higher rebirth" mean? If we take rebirth as a hell being, hungry ghost or animal we have no opportunity to understand and practice pure spiritual teachings, which lead us to pure and everlasting happiness. From this point of view they are called "lower rebirths." On the other hand if we take rebirth as a human being, demigod or god we have the opportunity to understand and practice pure spiritual teachings, so from this point of view these rebirths are called "higher rebirths." If we have no opportunity to understand, contemplate and meditate on the meaning of spiritual teachings we will have to remain with an empty life in this life, and in life after life, endlessly, without any meaning and experiencing only suffering.

NON-ATTACHMENT

Non-attachment in this context is the mind of renunciation, which is the opponent of attachment, or uncontrolled desire. Renunciation is not a wish to abandon our family, friends, home, job and so forth, and become like a beggar; instead, it is a mind that functions to stop attachment to worldly pleasures and that seeks liberation from contaminated rebirth.

We must learn to stop our attachment through the practice of renunciation or it will be a serious obstacle to our pure spiritual practice. Just as a bird cannot fly if it has stones tied to its legs, so we cannot make progress on the spiritual path if we are tightly tied down by the chains of attachment.

The time to practice renunciation is now, before our death. We need to reduce our attachment to worldly pleasures by realizing that they are deceptive and cannot give real satisfaction. In reality, they cause us only suffering. This human life with all its suffering and problems is a great opportunity for us to improve both our renunciation and our compassion. We should not waste this precious opportunity. The realization of renunciation is the gateway through which we enter the spiritual path to liberation, or nirvana. Without renunciation, it is impossible even to enter the path to the supreme happiness of nirvana, let alone progress along it.

To develop and increase our renunciation, we can repeatedly contemplate the following:

Because my consciousness is beginningless, I have taken countless rebirths in samsara. I have already had countless bodies. If they were all gathered together, they would fill the entire world; and all the blood and other bodily fluids that have flowed through them would form an ocean. So great has been my suffering in all these previous lives that I have shed enough tears of sorrow to form another ocean.

In every single life, I have experienced the sufferings of sickness, aging, death, being separated from those I love and being unable to fulfill my wishes. If I do not attain permanent liberation from suffering now, I will have to experience these sufferings again and again in countless future lives.

Contemplating this, from the depths of our heart we make a strong determination to abandon attachment to worldly pleasures and attain permanent liberation from the cycle of contaminated rebirth, samsara. By putting this determination into practice, we can control our attachment, or uncontrolled desire, and thereby solve our daily problems.

NON-HATRED

Non-hatred in this context is affectionate love, which is the opponent of hatred. Many people experience problems because their love is mixed with attachment; for such people, the more their "love" increases, the more their desirous attachment grows. If their desires are not fulfilled, they become upset and angry. If the object of their attachment, such as their lover, even so much as talks to another person, they may become jealous or aggressive. This clearly indicates that their "love" is not real love but attachment. Real love can never be a cause of anger; it is the opposite of anger and can never cause problems. If we love everyone as a mother loves her dearest child, there will be no basis for any problems to arise because our mind will always be at peace. Love is the real inner protection against suffering.

What is affectionate love? When, from the depths of our heart, without attachment, we feel very close, warm and happy toward someone, this is affectionate love. It makes our mind peaceful and balanced, free from anger and attachment. Thus, it is also called "equanimity."

Developing equanimity is like plowing a field—clearing our mind of the rocks and weeds of anger and attachment, thereby making it possible for true love to grow. We need to learn to develop affectionate love for everyone, so that our own problems of anger and attachment will cease and we can benefit others effectively. Whenever we meet anyone, we should be happy to see them and try to generate a warm feeling toward them. Through continual training we should try to become familiar with this practice. In this way we will maintain a good heart all the time, and this will give us good results in this life and in our countless future lives.

On the basis of this feeling of affectionate love, we should develop cherishing love so that we genuinely come to feel that they are precious and important. If we cherish others in this way, it will not be difficult to develop wishing love, wanting to give them happiness. Through learning to love everyone, we can solve all our daily problems of anger and jealousy and our life will become happy and meaningful. A more detailed explanation of how to develop and increase our love will be given in later chapters.

NON-IGNORANCE

Non-ignorance, in this context, is the wisdom that realizes emptiness, which is the opponent of the ignorance of self-grasping. Emptiness is not nothingness but the ultimate nature of phenomena, and is a very meaningful object. A detailed explanation of this can be found in the chapter *Ultimate Bodhichitta*.

We should know that normally when ordinary people see things that are attractive or beautiful they develop attachment, when they see things that are unattractive or unpleasant they develop hatred, and when they see things that are neutral, neither attractive nor unattractive, they develop the ignorance of self-grasping. On the other hand, when those who engage in pure spiritual practice see things that are attractive or beautiful they develop and maintain non-attachment, when they see things that are unattractive or unpleasant they develop and maintain non-hatred, and when they see things that are neutral, neither attractive nor unattractive, they develop and maintain non-ignorance.

EFFORT

If we do not apply ourself to our spiritual practice, no one can grant us liberation from suffering. We are often unrealistic in our expectations. We wish we could accomplish high attainments swiftly without having to apply any effort, and we want to be happy without having to create the cause of happiness. Unwilling to endure even the slightest discomfort we want all our suffering to cease, and while living in the jaws of the Lord of Death we wish to remain like a long-life god. No matter how much we long for these wishes to be fulfilled, they never will be. If we do not apply energy and effort to our spiritual practices, all the hopes we have for happiness will be in vain.

Effort in this context is a mind that delights in virtuous practice. Its function is to make our mind happy to engage in virtuous actions. With effort we delight in actions such as listening to, reading, contemplating and meditating on spiritual teachings, and engaging in the path to liberation. Through effort we will eventually attain the ultimate supreme goal of human life.

By applying effort in our meditation, we develop mental suppleness. Even though we may experience problems such as heaviness, tiredness or other forms of mental or physical discomfort when we first begin to meditate, we should nevertheless patiently persevere and try to become familiar with our practice. Gradually, as our meditation improves, it will induce mental suppleness—our mind and body will feel light, healthy and tireless, and be free from obstacles to concentration. All our meditations will become easy and effective, and we will have no difficulty in making progress.

However difficult meditation may be at the beginning, we should never give up hope. Instead, we should engage in the practice of moral discipline, which protects us from gross distractions and acts as the basis for developing pure concentration. Moral discipline also strengthens mindfulness, which is the life of concentration.

We need to abandon laziness—laziness arising from attachment to worldly pleasures, laziness arising from attachment to distracting activities and laziness arising from discouragement. With laziness, we will accomplish nothing. As long as we remain with laziness, the door to spiritual attainments is closed to us. Laziness makes our human life meaningless. It deceives us and causes us to wander aimlessly in samsara. If we can break free from the influence of laziness and immerse ourself deeply in spiritual training, we will quickly attain our spiritual goal. Training in spiritual paths is like constructing a large building—it demands continuous effort. If we allow our effort to be interrupted by laziness, we will never see the completion of our work.

Our spiritual attainments therefore depend upon our own effort. An intellectual understanding of spiritual teachings is not sufficient to carry us to the supreme happiness of liberation—we must overcome our laziness and put our knowledge into practice. Buddha said:

If you have only effort you have all attainments,
But if you have only laziness you have nothing.

A person without great spiritual knowledge who nevertheless applies effort consistently will gradually attain all virtuous qualities. However, someone who knows a great deal and has only one fault—laziness—will not be able to increase his or her good qualities and gain experience of spiritual paths. Understanding all of this, we should apply joyful effort to the study and practice of pure spiritual teachings in our everyday life.

Be victorious over the enemy of your delusions

Meaningful Objects

*A*ny object that through our understanding of it gives us great meaning is a meaningful object.

To solve our human problems and to enable us to find everlasting peace and happiness, we should first know what is the real nature of our problems and what are their main causes. Our problems do not exist outside our mind. The real nature of our problems is our unpleasant feelings, which are part of our mind. When our car, for example, has a problem, we often say, "I have a problem," but in reality it is not our problem but the car's problem, which is an outer problem. Our problem is an inner problem. By differentiating between inner and outer problems in this way, we can understand that the real nature of our problems is our own feelings, which are part of our mind.

All our problems—our unpleasant feelings—come from our delusions of attachment and self-grasping ignorance; therefore these delusions are the main causes of our problems. We have strong attachment to the fulfillment of our own wishes and for this aim we work very hard throughout our life, experiencing many difficulties and problems. When our wishes are not fulfilled we experience unhappiness and depression, which often causes us to become angry, creating more problems for both ourself and others. We can understand this clearly through our own experience. When we lose our friends, job, status, or reputation and so forth, we experience pain and many difficulties. This is because of our strong attachment to these things. If we had no such attachment, there would be no basis for experiencing suffering and problems at their loss.

Due to strong attachment to our own views, we immediately experience the inner problem of unpleasant feelings when someone opposes them. This causes us to become angry, which leads to arguments and conflicts with others, and this in turn gives rise to further problems such as those arising from fighting and even war. Most political problems experienced throughout the world are caused by people with strong attachment to their own views. Many problems are also caused by people's attachment to their religious views.

In previous lives, because of our attachment to fulfilling our own wishes we performed many different actions that harmed other living beings. As a result of these actions, we now experience many different problems and sufferings in our life.

If we look with wisdom in the mirror of our mind, we can see how our attachment, anger and especially our self-grasping ignorance are the causes of all our problems and sufferings. We will definitely realize that unless we control these delusions there is no other method to solve our human problems. Pure spiritual teachings, or Dharma, are the only method to control our delusions of attachment, anger and self-grasping ignorance. If we sincerely put these teachings into practice, we will definitely solve our human problems and find the real meaning of our life.

In general, everyone who has physical or mental pain, even animals, understands their own suffering. But what we really need to understand is the sufferings of our countless future lives. Through understanding this, we will develop a strong wish to liberate ourself from them. This is important for everybody because, if we have the wish to liberate ourself from the sufferings of future lives, we will definitely use our present human life for the freedom and happiness of our countless future lives. There is no greater meaning than this.

If we do not have this wish, we will waste our precious human life only for the freedom and happiness of this one short life. This would be foolish because our intention and actions would be no different from the intention and actions of animals who are concerned with this life alone. The great Yogi Milarepa once said to a hunter called Gonpo Dorje:

> Your body is human but your mind is that of an animal.
> You, a human being, who possess an animal's mind, please listen to my song.

Usually we believe that solving the problems and sufferings of our present life is most important, and we dedicate our whole life for this purpose. In reality, the duration of the problems and sufferings of this life is very short; if we die tomorrow they will end tomorrow. However, since the duration of the problems and sufferings of future lives is endless, the freedom and happiness of our future lives is vastly more important than the freedom and happiness of this one short life.

We may have the sincere wish to avoid suffering permanently, but we never think to abandon our delusions. However, without controlling and abandoning our delusions, it is impossible to attain permanent liberation from suffering and problems. This is because delusions, principally self-grasping ignorance, are the source of all our suffering and the main cause of all our problems.

First we should recognize that the principal delusion is our self-grasping, which always abides at our heart destroying our inner peace. Its nature is a wrong awareness that mistakenly believes ourself and others to be truly, or inherently, existent. This is an ignorant mind because in reality things do not exist inherently—they exist as mere imputations. Because the foolish mind of self-grasping believes or grasps at "I," "mine" and all other phenomena as truly existent, we develop attachment to those things we like and hatred for those we do not like. We then perform various actions that harm other living beings and, as a result, we experience various sufferings and problems throughout this life and in life after life; this is the fundamental reason why we experience so many problems. Because our sense of truly existent "I" and "mine" is so strong, our self-grasping also acts as the basis of all our daily problems.

Self-grasping can be likened to a poisonous tree, other delusions to its branches, and all our sufferings to its fruits; it is the fundamental source of all other delusions and all our suffering and problems. Understanding this, we should apply great effort to recognize, reduce and finally abandon this ignorance completely.

We know that generally, from time to time, everybody experiences a temporary cessation of particular sufferings. For instance, those who are physically healthy are experiencing a temporary cessation of sickness. However, this is not enough because it is only temporary. Later they will have to experience the suffering of sickness again and again, in this life and in countless future lives. Every living being without exception has to experience the cycle of the sufferings of sickness, aging, death and rebirth, in life after life, endlessly. Following Buddha's example, we should develop strong renunciation for this endless cycle of suffering. When Buddha was living in the palace with his family, he saw how his people were constantly experiencing these sufferings and he made the strong determination to attain enlightenment, the supreme permanent cessation of suffering, and to lead every living being to this state.

Buddha did not encourage us to abandon daily activities that provide necessary conditions for living, or that prevent poverty, environmental problems, particular diseases and so forth. However, no matter how successful we are in these activities, we will never achieve permanent cessation of such problems. We will still have to experience them in our countless future lives and, even in this life, although we work very hard to prevent these problems, the sufferings of poverty, environmental pollution and disease are increasing throughout the world. Furthermore, because of the power of modern technology there are now many great dangers developing in the world that have never been experienced before. Therefore, we should not be satisfied with a merely temporary freedom from particular sufferings, but apply great effort to attaining permanent freedom while we have this opportunity.

We should consider the preciousness of our human life. Because of their previous deluded views that denied the value of spiritual practice, those who have taken rebirth as animals, for example, have no opportunity to engage in spiritual practice that alone gives rise to a meaningful life. Since it is impossible for them to listen to, understand, contemplate and meditate on spiritual instructions, their present animal rebirth itself is an obstacle. Only human beings are free from such obstacles and have all the necessary conditions for engaging in spiritual paths, which alone lead to everlasting peace and happiness. This combination of freedom and possession of necessary conditions is the special characteristic that makes our human life so precious.

Because self-grasping is the root of suffering, if we do not attain the permanent cessation of self-grasping we will never attain the permanent cessation of suffering. How can we attain the permanent cessation of self-grasping? First we should know that there are nine different types of self-grasping. These are: self-grasping of the desire realm; self-grasping of the first, second, third and fourth form realms; and self-grasping of the first, second, third and fourth formless realms. The first is the most gross level of self-grasping, and they progressively become more and more subtle, so the ninth, called the "self-grasping of the Peak of Samsara" is the most subtle.

Through continually meditating on emptiness with the motivation of renunciation we will gradually abandon these nine types of self-grasping and finally, when we abandon the self-grasping of the Peak of Samsara, we will attain the permanent cessation of our self-grasping and all other delusions. At the same time we will attain the permanent cessation of all the sufferings of this life and countless future lives. This permanent cessation of suffering and its cause, self-grasping, is actual liberation and is known as "nirvana," the supreme permanent inner peace. Thus we will have accomplished the real meaning of human life.

Those who have attained liberation, or nirvana, always abide in a Pure Land in which they experience a pure environment, pure enjoyments, pure bodies and pure minds. This is because their minds are completely pure, free from the stains of all delusions. They also benefit living beings through their emanations.

Liberation cannot be attained without applying effort—just waiting and thinking that one day someone will bestow upon us permanent liberation from all problems. It is only through following the path to liberation that we will attain nirvana. The path to liberation is not an external path, but an inner path. We know that external paths lead from one place to another, whereas the path to liberation is an inner path that leads from samsara to a Pure Land. An inner path is a mental action, and is either virtuous or non-virtuous; it cannot be a neutral action. Mental actions that are non-virtuous lead us to any of the three lower rebirths: rebirth as an animal, hungry ghost or hell being. Mental actions that are contaminated virtue lead us to any of the three higher rebirths: rebirth as a human being, demigod or god. Mental actions motivated by renunciation lead us to the state of pure and everlasting happiness of liberation, nirvana.

Renunciation is the gateway through which we enter the path to liberation. The actual path to liberation has five levels: the path of accumulation, the path of preparation, the path of seeing, the path of meditation and the Path of No More Learning. The practice of these five paths are contained within the practice of three higher trainings: training in moral discipline, training in concentration or meditation, and training in the wisdom realizing emptiness, all motivated by renunciation—the sincere wish to permanently liberate ourself from suffering and its cause, self-grasping. We need to sincerely practice the three higher trainings because they are the main path to liberation.

The nature of moral discipline is abandoning inappropriate actions, maintaining pure behavior and performing every action correctly with a virtuous motivation. Moral discipline is most important for everybody in order to prevent future problems for oneself and for others. It makes us pure because it makes our actions pure. We ourself need to be clean and pure; just having a clean body is not enough, since our body is not our self. Moral discipline is like a great earth that supports and nurtures the crops of spiritual realizations, Dharma realizations. Without practicing moral discipline, it is very difficult to make progress in spiritual trainings. Training in higher moral discipline is learning to be deeply familiar with the practice of moral discipline, motivated by renunciation.

The second higher training is training in higher concentration. The nature of concentration is preventing distractions and concentrating on virtuous objects. It is very important to train in concentration, as with distractions we cannot accomplish anything. Training in higher concentration is learning to be deeply familiar with the ability to stop distractions and concentrate on virtuous objects, motivated by renunciation. With regard to any Dharma practice, if our concentration is clear and strong, it is very easy to make progress. Normally our main problem is distractions. The practice of moral discipline prevents gross distractions, and concentration prevents subtle distractions; together they give rise to quick results in our Dharma practice.

The third higher training is training in higher wisdom. The nature of wisdom is a virtuous intelligent mind whose functions are to dispel confusion and to understand meaningful objects. Many people are very intelligent in destroying their enemies, caring for their families, finding what they want and so forth, but this is not wisdom. Even animals have such intelligence. Worldly intelligence is deceptive, whereas wisdom will never deceive us. It is our inner Spiritual Guide that leads us to correct paths, and is the divine eye through which we can see past and future lives and the special connection between our actions and our experiences, known as "karma." The subject of karma is very extensive and subtle, and we can understand it only through wisdom. Training in higher wisdom is meditating on wisdom realizing emptiness, motivated by renunciation. Having realized emptiness we transform our mind into the wisdom realizing emptiness and remain on it single-pointedly for as long as possible.

The practice of the three higher trainings is the scientific method to attain the permanent cessation of suffering and its cause, self-grasping. This can be understood by the following analogy. When we cut a tree using a saw, the saw alone cannot cut the tree without the use of our hands, which in turn depends upon our body. Training in higher moral discipline is like our body, training in higher concentration is like our hands and training in higher wisdom is like the saw. By using these three together, we can cut the poisonous tree of our self-grasping ignorance, and automatically all other delusions – its branches – and all our sufferings and problems – its fruits – will cease completely. Then we will have attained the permanent cessation of the sufferings of this life and countless future lives. We will have solved all our human problems and accomplished the real meaning of our life.

PART TWO

Progress

Benefit others by turning the Wheel of Dharma

Learning to Cherish Others

From the depths of our heart we want to be happy all the time, but we are not usually very concerned with the happiness and freedom of others. In reality, however, our own happiness and suffering are insignificant compared to that of other living beings. Others are countless, whereas we ourself are just one single person. Understanding this, we must learn to cherish others and accomplish the ultimate, supreme goal of human life.

What is the ultimate, supreme goal of human life? We should ask ourself what we consider to be most important—what do we wish for, strive for or daydream about? For some people it is material possessions, such as a large house with all the latest luxuries, a fast car or a well-paid job. For others it is reputation, good looks, power, excitement or adventure. Many try to find the meaning of their life in relationships with people who are objects of their desire. All these things can make us superficially happy for a short while, but they can also cause us much worry and suffering. They can never give us the pure and everlasting happiness that all of us, in our heart of hearts, long for. Since we cannot take them with us when we die, if we have made them the principal meaning of our life they will eventually let us down. As an end in themselves worldly attainments are hollow; they are not the real meaning of human life.

Of all worldly possessions the most precious is said to be the legendary wish-granting jewel. It is impossible to find such a jewel in these degenerate times, but in the past, when human beings had abundant merit, there used to be magical jewels that had the power to grant wishes. These jewels, however, could only fulfill wishes for contaminated happiness—they could never bestow the pure happiness that comes from a pure mind. Furthermore, a wish-granting jewel only had the power to grant wishes in one life—it could not protect its owner in his or her future lives. Thus, ultimately even a wish-granting jewel is deceptive.

The only thing that will never deceive us is the attainment of full enlightenment. What is enlightenment? It is the inner light of wisdom that is completely free from all mistaken appearance, and whose function is to bestow mental peace upon each and every living being every day. It is the source of the happiness of all living beings. A person who possesses this wisdom is an enlightened being. The terms "enlightened being" and "Buddha" are synonymous. With the exception of enlightened beings, all beings experience mistaken appearances all the time, day and night, even during sleep.

Whatever appears to us, we perceive as existing from its own side. This is mistaken appearance. We perceive "I" and "mine" as being inherently existent, and we grasp strongly, believing this appearance to be true. Due to this we perform many inappropriate actions that lead us to experience suffering. This is the fundamental reason why we experience suffering. Enlightened beings are completely free from mistaken appearances and the sufferings they produce.

It is only by attaining enlightenment that we can fulfill our deepest wish for pure and lasting happiness, for nothing in this impure world has the power to fulfill this wish. Only when we become a fully enlightened Buddha will we experience the profound and lasting peace that comes from a permanent cessation of all delusions and their imprints. We will be free from all faults and mental obscurations, and will possess the qualities needed to help all living beings directly. We will then be an object of refuge for all living beings. Through this understanding, we can clearly see that the attainment of enlightenment is the ultimate, supreme goal and real meaning of our precious human life. Since our main wish is to be happy all the time and to be completely free from all faults and suffering, we must develop the strong intention to attain enlightenment. We should think, "I need to attain enlightenment because in samsara, the cycle of impure life, there is no real happiness anywhere."

The main cause of enlightenment is bodhichitta, the spontaneous wish to attain enlightenment that is motivated by compassion for all living beings. A person who possesses this precious mind of bodhichitta is called a "Bodhisattva." The root of bodhichitta is compassion. Since the development of compassion depends upon cherishing others, the first step to the sublime happiness of enlightenment is learning to cherish others. A mother cherishes her children, and we may cherish our friends to a certain degree, but this cherishing is not impartial and is usually mixed with attachment. We need to develop a pure mind that cherishes all living beings without bias or partiality.

Each and every living being has within them the seed, or potential, to become a Buddha, a fully enlightened being—this is our Buddha nature. In Buddha's teachings we have found the best method to ripen this seed, or potential. What we need to do now is to put these teachings into practice. This is something that only human beings can do. Animals can gather resources, defeat their enemies and protect their families, but they can neither understand nor engage in the spiritual path. It would be a great shame if we were to use our human life only to achieve what animals can also achieve, and thereby waste this unique opportunity to become a source of benefit for all living beings.

We are faced with a choice: either we can continue to squander our life in pursuing worldly enjoyments that give no real satisfaction and disappear when we die, or we can dedicate our life to realizing our full spiritual potential. If we make great effort to practice the instructions contained within this book we will definitely attain enlightenment, but if we make no effort enlightenment will never happen naturally, no matter how long we wait. To follow the path to enlightenment there is no need to change our external lifestyle. We do not need to abandon our family, friends or enjoyments, and retire to a mountain cave. All we need to do is change the object of our cherishing.

Until now we have cherished ourself above all others, and for as long as we continue to do this our suffering will never end. However, if we learn to cherish all beings more than ourself we will soon enjoy the bliss of enlightenment. The path to enlightenment is really very simple—all we need to do is stop cherishing ourself and learn to cherish others. All other spiritual realizations will naturally follow from this.

Our instinctive view is that we are more important than everyone else, whereas the view of all enlightened beings is that it is others who are more important. Which of these views is more beneficial? In life after life, since beginningless time, we have been slaves to our self-cherishing mind. We have trusted it implicitly and obeyed its every command, believing that the way to solve our problems and find happiness is to put ourself before everyone else. We have worked so hard and for so long for our own sake, but what do we have to show for it? Have we solved all our problems and found the lasting happiness we desire? No. It is clear that pursuing our own selfish interests has deceived us. After having indulged our self-cherishing for so many lives, now is the time to realize that it simply does not work. Now is the time to switch the object of our cherishing from ourself to all living beings.

All enlightened beings have discovered that by abandoning self-cherishing and cherishing only others they came to experience true peace and happiness. If we practice the methods they taught, there is no reason why we should not be able to do the same. We cannot expect to change our mind overnight, but through practicing patiently and consistently the instructions on cherishing others, while at the same time accumulating merit, purifying negativity and receiving blessings, we can gradually replace our ordinary self-cherishing attitude with the sublime attitude of cherishing all living beings.

To achieve this we do not need to change our lifestyle, but we do need to change our views and intentions. Our ordinary view is that we are the center of the universe and that other people and things derive their significance principally from the way in which they affect us. Our car, for example, is important simply because it is *ours*, and our friends are important because they make *us* happy. Strangers, on the other hand, do not seem so important because they do not directly affect our happiness, and if a stranger's car is damaged or stolen we are not that concerned. As we will see in later chapters, this self-centered view of the world is based on ignorance and does not correspond to reality. This view is the source of all our ordinary, selfish intentions. It is precisely because we think "I am important, I need this, I deserve that" that we engage in negative actions, which result in an endless stream of problems for ourself and others.

By practicing these instructions, we can develop a realistic view of the world, based on an understanding of the equality and interdependence of all living beings. Once we view each and every living being as important we will naturally develop good intentions toward them. Whereas the mind that cherishes only ourself is the basis for all impure, samsaric experience, the mind that cherishes others is the basis for all the good qualities of enlightenment.

Cherishing others is not so difficult—all we need to do is understand why we should cherish others and then make a firm decision to do so. Through meditating on this decision we will develop a deep and powerful feeling of cherishing for all beings. We then carry this special feeling into our daily life.

There are two main reasons why we need to cherish all living beings. The first is that they have shown us immense kindness, and the second is that cherishing them has enormous benefits. These will now be explained.

THE KINDNESS OF OTHERS

We should contemplate the great kindness of all living beings. We can begin by remembering the kindness of our mother of this life; and then, by extension, we can remember the kindness of all other living beings, who, as will be explained below, have been our mothers in previous lives. If we cannot appreciate the kindness of our present mother, how will we ever be able to appreciate the kindness of all our previous mothers?

It is very easy to forget our mother's kindness, or to take it for granted and remember only the times when we think she harmed us; therefore we need to remember in detail how kind our mother has been to us from the very beginning of this life.

In the beginning our mother was kind in offering us a place of rebirth. Before we were conceived in her womb, we wandered from place to place as an intermediate state being—a being who is between death and rebirth—with nowhere to rest. We were blown by the winds of our karma without freedom to choose where we would go, and all our acquaintances were fleeting. We experienced great pain and fear, but from this state we were able to enter the safety of our mother's womb. Although we were an uninvited guest, when she knew that we had entered her womb our mother let us stay there. If she had wanted to evict us, she could have done so and we would not have been alive today to enjoy all our present opportunities. We are now able to develop the aspiration to attain the supreme happiness of enlightenment only because our mother was kind enough to let us stay in her womb. In winter, when it is cold and stormy outside, if someone invites us into their warm home and entertains us well, we consider this person to be extremely kind. How much kinder is our mother, who let us enter her own body and offered us such good hospitality there!

When we were in our mother's womb she protected us carefully, more carefully than she would guard a most precious jewel. In every situation she thought of our safety. She consulted doctors, exercised, ate special foods and nurtured us day and night for nine months; she was also mindful not to do anything that might damage the development of our physical or mental faculties. Because she looked after us so well, we were born with a normal and healthy body that we can use to accomplish so many good things.

At the time of our birth our mother experienced great pain, but when she saw us she felt happier than if someone had presented her with a superb treasure. Even during the agony of childbirth our welfare was foremost in her mind. When we were newly born, although we looked more like a frog than a human being, our mother loved us dearly. We were completely helpless, even more helpless than a newborn foal, who can at least stand up and feed as soon as it is born. We were as if blind, unable to identify our parents and we could not understand anything. If someone had been preparing to kill us, we would not have known.

We had no idea what we were doing. We could not even tell when we were urinating.

Who cared for and protected this scarcely human thing? It was our mother. She clothed it, cradled it and fed it with her own milk. She removed the filth from its body without feeling any disgust. Sometimes mothers remove the mucus from their baby's nose by using their own mouths because they do not want to cause the baby any pain by using their rough hands. Even when our mother had problems, she always showed us a loving expression and called us sweet names. While we were small our mother was constantly watchful. If she had forgotten us for even a short time, we might have met our death or been disabled for life. Each day of our early childhood our mother rescued us from many disasters, and she always considered things from the point of view of our own safety and well-being.

In the winter she would make sure that we were warm and had good clothing, even when she herself was cold. She always selected the best things for us to eat, taking the worst for herself; and she would rather have been sick herself than see us sick. She would rather have died herself than see us die. Our mother naturally behaves toward us like someone who has gained the realization of exchanging self with others, cherishing us even more than she cherishes herself. She is able to put our welfare before her own, and she does so perfectly and spontaneously. If someone were to threaten to kill us she would offer herself to the killer instead. She has such compassion for us.

When we were small our mother would not sleep well. She slept lightly, waking every few hours and remaining alert for our cry. As we grew older our mother taught us how to eat, drink, speak, sit and walk. She sent us to school and encouraged us to do good things in life. If we have any knowledge and skills now, it is mainly as a result of her kindness. When we grew older and became adolescents, we preferred to be with our friends and we would completely forget our mother. While we enjoyed ourself it was as if our mother had ceased to exist, and we would remember her only when we needed something from her. Although we were forgetful and allowed ourself to become completely absorbed in the pleasures we enjoyed with our friends, our mother remained continuously concerned for us. She would often become anxious, and in the back of her mind there was always some worry about us. She had the kind of worry we normally have only for ourself. Even when we are grown up and have a family of our own, our mother does not cease to care for us. She may be old and weak and scarcely able to stand on her feet, and yet she never forgets her children.

By meditating in this way, recalling the kindness of our mother in great detail, we will come to cherish her very dearly. When we have this feeling of cherishing from the depths of our heart, we should extend it to all other living beings, remembering that every one of them has shown us the same kindness.

How are all living beings our mothers? Since it is impossible to find a beginning to our mental continuum it follows that we have taken countless rebirths in the past; and if we have had countless rebirths we must have had countless mothers. Where are all these mothers now? They are all the living beings alive today.

It is incorrect to reason that our mothers of former lives are no longer our mothers just because a long time has passed since they actually cared for us. If our present mother were to die today, would she cease to be our mother? No, we would still regard her as our mother and pray for her happiness. The same is true of all our previous mothers— they died, yet they remain our mothers. It is only because of the changes in our external appearance that we do not recognize each other. In our daily life we see many different living beings, both human and non-human. We regard some as friends, some as enemies and most as strangers. These distinctions are made by our mistaken minds; they are not verified by valid minds.

Because of changing our rebirth we do not recognize our former mothers, relatives and friends, and now because of this we see the majority of living beings as strangers and many even as our enemies. This mistaken appearance and conception is ignorance. Strangers and enemies are just creations of this ignorance. In truth there are no living beings who are strangers or our enemies because they are all our mothers, relatives or close friends. Our only real enemy is our delusions such as our uncontrolled desire, or attachment, our anger and jealousy, and especially our self-grasping ignorance. Understanding and believing this will give us great meaning in this life and in our countless future lives.

We can then meditate on the kindness of our mothers when we took other types of rebirth, considering, for example, how attentively a mother bird protects her eggs from danger and how she shields her young beneath her wings. When a hunter comes, she does not fly away and leave her chicks unprotected. All day long she searches for food to nourish them until they are strong enough to leave the nest.

There was once a robber in Tibet who stabbed a horse who was carrying a foal in her womb. His knife penetrated so deeply into the side of the horse that it cut open her uterus and the foal emerged through its mother's side. As she was dying, the mother spent her last strength licking her offspring with great affection. Seeing this, the robber was filled with remorse. He was amazed to see how, even in the pains of death, this mother had such compassion for her foal and how her only concern was for its welfare. He then ceased his non-virtuous way of life and began to follow spiritual paths purely.

Every single living being has shown us the same selfless concern, the perfect kindness of a mother. Moreover, even if we do not consider other living beings as our mother, still they have shown us tremendous kindness. Our body, for example, is the result of the kindness not only of our parents but of countless beings who have provided it with food, shelter and so forth. It is because we have this present body with human faculties that we are able to enjoy all the pleasures and opportunities of human life. Even simple pleasures such as going for a walk or watching a beautiful sunset can be seen as a result of the kindness of innumerable living beings. Our skills and abilities all come from the kindness of others; we had to be taught how to eat, how to walk, how to talk and how to read and write. Even the language we speak is not our own invention but the product of many generations. Without it we could not communicate with others or share their ideas. We could not read this book, learn spiritual practices or even think clearly. All the facilities we take for granted, such as houses, cars, roads, shops, schools, hospitals and the internet, are produced solely through others' kindness. When we travel by bus or car we take the roads for granted, but many people worked very hard to build them and make them safe for us to use.

The fact that some of the people who help us may have no intention of doing so is irrelevant. We receive benefit from their actions, so from our point of view this is a kindness. Rather than focusing on their motivation, which in any case we do not know, we should focus on the practical benefit we receive. Everyone who contributes in any way toward our happiness and well-being is deserving of our gratitude and respect. If we had to give back everything that others have given us, we would have nothing left at all.

We might argue that we are not given things freely but have to work for them. When we go shopping we have to pay, and when we eat in a restaurant we have to pay. We may have the use of a car, but we had to buy the car, and now we have to pay for gas, tax and insurance. No one gives us anything for free. But from where do we get this money? It is true that generally we have to work for our money, but it is others who employ us or buy our goods, and so indirectly it is they who provide us with money. Moreover, the reason we are able to do a particular job is that we have received the necessary training or education from other people. Wherever we look, we find only the kindness of others. We are all interconnected in a web of kindness from which it is impossible to separate ourself. Everything we have and everything we enjoy, including our very life, is due to the kindness of others. In fact, every happiness there is in the world arises as a result of others' kindness.

Our spiritual development and the pure happiness of full enlightenment also depend upon the kindness of living beings. Our opportunity to read, contemplate and meditate on spiritual teachings depends entirely upon the kindness of others. Moreover, as explained later, without living beings to give to, to test our patience or to develop compassion for, we could never develop the virtuous qualities needed to attain enlightenment.

In short, we need others for our physical, emotional and spiritual well-being. Without others we are nothing. Our sense that we are an island, an independent, self-sufficient individual, bears no relation to reality. It is closer to the truth to picture ourself as a cell in the vast body of life, distinct yet intimately bound up with all living beings. We cannot exist without others, and they in turn are affected by everything we do. The idea that it is possible to secure our own welfare while neglecting that of others, or even at the expense of others, is completely unrealistic.

Contemplating the innumerable ways in which others help us, we should make a firm decision: "I must cherish all living beings because they are so kind to me." Based on this determination, we develop a feeling of cherishing—a sense that all living beings are important and that their happiness and freedom are also important. We try to mix our mind single-pointedly with this feeling and maintain it for as long as we can without forgetting it. When we rise from meditation, we try to maintain this mind of love, so that whenever we meet or remember someone we naturally think, "This person is important, this person's happiness and freedom are important." In this way, we will make progress in our practice of learning to cherish others.

THE BENEFITS OF CHERISHING OTHERS

Another reason for cherishing others is that it is the best method to solve our own and others' problems. Problems, worry, pain and unhappiness are types of mind; they are feelings and do not exist outside the mind. If we cherish everyone we meet or think about, our mind will be at peace all the time so that we will be happy all the time and there will be no basis for developing jealousy, anger or other harmful thoughts. Jealousy, for example, is a state of mind that cannot bear another's good fortune; but if we cherish someone how can his or her good fortune disturb our mind? How can we wish to harm others if we regard everyone's happiness to be of paramount importance? By genuinely cherishing all living beings we will always act with loving kindness, in a friendly and considerate way, and they will return our kindness. Others will not act unpleasantly toward us, and there will be no basis for conflict or disputes. People will come to like us, and our relationships will be more stable and satisfying.

Cherishing others also protects us from the problems caused by desirous attachment. We often become strongly attached to another person who we feel will help us to overcome our loneliness by providing the comfort, security or excitement we crave. However, if we have a loving mind toward everyone we do not feel lonely. Instead of clinging onto others to fulfill our desires, we will want to help them fulfill their needs and wishes. Cherishing all living beings solves all our problems because all our problems come from our mind of self-cherishing. For example, at the moment if our partner left us for someone else we would probably feel very upset, but if we truly cherished them we would want them to be happy, and we would rejoice in their happiness. There would be no basis for us to feel jealous or depressed, so, although we might find the situation challenging, it would not be a problem for us. Cherishing others is the supreme protection from suffering and problems, and enables us to remain calm and peaceful all the time.

Cherishing our neighbors and the people in our local area will naturally lead to harmony in the community and society at large, and this will make everyone happier. We may not be a well-known or powerful figure, but if we sincerely cherish everyone we meet we can make a profound contribution to our community. This is true even for those who deny the value of religion. If a schoolteacher cherishes his or her students, and is free from self-concern, the students will respect him and learn not only the subject he teaches, but also the kind and admirable qualities he demonstrates. Such a teacher will naturally influence those around him in a positive way, and his presence will transform the whole school. It is said that there exists a magic crystal that has the power to purify any liquid in which it is placed. Those who cherish all living beings are like this crystal—by their very presence they remove negativity from the world and give back love and kindness.

Even if someone is clever and powerful, if he does not love others, sooner or later he will encounter problems and find it difficult to fulfill his wishes. If the leader of a country does not cherish his or her people but is concerned only with his own interests, he will be criticized and mistrusted, and eventually lose his position. If a Spiritual Teacher does not cherish and have a good relationship with his or her students, the students will find it difficult to develop faith in him, and this will make his teachings powerless.

If an employer is concerned only with his own interests and does not look after the welfare of his employees, the employees will be unhappy. They will probably work inefficiently and will certainly not be enthusiastic about fulfilling their employer's wishes. Thus, the employer will suffer from his own lack of consideration toward his employees. Similarly, if the employees are concerned only with what they can get out of the company, this will anger their employer, who may reduce their salary or ask them to leave. The company may even go bankrupt, causing them all to lose their jobs. In this way, the employees will suffer from their lack of consideration toward their employer. In every field of activity the best way to ensure success is for the people involved to reduce their self-cherishing and to have a greater sense of consideration for others.

There may sometimes appear to be short-term advantages to self-cherishing, but in the long term there are always only problems. The solution to all the problems of daily life is to cherish others.

All the suffering we experience is the result of negative karma, and the source of all negative karma is self-cherishing. It is because we have such an exaggerated sense of our own importance that we frustrate other people's wishes in order to fulfill our own. Driven by our selfish desires, we think nothing of destroying others' peace of mind and causing them distress. Such actions only sow the seeds for future suffering. If we sincerely cherish others we will have no wish to hurt them and will stop engaging in destructive and harmful actions. We will naturally observe pure moral discipline and refrain from killing or being cruel to other living beings, stealing from them or interfering with their relationships. As a result, we will not have to experience the unpleasant effects of these negative actions in the future. In this way, cherishing others protects us from all future problems caused by negative karma.

By cherishing others we continuously accumulate merit, and merit is the main cause of success in all our activities. If we cherish all living beings we will naturally perform many virtuous and helpful actions. Gradually all our actions of body, speech and mind will become pure and beneficial, and we will become a source of happiness and inspiration for everyone we meet. We will discover through our own experience that this precious mind of love is the real wish-granting jewel, for it fulfills the pure wishes of both ourself and all living beings.

The mind that cherishes all living beings is extremely precious. Keeping such a good heart will result only in happiness for ourself and all those around us. This good heart gives rise to universal compassion—the spontaneous wish to permanently liberate all living beings from fear and suffering. This eventually transforms into the universal compassion of an enlightened Buddha, which actually has the power to protect all living beings from suffering. In this way, cherishing others leads us to the ultimate, supreme goal of human life.

Through contemplating all these advantages of cherishing others we arrive at the following determination:

I will cherish all living beings without exception because this precious mind of love is the supreme method for solving all problems and fulfilling all wishes. Eventually it will give me the supreme happiness of enlightenment.

We meditate on this determination single-pointedly for as long as possible and develop a strong feeling of cherishing each and every living being. When we rise from meditation we try to maintain this feeling and put our resolution into practice. Whenever we are with other people we should be continuously mindful that their happiness and freedom are at least as important as our own. Of course we cannot cherish all living beings right away, but by training our mind in this attitude, beginning with our family and friends, we can gradually extend the scope of our love until it embraces all living beings. When in this way we sincerely cherish all living beings, we are no longer an ordinary person but have become a great being, like a Bodhisattva.

How to Enhance
Cherishing Love

The way to deepen our love for others is to familiarize ourself with the practice of cherishing others. To strengthen our determination to cherish all living beings, we need to receive further instructions on enhancing cherishing love.

We all have someone whom we regard as especially precious, such as our child, our partner or our mother. This person seems to be imbued with unique qualities that make him or her stand out from others. We treasure and want to take special care of this person. We need to learn to regard all living beings in a similar way, recognizing each and every one as special and uniquely valuable. Although we already cherish our family and close friends, we do not love strangers, and we certainly do not love our enemies. For us the vast majority of living beings are of no particular significance. By practicing the instructions on cherishing others, we can remove this bias and come to treasure each and every living being, just as a mother regards her dearest child. The more we can deepen and enhance our love in this way, the stronger our compassion and bodhichitta will become, and the quicker we will attain enlightenment.

RECOGNIZING OUR FAULTS IN THE MIRROR OF DHARMA

One of the main functions of Buddha's teachings, or Dharma, is to serve as a mirror in which we can see our own faults. For example, when anger arises in our mind, instead of making excuses we need to say to ourself, "This anger is the inner poison of delusion. It has no value or justification; its only function is to harm. I will not tolerate its presence in my mind." We can also use the mirror of Dharma to distinguish between desirous attachment and love. These two are easily confused, but it is vital to discriminate between them, for love will bring us only happiness whereas the mind of attachment will bring us only suffering and bind us ever more tightly to samsara. The moment we notice attachment arising in our mind, we should be on our guard—no matter how pleasant it may seem to follow our attachment, it is like licking honey off a razor's edge and in the long run invariably leads to more suffering.

The main reason why we do not cherish all living beings is that we are so preoccupied with ourself, and this leaves very little room in our mind to appreciate others. If we wish to cherish others sincerely, we have to reduce our obsessive self-concern. Why is it that we regard ourself as so precious, but not others? It is because we are so familiar with self-cherishing. Since beginningless time we have grasped at a truly existent I. This grasping at I automatically gives rise to self-cherishing, which instinctively feels, "I am more important than others." For ordinary beings, grasping at one's own I and self-cherishing are like two sides of the same coin: I-grasping grasps at a truly existent I, whereas self-cherishing feels this I to be precious and cherishes it. The fundamental reason for this is our constant familiarity with our self-cherishing, day and night, even during our sleep.

Since we regard our self or I as so very precious and important, we exaggerate our own good qualities and develop an inflated view of ourself. Almost anything can serve as a basis for this arrogant mind, such as our looks, possessions, knowledge, experiences or status. If we make a witty remark we think, "I'm so clever!" or if we have traveled around the world we feel that this automatically makes us a fascinating person. We can even develop pride on the basis of things we ought to be ashamed of, such as our ability to deceive others, or on qualities that we merely imagine we possess. On the other hand, we find it very hard to accept our mistakes and shortcomings. We spend so much time contemplating our real or imagined good qualities that we become oblivious to our faults. In reality our mind is full of gross delusions but we ignore them and may even fool ourself into thinking that we do not have such repulsive minds. This is like pretending that there is no dirt in our house after sweeping it under the rug.

It is often so painful to admit that we have faults that we make all manner of excuses rather than alter our exalted view of ourself. One of the most common ways of not facing up to our faults is to blame others. For instance, if we have a difficult relationship with someone, we naturally conclude that it is entirely their fault—we are unable to accept that it is at least partly ours. Instead of taking responsibility for our actions and making an effort to change our behavior, we argue with them and insist that it is they who must change. An exaggerated sense of our own importance thus leads to a critical attitude toward other people and makes it almost impossible to avoid conflict. The fact that we are oblivious to our faults does not prevent other people from noticing them and pointing them out, but when they do we feel that they are being unfair. Instead of looking honestly at our own behavior to see whether or not the criticism is justified, our self-cherishing mind becomes defensive and retaliates by finding fault with them.

Another reason why we do not regard others as precious is that we pay attention to their faults while ignoring their good qualities. Unfortunately we have become very skilled in recognizing the faults of others, and we devote a great deal of mental energy to listing them, analyzing them and even meditating on them! With this critical attitude, if we disagree with our partner or colleagues about something, instead of trying to understand their point of view we repeatedly think of many reasons why we are right and they are wrong. By focusing exclusively on their faults and limitations, we become angry and resentful and, rather than cherishing them, we develop the wish to harm or discredit them. In this way, small disagreements can easily turn into conflicts that simmer for months.

Nothing good ever comes from dwelling on our own qualities and others' faults. All that happens is that we develop a highly distorted, self-important view of ourself, and an arrogant, disrespectful attitude toward others. As the great scholar Shantideva says in *Guide to the Bodhisattva's Way of Life*:

> If we hold ourself in high esteem, we shall be reborn
> in the lower realms
> And later, as a human, experience low status and a
> foolish mind.

As a result of regarding ourself as superior and others as inferior, we perform many negative actions that will later ripen as rebirth in the lower realms. Due to this haughty attitude, even when we finally take rebirth again as a human being we will be of a low social status, living like a servant or slave. Out of pride we may regard ourself as highly intelligent, but in reality our pride makes us foolish and fills our mind with negativity. There is no value in viewing ourself as more important than others and thinking only of our own qualities. It neither increases our qualities nor reduces our faults, and it does not cause others to share our exalted opinion of ourself.

If instead we focus on the good qualities of others, our deluded pride will decrease and we will come to regard them as more important and precious than ourself. As a result, our love and compassion will increase and we will naturally engage in virtuous actions. Due to this we will be reborn in the higher realms, as a human or god, and we will gain the respect and friendship of many people. Only good can come from contemplating the good qualities of others. Therefore, whereas ordinary beings look for faults in others, Bodhisattvas look solely for good qualities.

In *Advice from Atisha's Heart* it says:

> Do not look for faults in others, but look for faults in yourself, and purge them like bad blood.

> Do not contemplate your own good qualities, but contemplate the good qualities of others, and respect everyone as a servant would.

We need to think about our own faults because if we are not aware of them we will not be motivated to overcome them. It was through constantly examining their minds for faults and imperfections, and then applying great effort to abandon them, that those who are now enlightened were able to release their minds from delusions, the source of all faults. Buddha said that those who understand their own faults are wise, whereas those who are unaware of their own faults yet look for faults in others are fools. Contemplating our own qualities and others' faults serves only to increase our self-cherishing and diminish our love for others; yet all enlightened beings agree that self-cherishing is the root of all faults and cherishing others is the source of all happiness. The only people who disagree with this view are those who are still in samsara. We can keep our ordinary view if we wish, or we can adopt the view of all the holy beings. The choice is ours, but we would be wise to adopt the latter if we wish to enjoy real peace and happiness.

Some people argue that one of our main problems is a lack of self-esteem, and that we need to focus exclusively on our good qualities in order to boost our self-confidence. It is true that to make authentic spiritual progress we need to develop confidence in our spiritual potential, and to acknowledge and improve our good qualities. However, we also need a keen and realistic awareness of our present faults and imperfections. If we are honest with ourself, we will recognize that at the moment our mind is filled with defilements such as anger, attachment and ignorance. These mental diseases will not go away just by our pretending they do not exist. The only way we can ever get rid of them is by honestly acknowledging their existence and then making the effort to eliminate them.

Although we need to be acutely aware of our faults we must never allow ourself to become overwhelmed or discouraged by them. We may have a lot of anger in our mind but this does not mean that we are an inherently angry person. No matter how many delusions we may have or how strong they are, they are not an essential part of our mind. They are defilements that temporarily pollute our mind but do not sully its pure, essential nature. They are like mud that dirties water but never becomes an intrinsic part of it. Just as mud can always be removed to reveal pure, clear water, so delusions can be removed to reveal the natural purity and clarity of our mind. While acknowledging that we have delusions, we should not identify with them, thinking, "I am a selfish, worthless person" or "I am an angry person." Instead, we should identify with our pure potential and develop the wisdom and courage to overcome our delusions.

When we look at external things, we can usually distinguish those that are useful and valuable from those that are not. We must learn to look at our mind in the same way. Although the nature of our root mind is pure and clear, many conceptual thoughts arise from it, like bubbles arising within an ocean or rays of light arising from a single flame. Some of these thoughts are beneficial and lead to happiness both now and in the future, whereas others lead to suffering and the extreme misery of rebirth in the lower realms. We need to keep a constant watch over our mind and learn to distinguish between the beneficial and harmful thoughts that are arising moment by moment. Those who are able to do this are truly wise.

Once an evil man who had killed thousands of people met a Bodhisattva called King Chandra, who helped him by teaching him Dharma and showing him the error of his ways. The man said, "Having looked into the mirror of Dharma I now understand how negative my actions have been, and I feel great regret for them." Motivated by deep remorse, he engaged sincerely in purification practices and eventually became a highly realized Yogi. This shows that by recognizing one's own faults in the mirror of Dharma and then making a concerted effort to remove them, even the most evil person can become a completely pure being.

In Tibet there was once a famous Dharma practitioner called Geshe Ben Gungyal, who neither recited prayers nor meditated in the traditional meditation posture. His sole practice was to observe his mind very attentively and counter delusions as soon as they arose. Whenever he noticed his mind becoming even slightly agitated, he was especially vigilant and refused to follow any negative thoughts. For instance, if he felt self-cherishing was about to arise, he would immediately recall its disadvantages and then he would stop this mind from manifesting by applying its opponent, the practice of love. Whenever his mind was naturally peaceful and positive, he would relax and allow himself to enjoy his virtuous states of mind.

To gauge his progress he would put a black pebble down in front of him whenever a negative thought arose, and a white pebble whenever a positive thought arose, and at the end of the day he would count the pebbles. If there were more black pebbles he would reprimand himself and try even harder the next day, but if there were more white pebbles he would praise and encourage himself. At the beginning, the black pebbles greatly outnumbered the white ones, but over the years his mind improved until he reached the point when entire days went by without any black pebbles. Before becoming a Dharma practitioner, Geshe Ben Gungyal had had a reputation for being wild and unruly, but by watching his mind closely all the time, and judging it with complete honesty in the mirror of Dharma, he gradually became a very pure and holy being. Why can we not do the same?

The Kadampa Masters, or Geshes, taught that the function of a Spiritual Guide is to point out his or her disciples' faults, for then the disciples have a clear understanding of these shortcomings and the opportunity to overcome them. These days, however, if a Teacher were to point out his or her disciples' faults they would probably become upset, and might even lose their faith, and so the Teacher usually has to adopt a gentler approach. However, even though our Spiritual Guide may tactfully be refraining from directly pointing out our faults, we still need to become aware of them by examining our mind in the mirror of his or her teachings. By relating our Spiritual Guide's teachings on karma and delusions to our own situation, we will be able to understand what we need to abandon and what we need to practice.

A sick person cannot be cured of his illness just by reading the instructions on a bottle of medicine, but he can be cured by actually taking the medicine. Similarly, Buddha gave Dharma instructions as supreme medicine to cure the inner disease of our delusions, but we cannot cure this disease just by reading or studying Dharma books. We can only solve our daily problems by taking Dharma into our heart and practicing it sincerely.

VIEWING ALL LIVING BEINGS AS SUPREME

The great Bodhisattva Langri Tangpa made the prayer:

> With a perfect intention,
> May I cherish others as supreme.

If we wish to attain enlightenment, or to develop the superior bodhichitta that comes from exchanging self with others, we must definitely adopt the view that others are more precious than ourself. This view is based on wisdom and leads us to our final goal, whereas the view that regards ourself as more precious than others is based on self-grasping ignorance and leads us to lower rebirth.

What exactly does it mean to say that something is precious? If we were asked which was more precious, a diamond or a bone, we would say a diamond. This is because a diamond is more useful to us. However, for a dog a bone would be more precious because he can eat a bone whereas he cannot do anything with a diamond. This indicates that preciousness is not an intrinsic quality of an object but depends upon an individual's needs and wishes, which in turn depend upon his or her karma. For someone whose main wish is to achieve the spiritual realizations of love, compassion, bodhichitta and great enlightenment, living beings are more precious than a universe filled with diamonds or even wish-granting jewels. Why is this? It is because living beings help that person to develop love and compassion and to fulfill their wish for enlightenment, which is something that a whole universe filled with jewels could never do.

No one wants to remain an ordinary, ignorant being forever; indeed, all of us have the wish to improve ourself and to progress to higher and higher states. The highest state of all is full enlightenment, and the main road leading to enlightenment is the realizations of love, compassion, bodhichitta and the practice of the six perfections—the perfections of giving, moral discipline, patience, effort, concentration and wisdom. We can only develop these qualities in dependence upon other living beings. How can we learn to love with no one to love? How can we practice giving with no one to give to, or patience with no one to irritate us? Whenever we see another living being we can increase our spiritual qualities such as love and compassion, and in this way we come closer to enlightenment and the fulfillment of our deepest wishes. How kind living beings are to act as the objects of our love and compassion. How precious they are!

When Atisha was in Tibet he had an Indian assistant who was always criticizing him. When the Tibetans asked him why he kept this assistant when there were many faithful Tibetans who would be more than happy to serve him, Atisha replied, "Without this man, there would be no one with whom I could practice patience. He is very kind to me. I need him!" Atisha understood that the only way to fulfill his deepest wish to benefit all living beings was to achieve enlightenment, and that to do this he needed to perfect his patience. For Atisha, his bad-tempered assistant was more precious than material possessions, praise or any other worldly attainment.

Our spiritual realizations are our inner wealth for they help us in all situations and are the only possessions we can take with us when we die. Once we learn to value the inner wealth of patience, giving, love and compassion above external conditions, we will come to regard each and every living being as supremely precious, no matter how they treat us. This will make it very easy for us to cherish them.

In our meditation session, we contemplate the reasons given above until we reach the following conclusion:

Sentient beings are extremely precious because without them I cannot gather the inner wealth of spiritual realizations that will eventually bring me the ultimate happiness of full enlightenment. Since without this inner wealth I will have to remain in samsara forever, I will always regard sentient beings as supremely important.

We meditate on this determination single-pointedly for as long as possible. When we rise from meditation we try to maintain this determination all the time, recognizing how much we need each and every sentient being for our spiritual practice. By maintaining this recognition, our problems of anger, attachment, jealousy and so forth will subside, and we will naturally come to cherish others. In particular, whenever people interfere with our wishes or criticize us, we should remember that we need these people in order to develop the spiritual realizations that are the true meaning of our human life. If everyone treated us with the kindness and respect our self-cherishing feels we deserve, this would only reinforce our delusions and deplete our merit. Imagine what we would be like if we always got what we wanted! We would be just like a spoiled child who feels that the world revolves around him, and who is unpopular with everyone. In fact, we all need someone like Atisha's assistant, for such people give us the opportunity to destroy our self-cherishing and train our mind, thereby making our life truly meaningful.

Since the above reasoning is the exact opposite to our normal way of thinking, we need to contemplate it very carefully until we are convinced that each and every sentient being is indeed more precious than any external attainment. In reality Buddhas and sentient beings are equally precious—Buddhas because they reveal the path to enlightenment, and sentient beings because they act as the objects of the compassion that we need in order to attain enlightenment. Because their kindness in enabling us to attain our supreme goal, enlightenment, is equal, we should regard Buddhas and sentient beings as equally important and precious. As Shantideva says in *Guide to the Bodhisattva's Way of Life*:

> Since living beings and enlightened beings are alike
> In that the qualities of a Buddha arise in
>   dependence upon them,
> Why do we not show the same respect to living
>   beings
> As we do to the enlightened beings?

LIVING BEINGS HAVE NO FAULTS

We might object that while it is true that we depend upon sentient beings as the objects of our patience, compassion and so forth, it is nevertheless impossible to see them as precious when they have so many faults. How can we regard as precious someone whose mind is pervaded by attachment, anger and ignorance? The answer to this objection is quite profound. Although sentient beings' minds are filled with delusions, sentient beings themselves are not faulty. We say that sea water is salty, but in fact it is the salt in the water that makes it salty. However, the real nature of water is not salty because salt can be removed from it. Similarly, all the faults we see in people are actually the faults of their delusions, not of the people themselves. Buddhas see that delusions have many faults but they never see people as faulty, because they distinguish between people and their delusions. If someone is angry we think, "He is a bad and angry person," whereas Buddhas think, "He is a suffering being afflicted with the inner disease of anger." If a friend of ours were suffering from cancer we would not blame him for his physical disease, and, in the same way, if someone is suffering from anger or attachment we should not blame him for the diseases of his mind.

Delusions are the enemies of sentient beings, and just as we would not blame a victim for the faults of his attacker, why should we blame sentient beings for the faults of their enemies? When someone is temporarily overpowered by the enemy of anger it is inappropriate to blame him, because in reality he is a victim. Just as a fault of a microphone is not that of a book, and a fault of a cup is not that of a teapot, so the faults of delusions are not those of a person. The only appropriate response to those who are driven by their delusions to harm others is compassion. Sometimes it is necessary to force those who are behaving in very deluded ways to stop, both for their own sake and to protect other people, but it is never appropriate to blame or become angry with them.

We normally refer to our body and mind as "my body" and "my mind," in the same way as we refer to our other possessions. This indicates that they are different from our I. The body and mind are the basis upon which we establish our I, not the I itself. Delusions are characteristics of a person's mind, not of the person. Since we can never find faults in sentient beings themselves, we can say that in this respect sentient beings are like Buddhas.

From this point of view sentient beings are like enlightened beings. Their root mind, their own mind, is completely pure. Their own mind is like a blue sky and their delusions and all other conceptions are like clouds that temporarily arise. From another point of view sentient beings mistakenly identify themselves and are harmed by delusions. They endlessly experience immense suffering as hallucinations. Therefore we need to develop compassion for them, and liberate them from their deep hallucination of mistaken appearance by showing them the real nature of things, which is the emptiness of all phenomena.

Just as we distinguish between a person and his or her delusions, so we should also remember that the delusions are only temporary, adventitious characteristics of that person's mind and not its real nature. Delusions are distorted conceptual thoughts that arise within the mind, like waves on the ocean—just as it is possible for waves to die down without the ocean disappearing, so it is possible for our delusions to end without our mental continuum ceasing.

It is because they distinguish between delusions and persons that Buddhas are able to see the faults of delusions without ever seeing a single fault in any sentient being. Consequently, their love and compassion for sentient beings never diminish. Failing to make this distinction, we, on the other hand, are constantly finding fault with other people but do not recognize the faults of delusions, even those within our own mind.

There is a prayer that says:

This fault I see is not the fault of the person
But the fault of delusion, or his actions.
Realizing this, may I never view others' faults,
But see all beings as supreme.

Focusing on other people's faults is the source of much of our negativity and one of the main obstacles to viewing others as supremely precious. If we are genuinely interested in developing cherishing love, we need to learn to discriminate between a person and his or her delusions, and realize that it is the delusions that are to blame for all the faults we perceive.

There may appear to be a contradiction between this and the earlier section where we are advised to recognize our own faults. Surely if we have faults, so too do other people! But there is no contradiction. For the effectiveness of our purification practice we need to recognize our own faults, which are our delusions and our non-virtuous actions. This also applies to others. And for the effectiveness of the practice of loving kindness towards all living beings, we need to understand that the faults that we see in the actions of living beings are not the faults of living beings, but the faults of their enemy—their delusions. We should practically appreciate these teachings; we do not need meaningless debate.

When a mother sees her child throwing a tantrum, she knows that the child is acting in a deluded way, but this does not diminish her love for him or her. Although she is not blind to the anger in her child, this does not lead her to the conclusion that the child is evil or intrinsically angry. Distinguishing between the delusion and the person, she continues to see her child as beautiful and full of potential. In the same way, we should regard all sentient beings as supremely precious, while clearly understanding that they are afflicted by the sickness of delusion.

We can also apply the above reasoning to ourself, recognizing that our faults are really the faults of our delusions and not of our self. This prevents us from identifying with our faults and thus feeling guilty and inadequate, and it helps us to view our delusions in a realistic and practical way. We need to acknowledge our delusions and take responsibility for overcoming them, but to do this effectively we need to distance ourself from them. For example, we can think, "Self-cherishing is presently in my mind, but it is not myself. I can destroy it without destroying myself." In this way, we can be utterly ruthless with our delusions but kind and patient with ourself. We do not need to blame ourself for the many delusions we have inherited from our previous life, but, if we wish for our future self to enjoy peace and happiness, it is our responsibility to remove these delusions from our mind.

As mentioned before, one of the best ways to regard others as precious is to remember their kindness. Once again we may object, "How can I see others as kind when they engage in so many cruel and harmful actions?" To answer this we need to understand that when people harm others they are controlled by their delusions. Delusions are like a powerful hallucinogenic drug that forces people to act in ways that are contrary to their real nature. A person under the influence of delusions is not in his right mind, because he is creating terrible suffering for himself and no one in his right mind would create suffering for himself. All delusions are based on a mistaken way of seeing things. When we see things as they really are, our delusions naturally disappear and virtuous minds naturally manifest. Minds such as love and kindness are based on reality and are an expression of our pure nature. Thus, when we view others as kind, we are seeing beyond their delusions and are relating to their pure nature, their Buddha nature.

Buddha compared our Buddha nature to a gold nugget in dirt, for, no matter how disgusting a person's delusions may be, the real nature of their mind remains undefiled, like pure gold. In the heart of even the cruelest and most degenerate person exists the potential for limitless love, compassion and wisdom. Unlike the seeds of our delusions, which can be destroyed, this potential is utterly indestructible and is the pure, essential nature of every living being. Whenever we meet other people, rather than focusing on their delusions we should focus on the gold of their Buddha nature. This will not only enable us to regard them as special and unique, but also help to bring out their good qualities. Recognizing everyone as a future Buddha, out of love and compassion we will naturally help and encourage this potential to ripen.

Because we are so familiar with cherishing ourself more than others, the view that all sentient beings are supremely important does not arise easily and we need to train our mind patiently for many years before it becomes natural. Just as an ocean is formed by many tiny drops of water gathering over a long period of time, so the realizations of love and compassion of advanced practitioners are the result of constant training. We should begin by trying to cherish our parents, family and close friends, and then extend this feeling to the people in our community. Gradually we can increase the scope of our cherishing until it includes all sentient beings.

It is important to begin with our immediate circle because if we try to love all sentient beings in a general way, while neglecting to cherish the specific individuals with whom we associate, our cherishing will be abstract and inauthentic. We may develop some good feelings in meditation, but these will quickly disappear once we rise from meditation, and our mind will remain basically unchanged. However, if at the end of each meditation session we make a special determination to cherish those with whom we are going to spend our time, and then put this determination into practice, our cherishing will be grounded and sincere. Through making a concerted effort to love our immediate circle, even when they are making life difficult for us, our self-cherishing will be continuously eroded and we will gradually build in our mind a firm foundation of cherishing others. With this foundation it will not be difficult to extend our love to more and more sentient beings until we develop the universal love and compassion of a Bodhisattva.

Our ability to help others also depends upon our karmic connection with them from this and previous lives. We all have a close circle of people with whom we have a special karmic connection in this life. Though we need to learn to cherish all living beings equally, this does not mean that we have to treat everyone in exactly the same way. For example, it would be inappropriate to treat people who do not like us in the same way as we treat our close friends and family; this is because they may not accept this. There are also people who just want to be left alone or who dislike any display of affection. Loving others is principally an attitude of mind, and the way in which we express it depends upon the needs, wishes and situations of each individual, as well as our karmic connection with them. We cannot physically care for everyone, but we can develop a caring attitude toward all beings. This is the main point of training the mind. By training our mind in this way we will eventually become a Buddha with the actual power to protect all sentient beings.

Through carefully contemplating all the above points, we arrive at the following conclusion:

Because all sentient beings are very precious to me, I must cherish them and hold them dear.

We should regard this determination as a seed and hold it continuously in our mind, nurturing it until it grows into the spontaneous feeling of cherishing ourself and all sentient beings equally. This realization is called "equalizing self and others." Just as we value our own peace and happiness, so too should we value the peace and happiness of all living beings; and just as we work to free ourself from suffering and problems, so too should we work to free others.

DEVELOPING HUMILITY

Bodhisattva Langri Tangpa said:

> Whenever I associate with others,
> May I view myself as the lowest of all.

With these words, Langri Tangpa is encouraging us to develop the mind of humility and to see ourself as lower and less precious than others. As mentioned before, preciousness is not an inherent quality of an object but depends upon an individual's karma. It is due to a mother's special karmic connection with her children that they naturally appear precious to her. For a practitioner who is seeking enlightenment, all sentient beings are equally precious, both because they are immensely kind and because they act as supreme objects for developing and increasing his or her spiritual realizations. For such a practitioner, no single being is inferior or less important, not even an insect. We may wonder, if preciousness depends on karma, is it because a practitioner seeking enlightenment has a karmic connection with all beings that he sees them as precious? The practitioner develops this special view through contemplating correct reasons that cause to ripen his karmic potential to see all beings as his precious mother. In reality all sentient beings are our mothers, so of course we have a karmic connection with them; but due to our ignorance we have no idea that they are our precious mothers.

In general, we would all prefer to enjoy high status and a good reputation, and we have little or no interest in being humble. Practitioners like Langri Tangpa are the complete opposite. They actually seek out subordinate positions and wish for others to enjoy the happiness of higher status. There are three reasons why such practitioners strive to practice humility. Firstly, by practicing humility we are not using up our merit on worldly attainments but saving it for the development of internal realizations. We only have a limited supply of merit, so if we waste it on material possessions, reputation, popularity or power there will not be enough positive energy left in our mind to effect deep spiritual realizations. Secondly, by practicing humility and wishing for others to enjoy higher status, we accumulate a vast amount of merit. We should understand that now is the time to accumulate merit, not to waste it on worldly attainments. Thirdly, we need to practice humility because there is no self or I that we normally see. We should view our self or I—the object of our self-cherishing—as the lowest of all, as something we need to neglect or forget. In this way our self-cherishing will become weaker and our love for others will increase.

Although many practitioners practice humility, they will nonetheless accept whatever social position enables them to benefit the most sentient beings. Such a practitioner may become a wealthy, powerful and respected member of society, but his or her motivation for doing so would be solely for the benefit of others. Worldly attainments do not attract him in the least, for he recognizes them as deceptive and a waste of his merit. Even if he were to become a king he would consider all his wealth as belonging to others, and in his heart would continue to view others as supreme. Because he would not grasp at his position or possessions as his own, they would not serve to exhaust his merit.

We need to practice humility even when we associate with those who according to social conventions are equal or inferior to us. Because we cannot see others' minds, we do not know who is actually a realized being and who is not. Someone may not have a high position in society, but if in his heart he maintains loving kindness toward all living beings, in reality he is a realized being. Moreover, Buddhas are able to manifest in any form to help living beings, and unless we are a Buddha ourself we have no means of knowing who is an emanation of a Buddha and who is not. We cannot say for sure that our closest friend or worst enemy, our mother or even our dog, is not an emanation. The fact that we feel we know someone very well and have seen him or her behaving in deluded ways does not mean that he or she is an ordinary person. What we see is a reflection of our own mind. An ordinary, deluded mind will naturally perceive a world filled with ordinary, deluded people.

Only when we purify our mind will we be able to see pure, holy beings directly. Until then we cannot know for sure whether or not someone is an emanation. Perhaps everyone we know is an emanation of a Buddha! This may seem rather improbable, but only because we are so used to seeing people as ordinary. We simply do not know. All we can realistically say is that maybe someone is an emanation, maybe he or she is not. This is a very useful way of thinking, for if we think that someone may be an emanation of a Buddha we will naturally respect him and avoid harming him. From the point of view of the effect it has on our mind, thinking that someone may be a Buddha is almost the same as thinking that he or she is a Buddha. Since the only person we know for sure is not a Buddha is ourself, through training in this way of thinking we will gradually come to regard everyone else as superior to, and more precious than, ourself.

Viewing ourself as the lowest of all is not easy to accept at first. When we meet a dog, for example, are we supposed to view ourself as lower than the dog? We can consider the story of the Buddhist Master Asanga, who came across a dying dog that in reality turned out to be an emanation of

Buddha Maitreya. The dog before us may appear to be an ordinary animal, but the fact is that we do not know its real nature. Perhaps it too has been emanated by Buddha to help us develop compassion. Since we cannot know for sure one way or another, rather than wasting our time speculating whether the dog is an ordinary animal or an emanation, we should simply think, "This dog may be an emanation of Buddha." From this point of view we can think that we are lower than the dog, and this thought will protect us against any feelings of superiority.

One of the advantages of humility is that it enables us to learn from everyone. A proud person cannot learn from other people because he feels he already knows better than they. On the other hand, a humble person who respects everyone and recognizes that they may even be emanations of Buddha has the openness of mind to learn from everyone and every situation. Just as water cannot collect on mountain peaks, so good qualities and blessings cannot gather on the rocky peaks of pride. If, instead, we maintain a humble, respectful attitude toward everyone, good qualities and inspiration will flow into our mind all the time, like streams flowing into a valley.

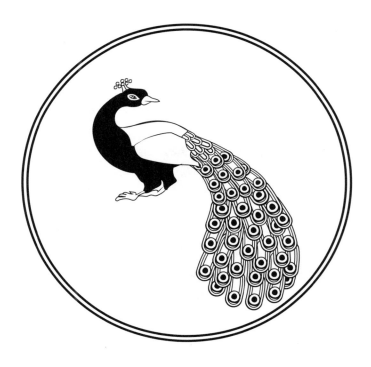

Just as peacocks are said to thrive on plants that are poisonous to other birds, sincere spiritual practitioners can make good use of whatever circumstances arise in their daily life.

Exchanging Self with Others

*W*hereas the two previous chapters explain the practice of what is called "equalizing self and others"—cherishing ourself and all other living beings equally—this chapter shows us how to exchange self with others. This means that we give up our self-cherishing and come to cherish only others. Because the main obstacles to gaining this realization are our delusions, I will now explain how we can overcome our delusions, and in particular our self-cherishing.

Normally we divide the external world into that which we consider to be good or valuable, bad or worthless, or neither. Most of the time these discriminations are incorrect or have little meaning. For example, our habitual way of categorizing people as friends, enemies and strangers depending on how they make us feel is both incorrect and a great obstacle to developing impartial love for all living beings. Rather than holding so tightly to our discriminations of the external world, it would be far more beneficial if we learned to discriminate between valuable and worthless states of mind.

To overcome a particular delusion, we need to be able to identify it correctly and distinguish it clearly from other states of mind. It is relatively easy to identify delusions such as anger or jealousy and to see how they are harming us. Delusions such as attachment, pride, self-grasping and self-cherishing, however, are more difficult to recognize and can easily be confused with other states of mind. For instance, we have many desires, but not all of these are motivated by desirous attachment. We can have the wish to sleep, to eat, to meet our friends or to meditate, without being influenced by attachment. A desire that is attachment necessarily disturbs our mind, but, since it may affect us in subtle, indirect ways, we may find it difficult to recognize when it arises in our mind.

WHAT IS SELF-CHERISHING?

Of all the innumerable conceptual thoughts that arise from the ocean of our root mind, the most harmful is self-cherishing and the most beneficial is the mind of cherishing others. What exactly is self-cherishing? Self-cherishing is our mind that thinks "I am important" while neglecting others. It is defined as a mind that considers oneself to be supremely important and precious, and that develops from the appearance of true existence of the self. The delusion of self-cherishing is functioning in our mind almost all the time, and is at the very core of our samsaric experience.

It is our self-cherishing that makes us feel that our happiness and freedom are more important than anyone else's, that our wishes and feelings matter more, and that our life and experiences are more interesting. Because of our self-cherishing we find it upsetting when we are criticized or insulted, but not when a stranger is criticized, and we may even feel happy when someone we dislike is insulted. When we are in pain we feel that the most important thing in the world is to stop our pain as quickly as possible, but we are far more patient when someone else is in pain. We are so familiar with self-cherishing that we find it difficult to imagine life without it—for us it is almost as natural as breathing. However, if we check with our wisdom, we will see that self-cherishing is a completely mistaken mind with no basis in reality. There are no valid reasons whatsoever for thinking that we are more important than others. For Buddhas, who have unmistaken minds and see things exactly as they are, all beings are equally important.

Self-cherishing is a wrong awareness because its observed object, the inherently existent self or I, does not exist. The inherently existent self or I, the self or I that we normally see, and the truly existent self or I, are synonymous. If we watch our mind when self-cherishing is manifesting strongly, such as when we are afraid, embarrassed or indignant, we will notice that we have a very vivid sense of I. Due to self-grasping ignorance, our I appears to us as a solid, real entity, existing from its own side, independently of our body or mind. This independent I is called the "inherently existent I," and it does not exist at all. The I that we grasp at so strongly, cherish so dearly, and devote our whole life to serving and protecting is merely a fabrication of our ignorance. If we reflect deeply on this point, we will realize how ridiculous it is to cherish something that does not exist. An explanation of how the inherently existent I does not exist is given in the chapter on ultimate bodhichitta.

Due to the imprints of self-grasping accumulated since beginningless time, whatever appears to our mind, including our I, appears to be inherently existent. Grasping at our own self as inherently existent, we grasp at the self of others as inherently existent, and then conceive self and others to be inherently different. We then generate self-cherishing, which instinctively feels, "I am supremely important and precious." In summary, our self-grasping apprehends our I to be inherently existent, and our self-cherishing then cherishes that inherently existent I above all others. For ordinary beings, self-grasping and self-cherishing are very closely related and almost mixed together. We can say that they are both types of ignorance because they both mistakenly apprehend a non-existent object, the inherently existent I. Because any action motivated by these minds is a contaminated action that causes us to be reborn in samsara, it is also correct to say that for ordinary beings both self-grasping and self-cherishing are the root of samsara.

There is a more subtle type of self-cherishing, which is not conjoined with self-grasping and which is therefore not a type of ignorance. This type of self-cherishing exists in the minds of Hinayana practitioners who have completely abandoned the ignorance of self-grasping and all other delusions, and achieved nirvana. However, they still have a subtle form of self-cherishing, which arises from the imprints of self-grasping and prevents them from working for the sake of all sentient beings. An explanation of this type of self-cherishing is not within the scope of this book. Here, self-cherishing refers to the self-cherishing of ordinary beings, which is a deluded mind that cherishes a non-existent self and regards it as supremely important.

THE FAULTS OF SELF-CHERISHING

It is impossible to find a single problem, misfortune or painful experience that does not arise from self-cherishing. As Bodhisattva Shantideva says:

All the happiness there is in this world
Arises from wishing others to be happy,
And all the suffering there is in this world
Arises from wishing ourself to be happy.

How should we understand this? As mentioned earlier, all our experiences are the effects of actions we have committed in the past: pleasant experiences are the effects of positive actions, and unpleasant experiences are the effects of negative actions. Sufferings are not given to us as a punishment. They all come from our self-cherishing mind, which wishes ourself to be happy while neglecting the happiness of others. There are two ways to understand this. First, the self-cherishing mind is the creator of all our suffering and problems; and second, self-cherishing is the basis for experiencing all our suffering and problems.

We suffer because in our previous lives we performed actions that caused others to experience suffering, motivated by selfish intention—our self-cherishing. As a result of these actions, we now experience our present suffering and problems. Therefore, the real creator of all our suffering and problems is our self-cherishing mind. If we never engaged in negative actions, it would be impossible for us to experience any unpleasant effects. All negative actions are motivated by delusions, which in turn arise from self-cherishing. First we develop the thought, "I am important," and because of this we feel that the fulfillment of our wishes is of paramount importance. Then we desire for ourself that which appears attractive and develop attachment, we feel aversion for that which appears unattractive and develop anger, and we feel indifference toward that which appears neutral and develop ignorance. From these three delusions, all other delusions arise. Self-grasping and self-cherishing are the roots of the tree of suffering, delusions such as anger and attachment are its trunk, negative actions are its branches and the miseries and pains of samsara are its bitter fruit.

By understanding how delusions develop, we can see that self-cherishing is at the very core of our negativity and suffering. Disregarding the happiness of others and selfishly pursuing our own interests, we perform many non-virtuous actions, the effects of which are only suffering. All the misery of disease, sickness, natural disasters and war can be traced back to self-cherishing. It is impossible to experience the suffering of sickness or any other misfortune if we have not at some time in the past created its cause, which is necessarily a non-virtuous action motivated by self-cherishing.

We should not take this to mean that a person's suffering is his own fault and that it is therefore inappropriate to feel compassion for him. Motivated by their delusions, living beings perform negative actions, and whenever they are under the influence of delusions they are not in control of their minds. If a mental patient were to injure his head by banging it against a wall, the doctors would not refuse to treat him by arguing that it was his own fault. In the same way, if in a previous life someone performed a negative action that has now resulted in his experiencing a serious illness, this is no reason for us not to feel compassion for him. Indeed, by understanding that living beings are not free from the delusions that are the cause of all their suffering, our compassion will become much stronger. To be able to help others effectively, we need a profoundly compassionate intention that wishes to free others from their manifest suffering *and* its underlying causes.

The self-cherishing mind is also the basis for experiencing all our suffering and problems. For example, when people are unable to fulfill their wishes, many experience depression, discouragement, unhappiness and mental pain, and some even want to kill themselves. This is because their self-cherishing believes that their own wishes are so important. It is therefore their self-cherishing that is mainly responsible for their problems. Without self-cherishing, there would be no basis for experiencing such suffering.

It is not difficult to see how the self-cherishing we have in this life causes us suffering. All disharmony, quarreling and fighting come from the self-cherishing of the people involved. With self-cherishing we hold our opinions and interests very strongly and are not willing to see a situation from another point of view. As a consequence we easily get angry and wish verbally or even physically to harm others. Self-cherishing makes us feel depressed whenever our wishes are not fulfilled, we fail in our ambitions or our life does not turn out the way we planned. If we examine all the times we have been miserable, we will discover that they are characterized by an excessive concern for our own welfare. If we lose our job, our home, our reputation or our friends we feel sad, but only because we deeply cherish ourself. We are not nearly so concerned when other people lose their jobs or are parted from their friends.

In themselves, external conditions are neither good nor bad. For example, wealth is generally thought of as desirable, but if we are strongly attached to wealth it will only cause us many worries and serve to deplete our merit. On the other hand, if our mind is governed principally by cherishing others, even losing all our money can be useful, for it gives us the opportunity to understand the suffering of those in similar situations and provides fewer distractions from our spiritual practice. Even if we did fulfill all the wishes of our self-cherishing, there is no guarantee that we would be happy, for every samsaric attainment brings with it new problems and invariably leads to new desires. The relentless pursuit of our selfish desires is like drinking salt water to quench our thirst. The more we indulge our desires, the greater our thirst.

When people kill themselves, it is usually because their wishes were not fulfilled, but this was unbearable to them only because their self-cherishing made them feel that their wishes were the most important thing in the world. It is because of self-cherishing that we take our wishes and plans so seriously and are unable to accept and learn from the difficulties that life brings us. We do not become a better person just by fulfilling our wishes for worldly success; we are as likely to develop the qualities that really matter—such as wisdom, patience and compassion—through our failures as through our successes.

We often feel that it is someone else who is making us unhappy, and we can become quite resentful. If we look at the situation carefully, however, we will find that it is always our own mental attitude that is responsible for our unhappiness. Another person's actions make us unhappy only if we allow them to stimulate a negative response in us. Criticism, for example, has no power from its own side to hurt us; we are hurt only because of our self-cherishing. With self-cherishing we are so dependent upon the opinions and approval of others that we lose our freedom to respond and act in the most constructive way.

We sometimes feel that the reason we are unhappy is that someone we love is in trouble. We need to remember that at the moment our love for others is almost invariably mixed with attachment, which is a self-centered mind. The love parents generally feel for their children, for example, is deep and genuine, but it is not always pure love. Mixed with it are feelings such as the need to feel loved and appreciated in return, the belief that their children are somehow part of them, a desire to impress other people through their children, and the hope that their children will in some way fulfill their parents' ambitions and dreams. It is sometimes very difficult to distinguish between our love and our attachment for others, but, when we are able to do so, we will see that it is invariably the attachment that is the cause of our suffering. Pure unconditional love never causes any pain or worry but only peace and joy.

All the problems of human society, such as war, crime, pollution, drug addiction, poverty, injustice and disharmony within families, are the result of self-cherishing. Thinking that human beings alone matter, and that the natural world exists to serve human desires, we have wiped out thousands of animal species and polluted the planet to such an extent that there is great danger it could soon be unfit even for human habitation. If everyone were to practice cherishing others, many of the major problems of the world would be solved in a few years.

Self-cherishing is like an iron chain that keeps us locked in samsara. The fundamental reason for our suffering is that we are in samsara, and we are in samsara because we continually create the deluded, self-centered actions that perpetuate the cycle of uncontrolled rebirth. Samsara is the experience of a self-centered mind. The six realms of samsara, from the god realm to the hell realm, are all the dream-like projections of a mind distorted by self-cherishing and self-grasping. By causing us to see life as a constant struggle to serve and protect our own I, these two minds impel us to perform innumerable destructive actions that keep us imprisoned in the nightmare of samsara. Until we destroy these two minds, we will never know true freedom or happiness, we will never really be in control of our mind and we will never be safe from the threat of lower rebirth.

Controlling our self-cherishing is of great value, even temporarily. All worries, anxiety and sadness are based on self-cherishing. The moment we let go of our obsessive concern for our own welfare, our mind naturally relaxes and becomes lighter. Even if we receive some bad news, if we manage to overcome our normal self-centered reaction our mind will remain at peace. On the other hand, if we fail to subdue our self-cherishing, even the most petty things disturb us. If a friend criticizes us we immediately become upset, and the frustration of even our smallest wishes leaves us dejected. If a Dharma Teacher says something we do not want to hear, we may become upset with him or her, or even lose our faith. Many people can get very agitated just because a mouse comes into their room. Mice do not eat people, so what reason is there to become upset? It is only the foolish mind of self-cherishing that disturbs us. If we loved the mouse as much as we loved ourself we would welcome the mouse into our room, thinking, "He has as much right to be here as I have!"

For those who aspire to become enlightened, the worst fault is self-cherishing. Self-cherishing is the main obstacle to cherishing others, failing to cherish others is the main obstacle to developing great compassion, and failing to develop great compassion is the main obstacle to developing bodhichitta and entering the path to enlightenment—the Mahayana path. Since bodhichitta is the main cause of great enlightenment, we can see that self-cherishing is also the main obstacle to the attainment of Buddhahood.

Although we might agree that objectively we are no more important than anyone else, and that self-cherishing has many faults, we may still feel that it is nevertheless indispensable. If we do not cherish and look after ourself, surely no one else will! This is a mistaken way of thinking. While it is true that we need to look after ourself, we do not need to be motivated by self-cherishing. Caring for ourself is not self-cherishing. We can take care of our health, have a job and look after our house and possessions solely out of concern for others' welfare. If we view our body as an instrument with which we can benefit others, we can feed it, clothe it, wash it and rest it—all without self-cherishing. Just as an ambulance driver can take care of his vehicle without regarding it as his own, so we can take care of our body and possessions for the benefit of others. The only way we can ever truly help all living beings is by becoming a Buddha, and the human form is the best possible vehicle for accomplishing this. Therefore, we need to take good care of our body. If we do this with bodhichitta motivation, all our actions of caring for our body become part of the path to enlightenment.

We may sometimes confuse self-cherishing with self-confidence and self-respect, but in reality they are completely unrelated. It is not out of self-respect that we always want the best for ourself, nor is it out of self-respect that we deceive or exploit others, or fail in our responsibilities to them. If we check honestly, we will see that it is our self-cherishing that causes us to act in ways that rob us of our self-respect and destroy our confidence. Some people are driven by their self-cherishing to the depths of alcoholism or drug addiction, completely losing any modicum of self-respect in the process. On the other hand, the more we cherish others and act to benefit them, the greater our self-respect and confidence will become. The Bodhisattva vow, for example, in which the Bodhisattva promises to overcome all faults and limitations, attain all good qualities and work until all living beings are liberated from the sufferings of samsara, is an expression of tremendous self-confidence, far beyond that of any self-centered being.

We might also ask, "If I had no self-cherishing, would that not mean that I dislike myself? Surely it is necessary to accept and love myself, for if I cannot love myself how can I love others?" This is an important point. In *Training the Mind in Seven Points*, Geshe Chekhawa explains a number of commitments that serve as guidelines for practitioners of training the mind. The first of these states: "Do not allow your practice of training the mind to cause inappropriate behavior." This commitment advises such practitioners to be happy with themselves. If we are excessively self-critical, we will turn in upon ourself and become discouraged, and this will make it very difficult for us to turn our mind to cherishing others. Although it is necessary to be aware of our faults, we should not hate ourself for them. This commitment also advises us to take care of ourself and look after our needs. If we try to live without basic necessities such as sufficient food and shelter we will probably damage our health and undermine our capacity to benefit others. Moreover, if people see us behaving in an extreme way, they may conclude that we are unbalanced and consequently will not trust us or believe what we say; and under such circumstances we will not be able to help them. Abandoning self-cherishing completely is not easy and will take a long time. If we are not happy with ourself, or foolishly neglect our own well-being, we will have neither the confidence nor the energy to effect such a radical spiritual transformation.

Once we are free from self-cherishing we do not lose our wish to be happy, but we understand that real happiness is to be found in benefiting others. We have discovered an inexhaustible fountain of happiness within our own mind—our love for others. Difficult external conditions do not depress us and pleasant conditions do not overexcite us, for we are able to transform and enjoy both. Rather than focusing on gathering good external conditions, our desire for happiness is channeled into a determination to attain enlightenment, which we recognize as the only means of achieving pure happiness. Though we long to enjoy the ultimate bliss of full enlightenment, we do so solely for the sake of others, for attaining enlightenment is merely the means to fulfill our real wish, which is to bestow the same happiness on all living beings. When we become a Buddha our happiness radiates eternally as compassion, nourishing all living beings and gradually drawing them into the same state.

In short, self-cherishing is an utterly worthless and unnecessary mind. We may be highly intelligent, but if we are concerned only with our own welfare we can never fulfill our basic wish to find happiness. In reality, self-cherishing makes us stupid. It causes us to experience unhappiness in this life, leads us to perform countless negative actions that cause suffering in future lives, binds us to samsara and blocks the path to enlightenment. Cherishing others has the opposite effects. If we cherish only others we will be happy in this life, we will perform many virtuous actions that lead to happiness in future lives, we will become free from the delusions that keep us in samsara and we will quickly develop all the qualities needed to attain full enlightenment.

HOW TO STOP DEVELOPING SELF-CHERISHING

If we have realized emptiness, the mere absence of things that we normally see—of which there is a detailed explanation in the chapter *Ultimate Bodhichitta*—we should think from our heart, "The object of my self-cherishing is only my self that I normally see, which actually does not exist. Thus, I must stop developing self-cherishing because its object —my self that I normally see—does not exist." We then meditate on this determination again and again. Out of meditation we do not allow ourself to cherish ourself that we normally see by remembering that it does not exist. Through continually applying effort to practice this special method, which is an oral instruction, we can easily stop developing self-cherishing.

However, as I previously said, in general abandoning self-cherishing is not easy, so there now follows a detailed explanation of how to stop developing self-cherishing. From our heart we mentally repeat again and again the instructions explained above on the faults of self-cherishing and the benefits of cherishing others. Having deep familiarity with contemplating the meaning of these instructions, we make a strong determination not to allow ourself to think and believe that we are more important than others. We then meditate on this determination. We should practice this contemplation and meditation continually. Between meditation sessions we should apply effort to putting our determination into practice.

Having made the determination to overcome our self-cherishing, the next step is to recognize it the moment it arises in our mind. To do this we need to examine our mind throughout the day and the night. This means that we should practice like Geshe Ben Gungyal and watch our own mind in everything we think and believe. Usually we keep an eye on what other people are doing, but it would be far better if we kept an eye all the time on what our mind is thinking and believing. Whenever we are working, talking, relaxing or studying Dharma, one part of our mind should always be watching to check what thoughts are arising in our mind. As soon as a delusion of self-cherishing is about to arise, we should try to stop it immediately. If we catch a delusion in its early stages, it is quite easy to stop, but if we allow it to develop fully it becomes very difficult to control.

One of our most destructive delusions is self-cherishing. The reason we naturally develop self-cherishing is that we have never applied effort in learning to stop the initial development of self-cherishing. If we catch our mind as soon as it starts to focus on on the object of our self-cherishing, our inherently existent self or I, it is quite easy to prevent self-cherishing from arising and to channel our thoughts in a more constructive direction. All we need to do is say to ourself, "This is an inappropriate way of thinking and will soon give rise to self-cherishing, which has many faults." However, if we fail to catch our self-cherishing early on and allow it to grow, it will soon become extremely powerful and very difficult to overcome. The same is true of all other delusions. If we become aware of a deluded train of thought early on, we can easily avert it, but, if we allow it to continue, it will gather momentum until it becomes almost impossible to stop.

There are three levels of abandoning delusions. The first is to recognize a particular delusion as it is about to arise and, remembering its disadvantages, to prevent it from manifesting. As long as we keep a watch over our mind, this is quite straightforward and is something we should try to practice all the time, whatever we are doing. In particular, as soon as we notice that our mind is becoming tense or unhappy we should be especially vigilant, for such a mind is a perfect breeding ground for delusions. For this reason, in *Training the Mind in Seven Points* Geshe Chekhawa says, "Always rely upon a happy mind alone."

The second level of abandoning our delusions is to subdue them by applying their specific opponents. For example, to subdue our attachment, we can meditate on the faults of samsara and replace our attachment with the opposite mind of renunciation. Through meditating on the path to enlightenment in a regular, systematic way, we not only prevent deluded patterns of thinking and feeling from arising but we also replace them with strong and stable virtuous patterns, based on wisdom rather than ignorance. In this way, we can prevent most delusions from arising in the first place. For instance, through deep familiarity with the view that others are more important than ourself, self-cherishing will rarely arise.

The third level of abandoning our delusions is to abandon them completely, together with their seeds, by gaining a direct realization of emptiness. In this way we destroy self-grasping, which is the root of all delusions.

In the practice of equalizing self and others that was explained earlier, we think, "Just as my happiness is important, so too is the happiness of everyone else"; and in this way we share our feeling of cherishing. Because this appeals to our sense of fairness and does not directly challenge our self-cherishing mind, it is easier to accept and practice. We can also reflect that, no matter how much we may suffer, we are only one single person whereas other living beings are countless, so it is obviously important for them to experience peace and happiness. Although we regard each of our fingers and thumbs as precious, we would be prepared to sacrifice one to save the other nine, whereas sacrificing nine to save one would be absurd. Similarly, nine people are more important than one, so of course countless living beings are more important than one self alone. It follows that it is logical to cherish others at least as much as we cherish ourself.

Having gained some familiarity with the practice of equalizing self and others, we are ready to confront the self-cherishing mind more directly. Because self-cherishing has so many faults, we should encourage ourself to confront and overcome it the moment it arises in our mind. By keeping a close watch over our mind all the time, we can train ourself to recognize self-cherishing the moment it arises and then immediately recall its disadvantages. Geshe Chekhawa advises us to "Gather all blame into one," by which he means that we should blame self-cherishing for all our problems and suffering. Normally when things go wrong we blame others, but the real cause of our problems is our self-cherishing mind. Once we have correctly identified self-cherishing, we should regard it as our worst enemy and blame it for all our suffering. Although it is good to be tolerant of others and to forgive their weaknesses, we should never tolerate our self-cherishing, for the more lenient we are with it the more it will harm us. It is far better to be utterly ruthless and blame it for everything that goes wrong. If we want to be angry with something, we should be angry with the "demon" of our self-cherishing. In reality, anger directed against self-cherishing is not real anger, for it is based on wisdom rather than ignorance and functions to make our mind pure and peaceful.

To practice in this way, we need to be very skillful. If, as a result of blaming our self-cherishing for all our problems, we find ourself feeling guilty and inadequate, this indicates that we have not made a clear distinction between blaming our self-cherishing and blaming ourself. Although it is true that self-cherishing is to blame for all our problems, this does not mean that we ourself are to blame. Once again, we have to learn to distinguish between ourself and our delusions. If we are attacked it is not our fault but the fault of our self-cherishing. How? Because it is the karmic effect of a non-virtuous action we performed in a previous life under the influence of self-cherishing. Moreover, our attacker harms us only because of his or her self-cherishing, and blaming him will not help, for it will only make us bitter. However, if we place all the blame on our self-cherishing mind and resolve to destroy it, we will not only remain undisturbed but also undermine the basis for all our future suffering.

This teaching on recognizing the faults of our self-cherishing and subsequently developing the desire to overcome it is not easy to put into practice, and so we need to be patient. A practice that is suitable for one person is not necessarily suitable for someone else, and a practice that is appropriate for one person at one time is not necessarily appropriate for that same person at another time. Buddha did not expect us to put all his teachings into practice right away; they are intended for a great variety of practitioners of different levels and dispositions. There are also some instructions that cannot be practiced while we are emphasizing other practices, just as it is not appropriate to drink tea and coffee together at the same time. Dharma instructions are like medicine and need to be administered skillfully, taking into account the nature of the individual and his or her particular needs. For example, to encourage us to develop renunciation, the wish to attain liberation from samsara, Buddha gave extensive teachings on how ordinary life is in the nature of suffering—but not everyone can apply these teachings right away. For some people, meditating on suffering only causes them to become despondent. Instead of developing a joyful mind of renunciation, they just get depressed. For these people it is better for the time being not to meditate on suffering but to come back to it later when their minds are stronger and their wisdom clearer.

If we practice advanced teachings and find that our pride or confusion increases, this indicates that we are not yet ready for such teachings and should first emphasize building a firm foundation of basic practices. If any meditation or practice is not having a good effect on our mind, is making us unhappy or is increasing our delusions, this is a clear sign that we are practicing incorrectly. Rather than stubbornly pushing at the practice, it may be better to put it to one side for the time being and seek advice from senior practitioners.

We can go back to that practice once we understand where we are going wrong and what is the correct way of practicing. What we should never do, however, is reject any Dharma instruction by thinking, "I will never practice this."

When we go shopping, we do not feel impelled to buy everything in the store, but it is useful to remember what the store stocks so that we can return later when we need something. In a similar way, when we listen to Dharma teachings, we may not immediately be able to practice all that we hear, but it is still important to remember everything so that we can build up a comprehensive understanding of Dharma. Later, when we are ready, we can put the instructions we have heard into practice. One of the great advantages of the instructions of Lamrim—the stages of the path to enlightenment—is that it gives us a structure, or storehouse, within which we can keep all the Dharma teachings we have heard.

If we remember only those teachings that we are immediately able to apply in our present situation, when our circumstances change we will have nothing to fall back on. However, if we can remember all the teachings we have received, we will have at our disposal a huge range of instructions that we can apply at the appropriate time. A practice that may seem obscure and of little significance to us now may later become an essential part of our spiritual practice. What is important is to proceed carefully and at our own pace, otherwise we might feel confused or discouraged and may even end up rejecting Dharma altogether.

There is no greater spiritual practice than recognizing self-cherishing whenever it arises and then blaming it for all our problems. It does not matter how long we spend on this; even if it takes years or our whole life, we need to continue until our self-cherishing is completely destroyed. We should not be in a hurry to see results, but instead practice patiently and sincerely. Expecting quick results is itself based on self-cherishing and is a recipe for disappointment. If we practice with joy and steadfastness, while at the same time purifying negativity, accumulating merit and receiving blessings, we will definitely succeed in reducing and finally abandoning our self-cherishing.

Even when our meditation is not going well, we can practice mindfulness and alertness in our daily life and stop self-cherishing as soon as it arises. This is a simple practice but it has great results. If we train in it continuously, our problems will disappear and we will naturally be happy all the time. There are people who have succeeded in completely abandoning their self-cherishing and who now cherish only others. As a result, all their problems have disappeared and their minds are always filled with joy. I guarantee that the less you cherish yourself and the more you cherish others the happier you will become.

We should keep a strong determination in our heart to abandon our self-cherishing mind. If we apply armor-like effort in this determination day by day, year by year, our self-cherishing will gradually diminish and eventually cease altogether. The early Kadampa Geshes would often say that to lead a virtuous life all we need to do is harm our delusions as much as possible and benefit others as much as possible. Understanding this, we should wage continuous warfare against our inner enemy of self-cherishing and strive to cherish and benefit others instead.

To destroy our self-cherishing completely, we need to rely upon the practice of exchanging self with others, in which we no longer grasp at our own happiness but instead feel that all living beings, and their needs and wishes, are of supreme importance. Our only concern is for the well-being of others.

Although someone who has completely exchanged himself with others has no self-cherishing, this does not mean that he does not look after himself. He does look after himself, but for the sake of others. He regards himself as a servant of all living beings and as belonging to them; but even servants need to eat and rest if they are to be effective. It would generally be very foolish, for example, if we were to give away all we owned, leaving ourself with nothing to live on or to sustain our spiritual practice. Since our real wish is to benefit all living beings, and the only way we can do this is by becoming a Buddha, we need to protect our spiritual practice by organizing our life so that we are able to practice in the most effective way. Moreover, when we help others, we should also make sure that in helping one person we are not undermining our capacity to help many people. Although in our hearts we would gladly give away everything we have to help one person, practically we need to manage our time and resources so that we can be of the greatest benefit to all living beings.

The practice of exchanging self with others belongs to the special wisdom lineage that came from Buddha Shakyamuni through Manjushri and Shantideva to Atisha and Je Tsongkhapa. The bodhichitta that is developed through this method is more profound and powerful than the bodhichitta developed through other methods. Although everyone with an interest in spiritual development can reduce their self-cherishing and learn to cherish others, a complete realization of exchanging self with others is a very profound attainment. To transform our mind in such a radical way, we need deep faith in this practice, an abundance of merit, and powerful blessings from a Spiritual Guide who has personal experience of these teachings. With all these conducive conditions, the practice of exchanging self with others is not difficult.

We may wonder why it is necessary to cherish others more than ourself. Rather than aiming for such high spiritual realizations, would it not be better just to emphasize helping people in a practical way right now? Without compassion and wisdom we do not know whether helping people in practical ways may benefit them or harm them. We should know that the happiness or peace of mind that comes from worldly enjoyments is not real happiness, but is just changing suffering or a reduction of previous suffering. People need the happiness and peace of mind that comes from wisdom. The wisdom realizing the meaning of the instructions on exchanging self with others will bring pure and everlasting happiness.

The reason why we need to train our mind in exchanging self with others is because our self-cherishing interferes with both our intention and our ability to benefit others. With self-cherishing, we do not have unbiased, universal love for all living beings, and for as long as our desire to help them is mixed with self-cherishing we can never be sure that our actions will actually benefit them. Although we may genuinely want to help some people, such as our family, our friends or those in need, we usually expect something back in return, and are hurt and disappointed if this is not forthcoming. Since our wish to benefit is mixed with selfish concerns, our help nearly always comes with the strings of expectation or personal reward. Because our intention is impure, our ability to help lacks power and remains limited.

If, while making no effort to eliminate our self-cherishing, we claim to be working for the benefit of all, our claim is coming from our mouth and not from our heart and our wisdom. Of course we should help others practically whenever we can, but we should always remember that our main intention is to develop our mind. By training in exchanging self with others we will finally experience the ultimate happiness of Buddhahood and possess complete power to benefit all living beings. Only then will we be in a position to say, "I am a benefactor of all living beings." In this way, our training in exchanging self with others accomplishes both our own and others' purpose.

Our most important task at the moment is to train our mind, and in particular to strengthen our intention to be of service to others. In his *Friendly Letter* Nagarjuna says that although we may not have the ability to help others now, if we keep the intention to do so in mind all the time, our ability to help them will gradually increase. This is because the more we cherish others, the more our merit, wisdom and capacity to actually benefit them will increase, and opportunities to help in practical ways will naturally present themselves.

HOW IS IT POSSIBLE TO EXCHANGE SELF WITH OTHERS?

Exchanging self with others does not mean that we become the other person—it means that we exchange the object of our cherishing from ourself to others. To understand how this is possible we should understand that the object of our self-cherishing mind is always changing. When we are young, the object of our self-cherishing is a young girl or boy, but later it changes to a teenager, then to a middle-aged person and finally to an old person. At the moment, we may cherish ourself as a particular human being called Maria or John, but after we die the object of our cherishing will completely change. In this way, the object of our cherishing is continually changing, both during this life and from one life to the next. Since our cherishing naturally changes from one object to another, it is definitely possible through training in meditation for us to change the object of our cherishing from self to others.

Due to our ignorance we grasp at our body very strongly, thinking, "This is my body." Identifying with this body as "mine," we cherish and love it dearly, feeling it to be our most precious possession. In reality, however, our body belongs to others; we did not bring it with us from our previous life but received it from our parents of this life. At the moment of conception our consciousness entered into the union of our father's sperm and mother's ovum, which gradually developed into our present body. Our mind then identified with this body and we began to cherish it. As Shantideva says in *Guide to the Bodhisattva's Way of Life*, our body is not really our own but belongs to others; it was produced by others, and after our death will be disposed of by others. If we contemplate this carefully, we will realize that we are already cherishing an object that in reality belongs to others, so why can we not cherish other living beings? Furthermore, whereas cherishing our body only leads to rebirth within samsara, cherishing others is a cause for attaining the nirvana of full enlightenment, the state beyond sorrow.

"Self" and "other" are relative terms, rather like "this mountain" and "that mountain" but not like "donkey" and "horse." When we look at a horse, we cannot say that it is a donkey, and likewise we cannot say that a donkey is a horse. However, if we climb a mountain in the east we call it "this mountain" and we call the mountain to the west "that mountain"; but if we climb down the eastern mountain and up the western mountain, we then refer to the western mountain as "this mountain" and to the eastern mountain as "that mountain." "This" and "that" therefore depend upon our point of reference. This is also true of self and other. By climbing down the mountain of self, it is possible to ascend the mountain of other, and thereby cherish others as much as we presently cherish ourself. We can do this by recognizing that, from another person's point of view, it is he or she who is self while it is we who are other.

Those who are skilled in Secret Mantra, or Tantra, have a profound experience of exchanging self with others. In the Tantric practice of self-generation, we exchange our present self with that of a Tantric Buddha. Suppose there is a Vajrayogini practitioner called Sarah. Whenever she is not engaged in Tantric practice, her ordinary body appears to her and she identifies with it and cherishes it. When she concentrates deeply on self-generation meditation, however, the sense of being Sarah and having Sarah's body completely disappears. Instead of identifying with Sarah's body, the practitioner identifies with the divine body of Buddha Vajrayogini and develops the thought, "I am Vajrayogini." The practitioner has now entirely changed the object of cherishing from the impure body of an ordinary being to the uncontaminated body of an enlightened being, Buddha Vajrayogini. Through training in meditation, the practitioner develops deep familiarity with the body of the Deity and comes to identify with it completely. Because Vajrayogini's body is a pure body, identifying with it and cherishing it is a cause of enlightenment. From this we can see that it is definitely possible to change our basis of identification—it just depends upon our motivation and our familiarity. A detailed explanation of Tantric practice can be found in the books *Modern Buddhism*, *The New Guide to Dakini Land* and *Tantric Grounds and Paths*.

THE ACTUAL PRACTICE OF
EXCHANGING SELF WITH OTHERS

We think:

I have worked for my own purpose since beginningless time, trying to find happiness for myself and avoid suffering, but what do I have to show for all my efforts? I am still suffering. I still have an uncontrolled mind. I still experience disappointment after disappointment. I am still in samsara. This is the fault of my self-cherishing. It is my worst enemy and a terrible poison that harms both myself and others.

Cherishing others, however, is the basis of all happiness and goodness. Those who are now Buddhas saw the futility of working for their own purpose and decided to work for others instead. As a result, they became pure beings, free from all the problems of samsara, and they attained the lasting happiness of full enlightenment. I must reverse my ordinary childish attitude—from now on I will stop cherishing myself and cherish only others.

With an understanding of the great disadvantages of cherishing ourself and the great advantages of cherishing all living beings, as explained above, and remembering that we have made the determination to abandon our self-cherishing and always cherish all living beings without exception, we think from the depths of our heart:

I must give up cherishing myself and instead cherish all other living beings without exception.

We then meditate on this determination. We should continually practice this meditation until we spontaneously believe that the happiness and freedom of each and every other living being are far more important than our own. This belief is the realization of exchanging self with others, and will give rise to a deep feeling of cherishing love for all living beings. We meditate on this feeling for as long as we can.

We try to carry this feeling with us during the meditation break. Whoever we meet, we think, "This person is important. Their happiness and freedom are important." Whenever self-cherishing begins to arise in our mind, we think, "Self-cherishing is poison; I will not allow it in my mind." In this way we can change our object of cherishing from ourself to all living beings. When we have developed spontaneous cherishing love for all living beings, we have gained the realization of exchanging self with others.

If our wishes are not fulfilled and we begin to feel unhappy, we should immediately remember that the fault lies not with the other person or the situation but with our own self-cherishing mind, which instinctively feels, "My wishes are of paramount importance." Remaining continually mindful of the dangers of our self-cherishing will strengthen our resolve to abandon it, and, instead of feeling sorry for ourself when we have problems, we can use our own suffering to remind us of the suffering of countless mother beings and develop love and compassion for them.

In *Guide to the Bodhisattva's Way of Life*, Shantideva explains a special method to enhance our experience of exchanging self with others. In meditation we imagine that we exchange places with another person, and we try to see the world from his or her point of view. Normally we develop the thought "I" on the basis of our own body and mind, but now we try to think "I" observing the body and mind of another person. This practice helps us to develop a profound empathy with other people, and shows us that they have a self that is also an I, and that is just as important as our own self or I. Because of her ability to identify with the feelings of her baby, a mother is able to understand her child's needs and wishes far better than other people. Similarly, as we become familiar with this meditation, our understanding of and empathy with other people will increase.

This technique is particularly powerful when we apply it to someone with whom we have a difficult relationship, such as someone we dislike or see as our rival. By imagining we are that person, and seeing the situation from his or her point of view, we will find it difficult to hold onto our deluded attitudes. Understanding the relativity of self and other from our own experience, and learning to see our "self" as "other," we will become far more objective and impartial toward our self, and our sense that we are the center of the universe will be shaken. We will become more open to others' point of view, more tolerant and more understanding; and we will naturally treat others with greater respect and consideration. More details on this practice are given in the book *Meaningful to Behold*.

In summary, through practicing the instructions of training the mind, Bodhisattva Langri Tangpa and countless other practitioners of the past have attained profound spiritual realizations, including the complete realization of exchanging self with others. At the beginning, these practitioners were self-centered people just like us, but through constant perseverance they managed to eliminate their self-cherishing completely. If we practice these instructions wholeheartedly and patiently, there is no reason why we too should not attain similar realizations. We should not expect to destroy our self-cherishing immediately, but through patient practice it will gradually become weaker and weaker until it eventually ceases altogether.

Great Compassion

*H*aving gained some experience of cherishing all living beings, we can now extend and deepen our compassion, and the method for doing so is revealed in this chapter. In general, everyone already has some compassion. We all feel compassion when we see our family or friends in distress, and even animals feel compassion when they see their offspring in pain. Our compassion is our Buddha seed or Buddha nature, our potential to become a Buddha. It is because all living beings possess this seed that they will all eventually become Buddhas.

When a dog sees her puppies in pain, she develops the wish to protect them and free them from pain, and this compassionate wish is her Buddha seed. Unfortunately, however, animals have no ability to train in compassion, and so their Buddha seed cannot ripen. Human beings, though, have a great opportunity to develop their Buddha nature. Through meditation we can extend and deepen our compassion until it transforms into the mind of universal, or great, compassion—the sincere wish to liberate all living beings permanently from suffering. Through improving this mind of universal compassion it will eventually transform into the compassion of a Buddha, which actually has the power to liberate all living beings. Therefore, the way to become a Buddha is to awaken our compassionate Buddha nature and complete the training in universal compassion. Only human beings can do this.

Compassion is the very essence of a spiritual life and the main practice of those who have devoted their lives to attaining enlightenment. It is the root of the Three Jewels—Buddha, Dharma and Sangha. It is the root of Buddha because all Buddhas are born from compassion. It is the root of Dharma because Buddhas give Dharma teachings motivated solely by compassion for others. It is the root of Sangha because it is by listening to and practicing Dharma teachings given out of compassion that we become Sangha, or Superior beings.

WHAT IS COMPASSION?

What exactly is compassion? Compassion is a mind that is motivated by cherishing other living beings and wishes to release them from their suffering. Sometimes out of selfish intention we can wish for another person to be free from their suffering; this is quite common in relationships that are based principally on attachment. If our friend is ill or depressed, for example, we may wish for him to recover quickly so that we can enjoy his company again; but this wish is basically self-centered and is not true compassion. True compassion is necessarily based on cherishing others.

Although we already have some degree of compassion, at present it is very biased and limited. When our family and friends are suffering, we easily develop compassion for them, but we find it far more difficult to feel sympathy for people we find unpleasant or for strangers. Furthermore, we feel compassion for those who are experiencing manifest pain, but not for those who are enjoying good conditions, and especially not for those who are engaging in harmful actions. If we genuinely want to realize our potential by attaining full enlightenment we need to increase the scope of our compassion until it embraces all living beings without exception, just as a loving mother feels compassion for all her children irrespective of whether they are behaving well or badly. Unlike our present, limited compassion, which already arises naturally from time to time, universal compassion must first be cultivated through training over a long period of time.

HOW TO DEVELOP COMPASSION

There are two essential stages to cultivating compassion. First we need to cherish others, and then, on the basis of cherishing others, we need to contemplate their suffering. Through this we will naturally develop compassion for them. Normally, when we see our enemy suffering we do not develop compassion because we do not cherish him or her. This is the opposite to the way in which we react when we see our friend suffering. This is because we cherish him or her. Cherishing others is the foundation for developing compassion. The way to develop and enhance our mind of cherishing love has already been explained. Now we must contemplate how each and every samsaric being is experiencing suffering.

To begin with, we can think about those who are suffering intense manifest pain right now. There are so many people experiencing terrible mental and physical suffering from illnesses such as cancer, AIDS and Parkinson's disease. How many people have lost a beloved child or friend through the scourge of cancer, watching him become weaker and weaker, knowing that it is difficult to cure? Every day, thousands of people experience the agony of dying from illnesses or in accidents. Without choice they are separated forever from everyone they love, and those they leave behind often experience inconsolable grief and loneliness. Imagine an old woman losing her husband and lifelong partner, sadly returning home after the funeral to an empty house to live out the rest of her days alone.

Throughout the world we can see how millions of people are suffering through the horrors of war and ethnic cleansing, from bombing, land mines and massacres. Suppose it was your child who went out to play in the fields and lost a limb, or even his very life, by stepping on a land mine. Hundreds of thousands of refugees throughout the world live in squalid camps, hoping someday to return to their ruined homes, many of them waiting to be reunited with their loved ones, every day not knowing if they are alive or dead.

Every year natural disasters such as floods, earthquakes and hurricanes devastate whole communities and leave people homeless and hungry. A few short seconds of an earthquake can kill thousands of people, destroy their homes and bury everything under tons of rubble. Think how we would feel if this were to happen to us. Famine and drought are endemic in many countries throughout the world. So many people live on a subsistence diet, barely scraping together one meager meal a day, while others who are less fortunate succumb and die of starvation. Imagine the torment of watching your loved ones slowly waste away, knowing that there is nothing you can do. Whenever we read, listen to or watch the news, we see living beings who are in terrible pain, and we all personally know people who are experiencing immense mental or physical suffering.

We can especially consider the plight of countless animals who experience extremes of heat and cold, and suffer great hunger and thirst. Every day, all around us, we can see the suffering of animals. Animals in the wild are in almost constant fear of being prey to others, and indeed many of them are eaten alive by predators. Just think of the terror and pain a field mouse experiences when caught and ripped to shreds by a hawk! Countless animals are kept by humans for labor, food or entertainment, and often live in disgusting conditions until they are slaughtered, butchered and packaged for human consumption. Hungry ghosts and hell beings have to experience far worse sufferings for inconceivably long periods of time.

We also need to remember that even those who are not presently experiencing manifest pain still experience other forms of suffering. Everyone in samsara experiences the suffering of not fulfilling their wishes. So many people find it difficult to satisfy even modest desires for adequate shelter, food or companionship; and, even if those desires are fulfilled, we have more to take their place. The more we get what we want, the stronger our attachment becomes; and the stronger our attachment, the more difficult it is to find satisfaction. The desires of samsaric beings are endless. There is no such thing as an ordinary person who has fulfilled all his or her wishes; only those who have transcended selfish minds can do this.

All suffering is the result of negative karma. If we develop compassion for those who are experiencing the effects of their previous negative actions, why can we not also develop compassion for those who are creating the cause to experience suffering in the future? In the long term a torturer is in a worse position than his victim, for his suffering is just beginning. If the victim can accept his or her pain without developing hatred, he will exhaust that particular negative karma and not create any more; and so his suffering has an end in sight. The torturer, on the other hand, will first have to endure many eons in hell, and then, when he is again reborn as a human being, will have to experience pain similar to that which he inflicted on the victim. For this reason it is entirely appropriate to develop strong compassion for such people.

If a child burns himself by putting his hand in a fire, this will not stop his mother from feeling compassion, even if the child has been previously warned about the dangers of fire. No one wants to suffer, yet out of ignorance living beings create the causes of suffering—non-virtuous actions—because they are controlled by their delusions. We should therefore feel equal compassion for all living beings—for those who are creating the causes of suffering, as much as for those who are already suffering the consequences of their unskillful actions. There is not a single living being who is not a suitable object of our compassion.

We may also find it difficult to feel compassion for the rich, healthy and well respected, who do not appear to be experiencing any manifest pain. In reality, however, they too experience a great deal of mental suffering and find it hard to maintain a peaceful mind. They worry about their money, their bodies and their reputation. Like all other samsaric beings, they suffer from anger, attachment and ignorance, and have no choice but to undergo the sufferings of birth, aging, sickness and death unceasingly and relentlessly, life after life. Moreover, their wealth and good conditions are utterly meaningless if, through their ignorance, they use them only to create the cause for future suffering.

If, on the basis of cherishing all living beings, we contemplate the fact that they experience the cycle of physical suffering and mental pain in life after life without end, their inability to liberate themselves from suffering, their lack of freedom and how, by engaging in negative actions, they create the causes of future suffering, we will develop deep compassion for them. We need to empathize with them and feel their pain as keenly as we feel our own. Finally, we concentrate on developing universal compassion, the sincere wish to permanently liberate all living beings from the sufferings of this life and countless future lives. We contemplate as follows:

All living beings suffer because they take contaminated rebirths. Human beings have no choice but to experience immense human sufferings because they have taken human rebirth, which is contaminated by the inner poison of delusions. Similarly, animals have to experience animal suffering, and hungry ghosts and hell beings have to experience all the sufferings of their respective realms. If living beings were to experience all this suffering for just one single life, it would not be so bad, but the cycle of suffering continues life after life, endlessly.

From the depths of our heart we should then understand and think:

I cannot bear the suffering of these countless mother beings. Drowning in the vast and deep ocean of samsara, the cycle of contaminated rebirth, they have to experience unbearable physical suffering and mental pain in this life and in countless future lives. I must liberate all living beings permanently from the cycle of suffering.

We should meditate continually on this determination, which is universal compassion, and apply great effort to fulfilling its aim.

THE SUPREME WEALTH OF COMPASSION

During the meditation break we should continually maintain our feeling of compassion for all living beings. Whenever we encounter anyone, we should recall how they are suffering and develop compassion for them. Then, just seeing a living being will be like finding a rare and precious treasure. This is because the compassion we experience upon meeting others is a supreme inner wealth that is an inexhaustible source of benefit for us in both this and future lives.

As mentioned earlier, external wealth cannot help us in our future lives, and even in this life it is not certain that it will bring us happiness for it is often the cause of much anxiety and can even endanger our life. Rich people have particular worries that poor people never have; for example, they often worry about thieves, about investments and interest rates, and about losing their money and social status. This is a heavy burden for them. Whereas most people can go out freely whenever they choose, many wealthy and famous people need bodyguards and may even worry about being kidnapped. Rich people have little freedom or independence and can never fully relax. The higher up we are in the world the further we have to fall; it is safer to be nearer the bottom.

No matter how much we succeed in improving our external conditions, they can never bring us pure happiness nor provide real protection from suffering. True happiness cannot be found in this impure world. Instead of striving to obtain external wealth, it would be far better if we sought the internal wealth of compassion and wisdom, for unlike external wealth, this can never deceive us and will definitely bring us the peace and happiness we desire.

If we are skillful, friends can be like treasure chests, from whom we can obtain the precious wealth of love, compassion, patience and so forth. For our friends to function in this way, however, our love for them must be free from attachment. If our love for our friends is mixed with strong attachment, it will be conditional upon their behaving in ways that please us, and, as soon as they do something we disapprove of, our liking for them may turn to anger. In fact, the most common objects of our anger are often our friends, not our enemies or strangers!

If we often get angry with our friends, we are transforming them into maras. A mara, or obstructing demon, is someone or something that interferes with our spiritual practice. No one is a mara from his or her own side, but if we allow people to stimulate deluded minds in us, such as anger, strong attachment or self-cherishing, we transform them into maras for us. A mara does not need to have horns and a terrifying expression; someone who appears to be a good friend, who flatters us and leads us into meaningless activities, can be a greater obstacle to our spiritual practice. Whether our friends are precious treasures or maras depends entirely upon us; if we are sincerely practicing patience, compassion and love, they can be like priceless jewels, but if we are often getting angry with them, they can become maras.

We would be delighted to find a treasure chest buried beneath the ground or to win a large amount of money, and would consider ourself very fortunate. However, if we consider the deceptiveness of external wealth and the superiority of the inner wealth of virtue, how much more fortunate should we feel whenever we meet another living being, the potential source of limitless inner wealth? For sincere, compassionate practitioners, just seeing other living beings, speaking with them or merely thinking about them is like finding buried treasure. All their encounters with other people serve to enhance their compassion, and even everyday activities such as shopping or talking to friends become causes of enlightenment.

Of all virtuous minds, compassion and wisdom are supreme. Compassion purifies our mind, and when our mind is pure its objects also become pure. There are many accounts of spiritual practitioners who, by developing strong compassion, purified their minds of the negativity that had long been obstructing their spiritual progress. For example, Asanga, a great scholar who lived in India in the fifth century AD, meditated in an isolated mountain cave in order to gain a vision of Buddha Maitreya. After twelve years he still had not succeeded and, feeling discouraged, abandoned his retreat. On his way down the mountain he came across an old dog lying in the middle of the path. Its body was covered in maggot-infested sores and it seemed close to death. This sight induced within Asanga an overwhelming feeling of compassion for all living beings trapped within samsara. As he was painstakingly removing the maggots from the dying dog, Buddha Maitreya suddenly appeared to him. Maitreya explained that he had been with Asanga since the beginning of his retreat, but, due to the impurities in Asanga's mind, Asanga had not been able to see him. It was Asanga's extraordinary compassion that had finally purified the karmic obstructions preventing him from seeing Maitreya. In reality the dog had been an emanation of Buddha Maitreya all along—Maitreya emanated as a suffering dog for the purpose of arousing Asanga's compassion. We can see from this how Buddhas manifest in many different ways to help living beings.

Anyone who dies with a mind of pure compassion will definitely be reborn in a Pure Land, where he or she will never again have to experience the sufferings of samsara. The Bodhisattva Geshe Chekhawa's main wish was to be reborn in hell so that he could help the beings suffering there. However, as he lay on his deathbed he perceived a vision of the Pure Land and realized that his wish would not be fulfilled. Instead of being reborn in hell, he had no choice but to go to the Pure Land! This was because his compassion had purified his mind to such an extent that, from the point of view of his own experience, impure objects such as hell realms no longer existed—for him everything was pure. However, although Geshe Chekhawa took rebirth in a Pure Land, he was able to help hell beings through his emanations.

We may find these stories difficult to believe, but this is because we do not understand the relationship between our mind and its objects. As Milarepa said, our mind and its objects are in truth the same nature, but due to ignorance we believe they are different natures. We feel that the world exists "out there," independent of the mind that perceives it, but in reality objects are totally dependent on the minds that perceive them. This impure world that we now experience exists only in relation to our impure mind. Once we have completely purified our mind through training in exchanging self with others, compassion and so forth, this impure world will disappear and we will perceive a new, pure world. Our sense that things exist separately from our mind, with their own fixed, inherent natures, comes from our ignorance. When we understand the true nature of things, we will see that our world is like a dream, in that everything exists as a mere appearance to mind. We will realize that we can change our world simply by changing our mind, and that if we wish to be free from suffering, all we need to do is purify our mind. Having purified our own mind, we will then be in a position to fulfill our compassionate wish by showing others how to do the same.

Considering all these benefits of compassion, we should resolve to make use of every opportunity to develop it. The most important thing is to put the teachings on compassion and wisdom into practice, for our own and others' purposes, otherwise for us they will remain just empty words. The nature and functions of wisdom are explained in the section on training in higher wisdom in the chapter *Meaningful Objects*.

Pure compassion is a mind that finds the suffering of others unbearable, but it does not make us depressed. In fact, it gives us tremendous energy to work for others and to complete the spiritual path for their sake. It shatters our complacency and makes it impossible to rest content with the superficial happiness of satisfying our worldly desires, yet in its place we will come to know a deep inner peace that cannot be disturbed by changing conditions. It is impossible for strong delusions to arise in a mind filled with compassion. If we do not develop delusions, external circumstances alone have no power to disturb us; so when our mind is governed by compassion it is always at peace. This is the experience of all those who have developed their compassion beyond the limited compassion normally felt for those we feel close to into a selfless compassion for all living beings.

Developing compassion and wisdom, and helping those in need whenever possible, is the true meaning of human life. By increasing our compassion we come closer to enlightenment and to the fulfillment of our deepest wishes. How kind living beings are to act as the objects of our compassion! How precious they are! If there were no suffering beings left for us to help, Buddhas would have to emanate them for us! Indeed, if we consider the story of Maitreya and Asanga, we will see that we have no way of knowing for sure whether those we are presently trying to help are not in fact emanations of Buddha manifested for our benefit. The indication that we have mastered the meditations on cherishing others and compassion is that whenever we meet another person, even someone who is harming us, we genuinely feel as if we have found a rare and precious treasure.

Through the mirror of Buddha's teachings, Dharma,
we can see our own faults and have the
opportunity to remove them.

Wishing Love

In general, there are three types of love: affectionate love, cherishing love and wishing love. For example, when a mother looks at her children she feels great affection for them and perceives them to be beautiful, no matter how they appear to other people. Because of her affectionate love, she naturally feels them to be precious and important; this feeling is cherishing love. Because she cherishes her children, she sincerely wishes for them to be happy; this wish is wishing love. Wishing love arises from cherishing love, which in turn arises from affectionate love. We need to develop these three types of love toward all living beings without exception.

HOW TO DEVELOP WISHING LOVE
FOR ALL LIVING BEINGS

Having developed experience of cherishing love for all living beings through practicing the previous instructions, if we contemplate how living beings lack pure happiness we will naturally develop a sincere wish to lead all living beings to a state of pure happiness. This is universal wishing love.

What is pure happiness? Pure happiness is happiness that comes from a peaceful mind. The happiness that comes from worldly enjoyments such as eating, drinking, sex and relaxing is not pure or real happiness. It is changing suffering, or just a reduction of our previous suffering. Through training we can develop and maintain peace of mind all the time, so that we will be happy all the time.

In *Four Hundred Verses* the great scholar Aryadeva says:

> The experience of suffering will never be changed by the same cause,
> But we can see the experience of happiness will be changed by the same cause.

This means that, for example, the suffering caused by fire will never be changed into happiness by that fire, but we can see that the happiness caused, for example, by eating will change into suffering just through eating. How can we understand this? When we eat our favorite food, it tastes wonderful, but if we were to continue plateful after plateful our happiness would soon change into discomfort, disgust and eventually pain. This proves that the experience of happiness will be changed into suffering by the same cause. From eating comes happiness, but also the suffering of sickness. This shows that worldly enjoyments such as eating are not real causes of happiness, and this implies that the pleasure that comes from worldly enjoyments is not real happiness. The reverse, however, does not happen with painful experiences. For instance, hitting our finger with a hammer again and again can never become pleasurable, because it is a true cause of suffering. Just as a true cause of suffering can never give rise to happiness, so a true cause of happiness can never give rise to pain. Since the pleasurable feelings resulting from worldly enjoyments do turn into pain, it follows that they cannot be real happiness. Prolonged indulgence in eating, sports, sex or any other ordinary enjoyment invariably leads to suffering. No matter how hard we try to find happiness in worldly pleasures, we will never succeed. As mentioned earlier, indulging in samsaric pleasures is like drinking salt water; rather than satiating our thirst, the more we drink the more thirsty we become. In samsara we never reach a point when we can say, "Now I am completely satisfied; I need nothing more."

Not only is worldly pleasure not true happiness, but it also does not last. People devote their lives to acquiring possessions and social standing, and building up a home, a family and a circle of friends; but when they die they lose everything. All they have worked for suddenly disappears, and they enter their next life alone and empty-handed. They long to form deep and lasting friendships with others, but in samsara this is impossible. The dearest lovers will eventually be torn apart, and when they meet again in a future life they will not recognize each other. We may feel that those who have good relationships and have fulfilled their ambitions in life are truly happy, but in reality their happiness is as fragile as a water bubble. Impermanence spares nothing and no one; in samsara all our dreams are broken in the end. As Buddha says in the *Vinaya Sutras*:

The end of collection is dispersion.
The end of rising is falling.
The end of meeting is parting.
The end of birth is death.

The nature of samsara, the cycle of impure life, is suffering. In this impure life we will never experience pure happiness unless we engage in pure spiritual practice. Buddha compared living in samsara to sitting on top of a pin—no matter how much we try to adjust our position it is always painful, and no matter how hard we try to adjust and improve our samsaric situation it will always irritate us and give rise to pain.

Pure happiness comes from wisdom, which in turn comes from practicing pure spiritual teachings, known as "Dharma." Each and every spiritual practice presented in this book gives us the ability to develop and maintain peace of mind. This inner peace is pure happiness because it comes from wisdom, not from worldly enjoyments. If we have deep knowledge understanding the great benefits of pure spiritual practice, which is wisdom, we will definitely engage in pure spiritual practice. Without this wisdom we will never do this, and so wisdom is the source of all pure spiritual practices. Without wisdom we are like a person who has no eyes who cannot see anything. Similarly, without wisdom we cannot understand meaningful objects.

The meaning of pure spiritual practice has previously been explained in the chapter on death. What is wisdom? Wisdom is a deep knowledge that understands meaningful objects. All the objects of meditation presented in this book are meaningful objects because the knowledge that understands these objects gives us great meaning in this life and in countless future lives. There are many levels of pure happiness. Of these the supreme is the happiness of enlightenment. For this reason, in this practice of developing wishing love for all living beings, we generate the object of meditation by making a strong determination to lead all living beings to the pure happiness of enlightenment. We do this by engaging in the following contemplation. Cherishing all living beings, from the depths of our heart, we should think:

> *Although all living beings, who are drowning in the deep ocean of suffering, are looking for happiness all the time none of them finds real happiness. I must lead them to the pure happiness of enlightenment.*

We meditate on this determination again and again until we develop a spontaneous wish to lead all living beings to the supreme happiness of enlightenment.

The term "ocean of suffering" has great significance. The ocean of suffering is very different from an ordinary ocean.

Each and every part of an ordinary ocean is the nature of water, but each and every part of the ocean of suffering is the nature of suffering. An ordinary ocean has an end, but the ocean of suffering is endless. All living beings are drowning in this endless ocean of suffering; although they are all looking for happiness day and night, in the ocean of suffering there is no happiness at all. Through thinking and contemplating this we generate wishing love, sincerely wishing to lead all living beings to the pure happiness of enlightenment. Although we normally use the term "ocean of samsara," if instead we sometimes use the term "ocean of suffering" it will powerfully touch our hearts.

Meditation on love is very powerful. Wishing love is also called "immeasurable love" because merely through meditating on wishing love we will receive immeasurable benefits in this life and in countless future lives, even if our concentration is not very strong. Based on Buddha's teachings, the great scholar Nagarjuna listed eight benefits of affectionate love and wishing love: (1) By meditating on affectionate love and wishing love for just one moment we accumulate greater merit, or good fortune, than we would by giving food three times every day to all those who are hungry in the world.

When we give food to those who are hungry we are not giving real happiness. This is because the happiness that comes from eating food is not real happiness, but just a temporary reduction of the suffering of hunger. However, meditation on affectionate love and wishing love leads us and all living beings to the pure and everlasting happiness of enlightenment.

The remaining seven benefits of meditating on affectionate love and wishing love are that in the future: (2) we will receive great loving kindness from humans and non-humans; (3) we will be protected in various ways by humans and non-humans; (4) we will be mentally happy all the time; (5) we will be physically healthy all the time; (6) we will not be harmed by weapons, poison and other harmful conditions; (7) we will obtain all necessary conditions without effort; and (8) we will be born in the superior heaven of a Buddha Land.

Having contemplated these benefits we should apply effort in meditating on wishing love many times every day.

Love is the great protector, protecting us from anger and jealousy and from harm inflicted by spirits. When Buddha Shakyamuni was meditating under the Bodhi Tree, he was attacked by all the terrifying demons of this world, but his love transformed their weapons into a rain of flowers. Ultimately our love will become the universal love of a Buddha, which actually has the power to bestow happiness on all living beings.

Most relationships between people are based on a mixture of love and attachment. This is not pure love for it is based on a desire for our own happiness—we value the other person because they make us feel good. Pure love is unmixed with attachment and stems entirely from a concern for others' happiness. It never gives rise to problems but only to peace and happiness for both ourself and others. We need to remove attachment from our minds, but this does not mean that we have to abandon our relationships. Instead, we should learn to distinguish attachment from love, and gradually try to remove all traces of attachment from our relationships and to improve our love until it becomes pure.

Taking and Giving

*T*hrough the practice of taking and giving, we can further improve our love and compassion. In dependence upon this practice we can develop superior bodhichitta, which is the gateway through which we can enter the path to enlightenment. As mentioned above, enlightenment is the inner light of wisdom that is permanently free from all mistaken appearance, and whose function is to bestow peace of mind upon each and every living being every day. It is the source of all happiness.

When we first meditate on taking and giving, we cannot actually take on the suffering of others nor give them our happiness, but by imagining that we are doing so now, we are training our mind to be able to do so in the future. At the moment we are unable to benefit all living beings but we have the potential for this ability, which is part of our Buddha nature. Through practicing the meditations on taking and giving with strong compassion for all living beings, the potential to be able to benefit all living beings will ripen, and when this happens we will become an enlightened being, a Buddha.

"Taking" in this context means taking others' sufferings upon ourself through meditation. When we start our practice of taking and giving we do not need to think too much about how it is possible to relieve others' suffering through the power of our imagination alone. Instead, we should simply practice taking and giving with a good motivation, understanding it to be a supreme method for increasing our merit, or good fortune, and the power of our concentration. This practice also causes our mind and actions to become pure, so that we can accomplish everything easily. Through sincere training, our meditation on taking and giving will become so powerful that we will develop the ability directly to take on the suffering of others and give them happiness.

There are many examples of accomplished practitioners using the power of their concentration to take on the suffering of other beings with whom they have a karmic connection. There is a story of a great scholar and meditator called Maitriyogi who took on the pain of a dog that was being beaten, so that the wounds appeared on his body instead of the dog's. The great Tibetan Yogi Milarepa had completely mastered the meditation on taking and giving. On one occasion he took on a man's suffering, but the man refused to believe that it was due to Milarepa that he was free from pain. To prove it, Milarepa returned the pain to him, and when the pain became too much Milarepa then transferred the pain to a door, which started to shake! Faithful Buddhist practitioners believe that when their Spiritual Guide is ill, in reality he or she is taking on the suffering of others. Many Christians also believe that by allowing himself to be crucified Jesus was taking on the sufferings of human beings. It is quite possible that Jesus was practicing taking while he was on the cross.

If Buddhas and high Bodhisattvas have the power directly to take on the suffering of others and bestow happiness upon them, we may wonder why living beings are still suffering. Because Buddhas have this power, they are continuously bestowing blessings on all living beings. As a direct result of receiving these blessings, each and every living being, including animals and hell beings, occasionally experiences peace of mind, and at these times they are happy and free from manifest suffering. However, the only way living beings can achieve permanent liberation from suffering is by actually putting Buddha's teachings into practice. Just as a doctor cannot cure a disease unless the sick person actually takes the medicine that the doctor has prescribed, so Buddhas cannot cure our inner disease of delusions unless we actually take the medicine of Dharma.

Even when the sun is shining, if our house is shuttered only a little light can enter and our house will remain cold and dark; but if we open the shutters, the warm rays of the sun will come pouring in. Similarly, even though the sun of Buddha's blessings is always shining, if our mind is shuttered by our lack of faith, few blessings can enter and our mind will remain cold and dark; but, by developing strong faith, our mind will open and the full sun of Buddha's blessings will come pouring in. Faith is the life force of spiritual practice. We need to have unshakable faith in Buddha's teachings, otherwise we will never apply effort to putting these teachings into practice.

TAKING BY MEANS OF COMPASSION

For non-humans, such as animals or even gods, suffering only causes them distress and unhappiness, and they cannot learn anything from their pain. By contrast, humans who have met Buddhadharma can learn a great deal from their suffering. For us, suffering can be a great incentive to develop renunciation, compassion and bodhichitta, and can encourage us to engage in sincere purification practice.

When the Buddhist Master Je Gampopa was a young lay man he was happily married to a beautiful young woman, but before long she fell ill and died. Because of his deep attachment to his wife, Gampopa was grief-stricken, but his loss made him realize that death and suffering are the very nature of samsara and this encouraged him to seek permanent liberation from samsara, the cycle of impure life, through practicing Dharma purely. First he relied upon a number of Kadampa Geshes and practiced Kadam Lamrim, and later he met Milarepa and received the Mahamudra instructions. Finally, by sincerely practicing all the teachings he had heard, he became a great Master who led many beings along spiritual paths. Thus, we can see that, for the qualified Dharma practitioner, suffering has many good qualities. For these practitioners, samsara's sufferings are like a Spiritual Guide who leads them along the path to enlightenment.

As Shantideva says:

Moreover, suffering has many good qualities.
Through experiencing it, we can dispel pride,
Develop compassion for those trapped in samsara,
Abandon non-virtue, and delight in virtue.

Also, Atisha, the founder of the Kadampa tradition, says:

If, through being encouraged by his or her own
suffering,
A person sincerely wishes to liberate others from
their suffering,
Such a practitioner is a person of great scope.

Understanding the good qualities of our own suffering, which is wisdom, we should develop great joy at our opportunity to practice taking by means of compassion.

TAKING ON OUR OWN FUTURE SUFFERING

To prepare ourself for the actual meditation on taking on others' suffering, we can begin by taking on our own future suffering. This meditation is a powerful method for purifying the negative karma, or actions, that is the main cause of our future suffering. If we remove the cause of our future suffering, there will be no basis to experience the effect. Freedom from future suffering is more important than freedom from present suffering because our future suffering is endless whereas our present suffering is just the suffering of one short life. Therefore, while we still have the opportunity to purify the causes of our future suffering, we should train in taking on this suffering. This practice also serves to reduce our self-cherishing, which is the main reason why we find our suffering so difficult to bear, and it also strengthens our patience. When through the practice of patiently accepting our own suffering we can happily endure our adversities, it will not be difficult to take on the suffering of others. In this way, we gain the ability to prevent our own suffering and to benefit others. Understanding this, we make a determination to purify our non-virtues by taking on their effects now.

We imagine that all the sufferings we will experience in the future as a human, god, demi-god, animal, hungry ghost or hell being gather together in the aspect of black smoke and dissolve into our ignorance of self-grasping and self-cherishing at our heart. We strongly believe that our ignorance of self-grasping and self-cherishing is completely destroyed, and that we have purified the negative potentialities in our mind, the cause of all our future suffering. We then meditate on this belief for as long as possible. We should repeat this meditation on taking on our future suffering many times, until we receive signs that our negative karma has been purified. From engaging in this meditation we will experience a joy that will encourage us to develop a sincere wish to take on the suffering of others by means of compassion.

We can also prepare for the actual meditation on taking others' suffering by making prayers. It is very easy to say prayers, and if we say them with a good heart and strong concentration they are very powerful. While concentrating on the meaning, and believing that the living Buddha Shakyamuni is present in front of us, we pray:

Therefore, O Compassionate Venerable Guru, I seek
your blessings
So that all the suffering, negativities and obstructions
of mother sentient beings
Will ripen upon me right now.

We feel joy at the thought of taking on the suffering of all living beings, and we hold this special feeling for as long as possible. By repeating this prayer day and night, we continually strengthen our sincere wish to take on the suffering of others. We then engage in the actual meditation on taking on others' suffering.

THE BENEFITS OF TAKING ON OTHERS' SUFFERING

There are four main benefits of the meditations on taking and giving: they are powerful methods (1) to purify the potentialities of non-virtuous actions that cause us to experience serious diseases such as cancer; (2) to accumulate a great collection of merit; (3) to ripen our potentiality to be able to benefit all living beings; and (4) to purify our mind.

When we purify our mind through the practices of taking and giving, every spiritual realization will grow easily in our mind. Through contemplating the four main benefits of meditating on taking and giving, we should encourage ourself to practice these meditations sincerely.

Through meditating on taking the sufferings of all living beings we will develop a very strong mind that can bear adversity with courage. At present our mind is like an open wound—at the slightest hint of hardship we recoil in dismay. With such a weak mind, even minor difficulties interfere with our Dharma practice. By training in taking, however, we can strengthen our mind until it becomes unshakable. The Kadampa Geshes used to pray to develop a mind that is as strong and stable as a blacksmith's anvil, which does not break however hard it is struck. We need a strong and stable mind, one that is undisturbed by any hardship that life throws at us. With such a mind, we are like a hero or heroine, and nothing can interfere with our progress toward enlightenment.

Those with deep experience of the practice of taking can easily fulfill their own and others' wishes. Why is this? It is because they have so much merit and because their wishes are always pure and motivated by compassion. They can even fulfill their wishes by means of prayer or simply by declaring the truth.

There are many stories of Bodhisattvas performing miraculous feats through the power of their declaration of truth. These declarations are very powerful because they are motivated by bodhichitta, and bodhichitta derives its power from great compassion. When I was a young monk at Jampaling Monastery in Western Tibet, I was seriously ill for a few months. When the pain got so bad that I could hardly bear it, my Teacher Geshe Palden came to see me. He had a blessed mala and would often tell us how special it was, but we used to think he was joking. However, on this occasion he stood by my bedside and said to me, "If it is true that my mala is blessed by the Wisdom Buddha Manjushri, may you soon be cured," and then blessed me by touching my crown with the mala. After this, I recovered completely.

THE ACTUAL MEDITATION ON TAKING

There are two ways of training in taking by means of compassion. The first is to focus on all living beings in general and imagine taking on their suffering, and the second is to focus on particular living beings and imagine taking on their sufferings.

To practice the first method, we visualize ourself surrounded by the assembly of all mother living beings without exception. For auspiciousness, and to help us relate to them more easily, we can visualize them all in human aspect, but we should remember that each of them is experiencing the suffering of their own particular realm. It is not necessary to perceive them clearly—a rough mental image will suffice.

Then, from the depths of our heart, we should think:

In their countless future lives all these mother living beings will have to experience the immeasurable sufferings of animals, hungry ghosts and hell beings, and the immeasurable sufferings of humans, demi-gods and gods, in life after life, endlessly. I cannot bear this! How wonderful it would be if they attained permanent liberation from these sufferings! May they attain this liberation. I myself will work for this liberation now.

Thinking in this way, we imagine that the sufferings of all living beings gather together in the aspect of black smoke. This dissolves into our ignorance of self-grasping and self-cherishing at our heart. We then strongly believe that all living beings are permanently freed from suffering, and that our ignorance of self-grasping and self-cherishing is completely destroyed. We meditate on this belief single-pointedly for as long as possible.

With compassion for all living beings we should continually practice this meditation until we experience signs that indicate our mind has been purified. These signs can include the curing of any sickness we may have had, the reducing of our delusions, our having a more peaceful and happy mind, the increasing of our faith, correct intention and correct view, and especially the strengthening of our experience of universal compassion.

We may think our belief that living beings have attained permanent liberation from suffering through our meditation is incorrect, because living beings have not actually attained this. Although it is true that living beings have not actually attained permanent liberation, our belief is still correct because it arises from our compassion and wisdom, and especially from the power of our concentration. Meditating on this belief will cause our potentiality of being able to liberate all living beings permanently from suffering to ripen quickly, so that we will attain enlightenment quickly. Therefore we should never abandon such a beneficial belief, which is the nature of wisdom.

It is true that at first we do not have the power directly to take on others' suffering, but through repeatedly meditating on the conviction that we have taken on their suffering, we will gradually develop the actual power to do so. Meditation on taking is the quick path to enlightenment, and is similar to the Tantric practice of bringing the result into the path, in which through strongly imagining that we are already a Buddha we gradually become a Buddha. The fact is that if we cannot even imagine attaining enlightenment we will never be able to attain it! According to the teachings of training the mind the practice of taking and giving is similar to the practice of Secret Mantra, or Tantra. It is said that Tantric realizations can be achieved simply through relying upon correct belief and imagination. This practice is very simple; all we need to do is to become deeply familiar with meditation on correct belief and imagination, as presented in Tantra, by applying continual effort.

How is it possible for something that exists only in our imagination to become a reality? It is a remarkable quality of the mind that we first create objects with our imagination and then bring them into our everyday reality. In fact, everything starts in the imagination. For example, the house we are presently living in was first created in the imagination of the architect. He or she then made a design on paper, which acted as the blueprint for the actual building. If no one had first imagined our house, it would never have been built. In reality, our mind is the creator of all we experience. All external creations such as money, cars and computers were developed in dependence upon someone's imagination; if no one had imagined them, they would never have been invented. In the same way, all inner creations and all Dharma realizations, even liberation and enlightenment, are developed in dependence upon correct imagination. Therefore, for both worldly and spiritual attainments, the imagination is of primary importance.

If we imagine something that could in theory exist, and then familiarize our mind with it for long enough, eventually it will appear directly to our mind, first to our mental awareness and then even to our sense awarenesses. For as long as the object is still just an imagined object, the mind that apprehends it is simply a belief. If the object is a beneficial one it is a correct belief, and if the object stimulates delusions it is an incorrect belief. A belief is a conceptual mind that apprehends its object by means of a generic, or mental, image of that object. If we meditate on a correct belief for long enough, the generic image will become progressively more transparent until eventually it disappears entirely and we perceive the object directly. The imagined object will then have become a real object. By meditating on the beneficial belief that we have liberated all sentient beings and destroyed our self-cherishing mind, eventually we will actually accomplish this. Our correct belief will have transformed into a valid cognizer, a completely reliable mind.

In the second way of training in taking by means of compassion we take on the sufferings of particular individuals or groups of living beings throughout infinite worlds. For example, we focus on the assembly of living beings who experience the suffering of sickness, and develop compassion. We then think:

These living beings experience the suffering of sickness in this life and in their countless future lives without end. How wonderful it would be if these living beings were permanently freed from sickness! May they achieve this. I myself will work for them to achieve this. I must do this.

Thinking in this way, we imagine that the suffering of sickness of all living beings gathers together in the aspect of black smoke. This dissolves into our ignorance of self-grasping and self-cherishing at our heart. We then strongly believe that all these living beings are permanently freed from sickness, and that our ignorance of self-grasping and self-cherishing is completely destroyed. We meditate on this belief single-pointedly for as long as possible.

In the same way, we can practice the meditation on taking while focusing on a particular individual or group of living beings who are experiencing other sufferings such as poverty, fighting and famine.

Whenever we are experiencing a particular problem, whether from sickness, lack of resources or our delusions, we can think about the countless sentient beings who are experiencing similar problems, and then with a compassionate motivation we imagine taking on their suffering. This will help us deal with our own problem, and, by purifying the negative karma that prolongs the problem, may even rid us of it. If we are suffering from strong attachment, for example, we can consider all those who are also suffering from attachment, develop compassion for them, and imagine that we take on all their attachment together with the suffering it causes. This is a powerful method for destroying our own attachment.

Taking, motivated by compassion, is an extremely pure mind, unstained by self-cherishing. When our mind is pure, this in turn makes all our actions pure so that we become a pure being. If we die with strong compassion for all living beings we will definitely be born in the Pure Land of a Buddha. This is because our compassion that manifests when we are dying will directly cause our potential for taking rebirth in the Pure Land of a Buddha to ripen. This is the good result of a good heart. The result of maintaining the good heart of sincerely wishing to liberate permanently all living beings from suffering is that we ourself will experience permanent liberation from suffering by taking rebirth in the Pure Land of a Buddha.

To conclude our meditation sessions on taking, we dedicate our merit to freeing all sentient beings from their suffering and problems, and to lasting peace in this world.

GIVING BY MEANS OF LOVE

"Giving" in this context means, with a pure mind of wishing love, giving our own happiness to others through meditation. In general, in the cycle of impure life, samsara, there is no real happiness at all. As mentioned previously, the happiness that we normally experience through eating, drinking, sex and so forth is not real happiness, but merely a reduction of a previous problem or dissatisfaction.

How do we meditate on giving? In *Guide to the Bodhisattva's Way of Life* Shantideva says:

> ... to accomplish the welfare of all living beings
> I will transform my body into an enlightened
>   wishfulfilling jewel.

We should understand and believe that our continuously residing body, our very subtle body, is the real wishfulfilling inner jewel; this is our Buddha nature through which the wishes of ourself and all other living beings will be fulfilled. We then think:

> *All living beings wish to be happy all the time, but they do not know how to do this. They never experience real happiness, because out of ignorance they destroy their own happiness by developing delusions such as anger and performing non-virtuous actions. How wonderful it would be if all these living beings experienced the pure and everlasting happiness of enlightenment! May they experience this happiness. I will now give my own future happiness of enlightenment to each and every living being.*

Thinking in this way we imagine that from our continuously residing body at our heart we emanate infinite rays of light, which are in nature our future happiness of enlightenment. These reach all living beings of the six realms, and we strongly believe that each and every living being experiences the pure and everlasting happiness of enlightenment. We meditate on this belief single-pointedly for as long as possible. We should continually practice this meditation until we spontaneously believe that all living beings have actually received our future happiness of enlightenment now.

If we wish to meditate on giving more extensively, we can imagine that the rays of light we emanate fulfill all the individual needs and wishes of each and every living being. Human beings receive pure environments, pure enjoyments and a pure body and mind, and a meaningful life. Animals receive food, secure and warm homes, and freedom from being used for enjoyment or work by human beings; hungry ghosts receive food and drink, and freedom from poverty; beings in the hot hells receive cooling breezes; and beings in the cold hells receive warm sunshine. The demi-gods receive peace and satisfaction and freedom from their problems of jealousy; and the gods receive uncontaminated happiness and a meaningful life. Through enjoying these objects of desire all living beings are completely satisfied and experience the uncontaminated bliss of enlightenment.

Although we are principally training in the thought of giving, we can also engage in taking and giving in practical ways whenever we have the opportunity. At our stage we cannot take on the suffering of others through the power of our concentration, but we can often be of practical benefit to them. We can ease the pain of sick people by taking good care of them, and we can look after those who are not able to care for themselves. Accepting hardship while engaged in helping others is also a form of giving. We can also give material help, our labor, our skills, Dharma teachings or good advice. When we meet people who are depressed and need cheering up we can give our time and love.

We can also give to animals. Saving insects from drowning or gently picking worms up from the road is an example of giving fearlessness, or protection. Even allowing a mouse to rummage through our wastepaper basket without getting irritated can be a form of giving. Animals want to be happy just as much as we do, and they need our help even more than humans. Most humans have some power to help themselves, but animals are so deeply enveloped in ignorance that they have no freedom whatsoever to improve their situation. Just as our life is important, so we should understand that the lives of animals, including insects, are also important. So we must therefore stop killing insects by crushing them without any thought of their suffering or loss of their life. Animals have taken rebirth in a lower state of existence than humans, but we should never regard them as less important.

Buddhas and Bodhisattvas have complete equanimity and cherish animals and human beings equally.

At the end of our meditation on giving, we dedicate our merit so that all living beings may find true happiness. We can also make specific dedications, praying that the sick be restored to health, the poor obtain wealth, the unemployed find good jobs, the unsuccessful meet with success, the anxious find peace of mind and so forth. Through the strength of our pure motivation and the power and blessings of Buddhadharma, our dedications can certainly help, especially if we have a strong karmic link with the people for whom we are praying. Dedicating our merit to others is itself a form of giving. We can also mentally practice giving in daily life. Whenever we see or read about people who are poor, unhealthy, fearful, unsuccessful or unhappy, we can increase our wishing love for them and dedicate our merit toward their happiness and freedom from suffering.

MOUNTING TAKING AND GIVING UPON THE BREATH

Once we have become familiar with the meditations on taking and giving, we can combine the two and practice them in conjunction with our breathing. We begin by meditating on compassion and love for all living beings, and developing a strong determination to take on their suffering and give them pure happiness. With this determination, we imagine that we inhale through our nostrils the suffering, delusions and non-virtues of all living beings in the form of black smoke, which dissolves into our heart and completely destroys our self-cherishing. As we exhale, we imagine that our breath in the aspect of wisdom light, its nature pure uncontaminated happiness, pervades the entire universe. Each and every living being receives whatever they need and desire, and in particular the supreme happiness of permanent inner peace. We practice this cycle of breathing day and night, with each breath taking on the suffering of all living beings and giving them pure happiness, until we gain a deep experience of this practice.

Once we are proficient at this meditation on mounting taking and giving upon the breath, it is very powerful because there is a close relationship between the breath and the mind. The breath is related to the inner energy winds that flow through the channels of our body, and which act as the vehicles, or mounts, for different types of awareness. By harnessing our breath for virtuous purposes, we purify our inner winds, and when pure winds are flowing through our channels, pure minds arise naturally.

Many people practice breathing meditation, but the most widely practiced type consists simply of concentrating on the sensation of the breath entering and leaving the nostrils. This serves to calm the mind temporarily and reduces distracting thoughts, but it does not have the power to effect a deep and lasting transformation of our mind. Combining breathing meditation with the practice of taking and giving, however, has the power to transform our mind from its present miserable and self-centered state into the blissful and altruistic mind of a Bodhisattva. It improves our concentration, makes our love and compassion very strong and accumulates vast merit. In this way, the simple act of breathing is transformed into a powerful spiritual practice. At first we do this practice only in meditation, but with familiarity we can do it at any time. Through deep familiarity with this practice, our mind will eventually transform into the compassion of a Buddha.

Meditating on taking and giving can also be very effective in curing disease. By taking on the sickness and suffering of others with a mind of compassion, we can purify the negative karma that causes the continuation of our disease. Although we should always seek medical advice when we are ill, there may be times when doctors are unable to help us. There are many stories in Tibet of people curing themselves of otherwise incurable diseases through sincerely meditating on taking and giving. There was a meditator called Kharak Gomchen who contracted a disease that doctors were unable to cure. Thinking that he was going to die, he gave away all his possessions as offerings to Avalokiteshvara, the Buddha of Compassion, and retired to a cemetery, where he intended to make the last few weeks of his life meaningful by meditating on taking and giving. However, through his practice of taking and giving he purified the karma that was perpetuating his illness, and, much to everyone's surprise, returned home completely cured. This shows us how powerful the practice of taking and giving can be.

If we purify our negative karma, it is easy to cure even the heaviest disease. My mother told me about a monk she met who had contracted leprosy. Hoping to purify his sickness, he made a pilgrimage to Mount Kailash in western Tibet, which Buddhists believe to be Buddha Heruka's Pure Land. He was extremely poor and so my mother helped him on his way by giving him food and shelter, which was very kind as most people avoided lepers out of fear of catching leprosy. He stayed around Mount Kailash for about six months, prostrating and circumambulating the holy mountain as his purification practice. Afterward, while he was sleeping near a lake, he dreamed that many worms crawled out of his body and into the water. When he awoke he felt extremely comfortable, and later discovered that he was completely cured. On his way home, he stopped to see my mother and told her what had happened.

We can reflect that since beginningless time we have had countless lives and countless bodies, but that we have wasted them all in meaningless activities. Now we have the opportunity to derive the greatest meaning from our present body by using it to engage in the path of compassion and wisdom. How wonderful it would be for our world if many modern-day practitioners could emulate the training the mind practitioners of ancient times and become actual Bodhisattvas!

*Like the sun dispelling clouds, we can develop the wisdom
that can remove all delusions from our mind*

The Supreme Good Heart

The supreme good heart in this context is bodhichitta. "Bodhi" means "enlightenment," and "chitta," "mind"; therefore "bodhichitta" literally means "mind of enlightenment." It is defined as a mind, motivated by compassion for all living beings, which spontaneously seeks enlightenment to benefit each and every living being. Bodhichitta is born from compassion, which itself depends on cherishing love. Cherishing love can be likened to a field, compassion to the seeds, taking and giving to the supreme methods for making the seeds grow and bodhichitta to the harvest. The cherishing love that is developed through the practice of exchanging self with others is more profound than that developed through other methods, and so the resultant compassion and bodhichitta are also more profound. If we have compassion for all living beings generated through exchanging self with others, bodhichitta will arise naturally. The strength of our bodhichitta depends entirely upon the strength of our compassion.

Of all Dharma realizations, bodhichitta is supreme. This profoundly compassionate mind is the very essence of the Bodhisattva's training. Developing and maintaining the good heart of bodhichitta enables us to perfect all our virtues into the path to enlightenment, solve all our problems, fulfill all our wishes, and develop the power to help others in the most appropriate and beneficial ways. Bodhichitta is the best friend we can have and the highest quality we can develop. The moment we develop bodhichitta we will become a Bodhisattva, a Son or Daughter of Conqueror Buddha.

Atisha had many Teachers, but the one he revered above all was Guru Serlingpa. Whenever he heard Serlingpa's name, he would prostrate. When Atisha's disciples asked him why he respected Serlingpa more than his other Teachers, he replied, "It is due to the kindness of Guru Serlingpa that I now have the good heart of bodhichitta." Through the power of his bodhichitta, Atisha was able to bring great joy and happiness to everyone he met, and whatever he did was of benefit to others.

How does bodhichitta solve all our problems and fulfill all our wishes? As already explained, problems do not exist outside the mind; they are our unpleasant feelings that necessarily come from our self-cherishing. If we had the compassionate mind of bodhichitta our self-cherishing would have no power to cause us to experience problems. With this supreme good heart we will be happy all the time. Furthermore, with the supremely altruistic mind of bodhichitta we will create a vast amount of merit, or good fortune, because we engage in all our actions for the benefit of others. With such an accumulation of merit our wishes will easily be fulfilled, we will develop a tremendous capacity to benefit others, and all our Dharma activities will be successful.

We need to contemplate the benefits of bodhichitta until we are deeply inspired to develop this rare and precious mind. An extensive presentation of these benefits can be found in the books *Meaningful to Behold* and *Joyful Path of Good Fortune*.

At the moment we have a very special opportunity to develop bodhichitta. However, we do not know how long our good fortune will last, and if we waste this opportunity it will not arise again. If we wasted an opportunity to make a lot of money, or to obtain a good job or an attractive partner, we would probably feel strong regret, but in reality we have not lost a great deal. These things are not so difficult to find, and even when found they do not bring us real happiness. Not taking advantage of this unique opportunity to develop such a good heart, however, is an irretrievable loss. Humans have the greatest opportunity for spiritual development, and of all the possible types of rebirth we could have taken we have been born human. Nowadays most humans have no interest in spiritual development, and of those who do, only a few have met

Buddhadharma. If we contemplate this carefully we will realize how very fortunate we are to have this precious opportunity to attain the supreme happiness of Buddhahood.

DEVELOPING BODHICHITTA

We should understand that, despite our strong wish to protect all living beings, we do not have the power to do so at present. Just as one drowning person cannot save another, no matter how fervently he or she may wish to do so, likewise it is only when we have freed ourself from suffering and mental limitations that we are able to free others. If we ask ourself who has the actual power to protect all living beings, we will realize that it is only a Buddha. Only a Buddha is free from all faults and limitations, and has both the omniscient wisdom and the skill to help each and every living being in accordance with his or her individual needs and dispositions. Only a Buddha has reached the shore of enlightenment and is in a position to release all mother beings from the cruel ocean of suffering.

When we attain a Buddha's enlightenment we will be able to benefit each and every living being every day through bestowing blessings and through our countless emanations. If we consider this deeply, bodhichitta will arise naturally in our mind. We contemplate:

I want to protect all living beings from suffering, but in my present, limited state I have no power to do this.

246

*Because only a Buddha has such power, I must become
a Buddha, an enlightened being, as quickly as possible.*

We meditate on this determination, which is bodhichitta,
single-pointedly again and again until we develop the spontaneous wish to attain enlightenment to benefit each and
every living being every day.

We need to have this precious mind of bodhichitta in our
heart. It is our inner Spiritual Guide, who leads us directly
to the state of supreme happiness of enlightenment; and it
is the real wishfulfilling jewel through which we can fulfill
our own and others' wishes. There is no greater beneficial
intention than this.

When we want a cup of tea, our main wish is to drink
tea, but to fulfill this wish we naturally develop the secondary wish to find a cup. In a similar way, the main wish of
those who have great compassion is to protect all living
beings from their suffering; but to fulfill this wish they
know that they must first attain Buddhahood themselves,
and so they naturally develop the secondary wish to attain
enlightenment. Just as finding a cup is the means to accomplish our goal of drinking tea, so attaining enlightenment
is the means to accomplish our ultimate goal of benefiting
all living beings.

At first our bodhichitta will be artificial, or fabricated,
bodhichitta, arising only when we make a specific effort to
generate it. The best way to transform this into spontaneous bodhichitta is to gain deep familiarity with it through

continual practice. As most of our time is spent out of meditation, it is vital that we make use of every opportunity to improve our training in bodhichitta during our daily life. We need to make our meditation sessions and meditation breaks mutually supportive. During our meditation session, we may experience a peaceful state of mind and develop many virtuous intentions; but if we forget them all as soon as we arise from meditation we will not be able to solve our daily problems of anger, attachment and ignorance, nor make progress in our spiritual practice. We must learn to integrate our spiritual practice into our daily activities so that day and night we can maintain the peaceful states of mind, pure intentions and pure view that we developed in meditation.

At the moment we may find that our meditations and our daily life are pulling in different directions. In meditation we try to generate virtuous minds, but, because we cannot stop thinking about our other activities, our concentration is very poor. The virtuous feelings we do manage to develop are then quickly dissipated in the busyness of daily life, and we return to our meditation seat tired, tense and filled with distracting thoughts. We can overcome this problem by transforming all our daily activities and experiences into the spiritual path through developing special ways of thinking. Activities such as cooking, working, talking and relaxing are not intrinsically mundane; they are mundane only if done with a mundane mind. By doing exactly the same actions with a spiritual motivation, they become pure spiritual practices. For example, when we talk to our friends our motivation is usually mixed with self-cherishing and we say whatever comes into our mind, regardless of whether or not it is beneficial. We can, however, talk to others with the sole purpose of benefiting them, encouraging them to develop positive states of mind and taking care not to say anything that will upset them. Instead of thinking about how we can impress people, we should think about how we can help them, recalling how they are trapped in samsara and lack pure happiness. In this way, talking with our friends can become a means of improving our love, compassion and other realizations. If we can skillfully transform all our daily activities in this way, instead of feeling drained and tired when we sit down to meditate we will feel joyful and inspired, and it will be easy to develop pure concentration.

Developing great compassion, compassion for all living beings, is the main, or substantial, cause of generating bodhichitta—it is like the seed of bodhichitta. To enable this seed to grow, we also need the cooperative conditions of accumulating merit, purifying negativity and receiving the blessings of the Buddhas and Bodhisattvas. If we gather all these causes and conditions together, it is not difficult to develop bodhichitta. To fulfill the wishes of our compassionate mind of bodhichitta, we need to engage sincerely in the practices of giving, moral discipline, patience, effort, concentration and wisdom. When these practices are motivated by bodhichitta, they are called "the six perfections." We especially need to apply great effort to training in the wisdom that realizes ultimate truth, emptiness. We should know that a direct realization of emptiness motivated by bodhichitta is ultimate bodhichitta, which is the nature of wisdom. The bodhichitta that has already been explained above is conventional bodhichitta, which is the nature of compassion. These two bodhichittas are like the two wings of a bird with which we can fly directly to the enlightened Pure Land.

Ultimate Bodhichitta

*W*hen we meditate on ultimate truth, or emptiness motivated by bodhichitta, we are training in ultimate bodhichitta. Actual ultimate bodhichitta is a wisdom that directly realizes emptiness motivated by bodhichitta. It is called "ultimate bodhichitta" because its object is ultimate truth, emptiness, and it is one of the main paths to enlightenment.

If we do not know the meaning of emptiness there is no basis for training in ultimate bodhichitta, because emptiness is the object of ultimate bodhichitta. What is the difference between empty and emptiness? In Buddhism, emptiness has great meaning. It is the real nature of things, and is a very profound and meaningful object. If we realize emptiness directly we will attain permanent liberation from all the sufferings of this life and countless future lives; there is no greater meaning than this. So emptiness is a very meaningful object, but an empty is just empty—it has no special meaning. There is an empty of inherent existence, but there is no emptiness of inherent existence because inherent existence itself does not exist.

Je Tsongkhapa said:

The knowledge of emptiness is superior to any other
    knowledge,
The Teacher who teaches emptiness unmistakenly is
    superior to any other teacher,
And the realization of emptiness is the very essence
    of Buddhadharma.

If we really do not wish to experience problems and suffering
we must realize emptiness, the selflessness of persons and
phenomena. Milarepa's Guru Marpa Lotsawa said:

In east India near the river Ganges
I met Venerable Maitripa, and through his great
    kindness
I realized that the things that I normally see do not
    exist.
Thus, all my experiences of problems and suffering
    have ceased.

We should know that since beginningless time our way of
identifying ourself has been mistaken. We believe that our
self that we normally see is our self. This belief is ignorance
because our self that we normally see does not exist. All the
things that we normally see do not exist. This will be explained in detail below. Because of this ignorance we develop
and experience various kinds of mistaken appearance, and
because of this we experience various kinds of suffering and

problems as hallucinations throughout this life, and in life after life, endlessly. On the other hand, if we identify our self as a mere appearance that is not other than the emptiness of all phenomena, the mere absence of all phenomena that we normally perceive, our mistaken appearance will reduce and finally cease completely. Then we will experience the supreme happiness of nirvana or enlightenment.

WHAT IS EMPTINESS?

Emptiness is the way things really are. It is the way things exist as opposed to the way they appear. We naturally believe that the things we see around us, such as tables, chairs and houses, are truly existent, because we believe that they exist in exactly the way that they appear. However, the way things appear to our senses is deceptive and completely contradictory to the way in which they actually exist. Things appear to exist from their own side, without depending upon our mind. This book that appears to our mind, for example, seems to have its own independent, objective existence. It seems to be "outside" whereas our mind seems to be "inside." We feel that the book can exist without our mind; we do not feel that our mind is in any way involved in bringing the book into existence. This way of existing independent of our mind is variously called "true existence," "inherent existence," "existence from its own side," and "existence from the side of the object."

Although things appear directly to our senses to be truly, or inherently, existent, in reality all phenomena lack, or are empty of, true existence. This book, our body, our friends, we ourself, and the entire universe are in reality just appearances to mind, like things seen in a dream. If we dream of an elephant, the elephant appears vividly in all its detail—we can see it, hear it, smell it and touch it—but when we wake up we realize that it was just an appearance to mind. We do not wonder, "Where is the elephant now?" because we understand that it was simply a projection of our mind and had no existence outside our mind. When the dream awareness that apprehended the elephant ceased, the elephant did not go anywhere—it simply disappeared, for it was just an appearance to the mind and did not exist separately from the mind. Buddha said that the same is true for all phenomena; they are mere appearances to mind, totally dependent upon the minds that perceive them.

The world we experience when we are awake and the world we experience when we are dreaming are both mere appearances to mind that arise from our mistaken conceptions. If we want to say that the dream world is false, we also have to say that the waking world is false; and if we want to say that the waking world is true, we also have to say that the dream world is true. The only difference between them is that the dream world is an appearance to our subtle dreaming mind whereas the waking world is an appearance to our gross waking mind. The dream world exists only for as long as the dream awareness to which it appears exists, and the waking world exists only for as long as the waking awareness to which it appears exists. Buddha said, "You should know that all phenomena are like dreams." When we die, our gross waking minds dissolve into our very subtle mind and the world we experienced when we were alive simply disappears. The world as others perceive it will continue, but our personal world will disappear as completely and irrevocably as the world of last night's dream.

Buddha also said that all phenomena are like illusions. There are many different types of illusion, such as mirages, rainbows or drug-induced hallucinations. In ancient times, there used to be magicians who would cast a spell over their audience, causing them to see objects, such as a piece of wood, as something else, such as a tiger. Those deceived by the spell would see what appeared to be a real tiger and develop fear, but those who arrived after the spell had been cast would simply see a piece of wood. What all illusions have in common is that the way they appear does not coincide with the way they exist. Buddha likened all phenomena to illusions, because through the force of the imprints of self-grasping ignorance accumulated since beginningless time, whatever appears to our mind naturally appears to be truly existent and we instinctively assent to this appearance, but in reality everything is totally empty of true existence. Like a mirage that appears to be water but is not in fact water, things appear in a deceptive way. Not understanding their real nature we are fooled by appearances, and grasp at books and tables, bodies and worlds as truly existent. The result of grasping at phenomena in this way is that we develop self-cherishing, attachment, hatred, jealousy and other delusions, our mind becomes agitated and unbalanced, and our peace of mind is destroyed. We are like travelers in a desert who exhaust themselves running after mirages, or like someone walking down a road at night mistaking the shadows of the trees for criminals or wild animals waiting to attack.

THE EMPTINESS OF OUR BODY

To understand how phenomena are empty of true, or inherent, existence we should consider our own body. Once we have understood how our body lacks true existence we can easily apply the same reasoning to other objects.

In *Guide to the Bodhisattva's Way of Life*, Bodhisattva Shantideva says:

Therefore, there is no body,
But, because of ignorance, we see a body within the hands and so forth,
Just like a mind mistakenly apprehending a person
When observing the shape of a pile of stones at dusk.

On one level we know our body very well—we know whether it is healthy or unhealthy, beautiful or ugly, and so forth. However, we never examine it more deeply, asking ourself, "What precisely is my body? Where is my body? What is its real nature?" If we did examine our body in this way we would not be able to find it—instead of finding our body the result of this examination would be that our body disappears. The meaning of the first part of Shantideva's verse, "Therefore, there is no body," is that if we search for our "real" body, there is no body; our body exists only if we do not search for a real body behind its mere appearance.

There are two ways of searching for an object. An example of the first way, which we can call a "conventional search," is searching for our car in a parking lot. The conclusion of this type of search is that we find the car, in the sense that we see the thing that everyone agrees is our car. However, having located our car in the parking lot, suppose we are still not satisfied with the mere appearance of the car and we want to determine exactly what the car is. We might then engage in what we can call an "ultimate search" for the car, in which we look within the object itself to find something that is the object. To do this we ask ourself, "Are any of the individual parts of the car, the car? Are the wheels the car? Is the engine the car? Is the chassis the car?" and so forth. When conducting an ultimate search for our car we are not satisfied with just pointing to the hood, wheels and so forth, and then saying "car"; we want to know what the car really is. Instead of just using the word "car" as ordinary people do, we want to know what the word really refers to. We want to mentally separate the car from all that is not car, so that we can say, "This is what the car really is." We want to find a car, but in truth there is no car; we can find nothing. In *Condensed Perfection of Wisdom Sutra*, Buddha says, "If you search for your body with wisdom you cannot find it." This also applies to our car, our house and all other phenomena.

In *Guide to the Bodhisattva's Way of Life*, Shantideva says:

When examined in this way,
Who is living and who is it who will die?
What is the future and what is the past?
Who are our friends and who are our relatives?

I beseech you who are just like me,
Please know that all things are empty, like space.

The essential meaning of these words is that when we search for things with wisdom, there is no person who is living or dying, there is no past or future and there is no present, such as our friends and relatives. We should know that all phenomena are empty, like space, which means we should know that all phenomena are not other than emptiness.

To understand Shantideva's claim that in reality there is no body, we need to conduct an ultimate search for our body. If we are ordinary beings, all objects, including our body, appear to exist inherently. As mentioned above, objects seem to be independent of our mind and independent of other phenomena. The universe appears to consist of discrete objects that have an existence from their own side. These objects appear to exist in themselves as stars, planets, mountains, people and so forth, "waiting" to be experienced by conscious beings. Normally it does not occur to us that we are involved in any way in the existence of these phenomena. For example, we feel that our body exists from its own side and does not depend upon our mind, or anyone else's, to bring it into existence. However, if our body did exist in the way that we instinctively grasp it—as an external object rather than just a projection of mind—we should be able to point to our body without pointing to any phenomenon that is not our body. We should be able to find it among its parts or outside its parts. Since there is no third possibility, if our body cannot be found either among its parts or outside its parts we must conclude that our body that we normally see does not exist.

It is not difficult to understand that the individual parts of our body are not our body—it is absurd to say that our back, our legs or our head are our body. If one of the parts, say our back, is our body, then the other parts are equally our body, and it would follow that we have many bodies. Furthermore, our back, legs and so forth cannot be our body because they are parts of our body. The body is the part-possessor, and the back, legs and so forth are the possessed parts; and possessor and possessed cannot be one and the same.

Some people believe that although none of the individual parts of the body is the body, the collection of all the parts assembled together is the body. According to them, it is possible to find our body when we search for it analytically because the collection of all the parts of our body is our body. However, this assertion can be refuted with many valid reasons. The force of these reasons may not be immediately obvious to us, but if we contemplate them carefully with a calm and positive mind we will come to appreciate their validity.

Since none of the individual parts of our body is our body, how can the collection of all the parts be our body? For example, a collection of dogs cannot be a human being, because none of the individual dogs is human. As each individual member is "non-human," how can this collection of non-humans magically transform into a human? Similarly, since the collection of the parts of our body is a collection of things that are not our body, it cannot be our body. Just as the collection of dogs remains simply dogs, so the collection of all the parts of our body remains simply parts of our body—it does not magically transform into the part-possessor, our body.

We may find this point difficult to understand, but if we think about it for a long time with a calm and positive mind, and discuss it with more experienced practitioners, it will gradually become clearer. We can also consult authentic books on the subject, such as *The New Heart of Wisdom* and *Ocean of Nectar*.

There is another way in which we can know that the collection of the parts of our body is not our body. If we can point to the collection of the parts of our body and say that this is, in itself, our body, then the collection of the parts of our body must exist independently of all phenomena that are not our body. Thus it would follow that the collection of the parts of our body exists independently of the parts themselves. This is clearly absurd—if it were true, we could remove all the parts of our body and the collection of the parts would remain. We can therefore conclude that the collection of the parts of our body is not our body.

Since the body cannot be found within its parts, either as an individual part or as the collection, the only possibility that remains is that it exists separately from its parts. If this is the case, it should be possible mentally or physically to remove all the parts of our body and still be left with the body. However, if we remove our arms, our legs, our head, our trunk and all the other parts of our body, no body is left. This proves that there is no body separate from its parts. It is because of ignorance that whenever we point to our body we are pointing only to a part of our body, which is not our body.

We have now searched in every possible place and have been unable to find our body either among its parts or anywhere else. We can find nothing that corresponds to the vividly appearing body that we normally grasp at. We are forced to agree with Shantideva that, when we search for our body, there is no body to be found. This clearly proves that our body that we normally see does not exist. It is almost as if our body does not exist at all. Indeed, the only sense in which we can say that our body does exist is if we are satisfied with the mere name "body" and do not expect to find a real body behind the name. If we try to find, or point to, a real body to which the name "body" refers, we will not find anything at all. Instead of finding a truly existent body, we will perceive the mere absence of our body that we normally see. This mere absence of our body that we normally see is the way our body actually exists. We will realize that the body we normally perceive, grasp at and cherish does not exist at all. This non-existence of the body we normally grasp at is the emptiness of our body, the true nature of our body.

The term "true nature" is very meaningful. Not being satisfied with the mere appearance and name "body" we examined our body to discover its true nature. The result of this examination was a definite non-finding of our body. Where we expected to find a truly existent body, we discovered the utter non-existence of that truly existent body. This non-existence, or emptiness, is the true nature of our body. Apart from the mere absence of a truly existent body, there is no other true nature of our body—every other attribute of the body is just part of its deceptive nature. Since this is the case, why do we spend so much time focusing on the deceptive nature of our body? At present we ignore the true nature of our body and other phenomena, and concentrate only on their deceptive nature; yet the result of concentrating all the time on deceptive objects is that our mind becomes disturbed and we remain in the miserable life of samsara. If we wish to experience pure happiness, we must acquaint our mind with the truth. Instead of wasting our energy focusing only on meaningless, deceptive objects, we should focus on the true nature of things.

Although it is impossible to find our body when we search for it analytically, when we do not engage in analysis our body appears very clearly. Why is this? Shantideva says that because of ignorance we see our body within the hands and other parts of our body. In reality, our body does not exist within its parts. Just as at dusk we might see a pile of stones as a man even though there is no man within the stones, so in the same way our ignorant mind sees a body within the collection of arms, legs and so forth, even though no body exists there. The body we see within the collection of arms and legs is simply a hallucination of our ignorant mind. Not recognizing it as such, however, we grasp at it very strongly, cherish it and exhaust ourself in trying to protect it from any discomfort.

The way to familiarize our mind with the true nature of the body is to use the above reasoning to search for our body, and then when we have searched in every possible place and not found it, to concentrate on the space-like emptiness that is the mere absence of the body that we normally see. This space-like emptiness is the true nature of our body. Although it resembles empty space, it is a meaningful emptiness. Its meaning is the utter non-existence of the body that we normally see, the body that we grasp at so strongly and have cherished all our life.

Through becoming familiar with the experience of the space-like ultimate nature of the body, our grasping at our body will be reduced. As a result we will experience far less suffering, anxiety and frustration in relation to our body. Our physical tension will diminish and our health will improve, and even when we do become sick our physical discomfort will not disturb our mind. Those who have a direct experience of emptiness do not feel any pain even if they are beaten or shot. Knowing that the real nature of their body is like space, for them being beaten is like space being beaten and being shot is like space being shot. Moreover, good and bad external conditions no longer have the power to disturb their mind, because they realize them to be like a magician's illusion, with no existence separate from the mind. Instead of being pulled about by changing conditions like a puppet on a string, their minds remain free and tranquil in the knowledge of the equal and unchanging ultimate nature of all things. In this way, a person who directly realizes emptiness, the true nature of phenomena, experiences peace and happiness day and night, life after life.

We need to distinguish between the conventionally existent body that does exist and the inherently existent body that does not exist; but we must take care not to be misled by the words into thinking that the conventionally existent body is anything more than a mere appearance to mind. It is perhaps less confusing simply to say that for a mind that directly sees the truth, or emptiness, there is no body. A body exists only for an ordinary mind to which a body appears.

Shantideva advises us that unless we wish to understand emptiness we should not examine conventional truths such as our body, possessions, places and friends, but instead be satisfied with their mere names, as are worldly people. Once a worldly person knows an object's name and purpose, he is satisfied that he knows the object and does not investigate further. We must do the same, unless we want to meditate on emptiness. However, we should remember that if we did examine objects more closely we would not find them, for they would simply disappear, just as a mirage disappears if we try to look for it.

The same reasoning that we have used to prove the lack of true existence of our body can be applied to all other phenomena. This book, for example, seems to exist from its own side, somewhere within its parts; but when we examine the book more precisely we discover that none of the individual pages nor the collection of the pages is the book, yet without them there is no book. Instead of finding a truly existent book we are left beholding an emptiness that is the non-existence of the book we previously held to exist. Because of our ignorance the book appears to exist separately from our mind, as if our mind were inside and the book outside, but through analyzing the book we discover that this appearance is completely false. There is no book outside the mind. There is no book "out there," within the pages. The only way the book exists is as a mere appearance to mind, a mere projection of the mind.

All phenomena exist by way of convention; nothing is inherently existent. This applies to mind, to Buddha and even to emptiness itself. Everything is merely imputed by mind. All phenomena have parts—physical phenomena have physical parts, and non-physical phenomena have various parts, or attributes, that can be distinguished by thought. Using the same type of reasoning as above, we can realize that any phenomenon is not one of its parts, not the collection of its parts and not separate from its parts. In this way we can realize the emptiness of all phenomena, the mere absence of all phenomena that we normally see or perceive.

It is particularly helpful to meditate on the emptiness of objects that arouse in us strong delusions like attachment or anger. By analyzing correctly we will realize that the object we desire, or the object we dislike, does not exist from its own side. Its beauty or ugliness, and even its very existence, are imputed by mind. By thinking in this way we will discover that there is no basis for attachment or anger.

THE EMPTINESS OF OUR MIND

In *Training the Mind in Seven Points*, after outlining how to engage in analytical meditation on the emptiness of inherent existence of outer phenomena such as our body, Geshe Chekhawa continues by saying that we should then analyze our own mind to understand how it lacks inherent existence.

Our mind is not an independent entity, but an ever-changing continuum that depends upon many factors, such as its previous moments, its objects and the inner energy winds upon which our minds are mounted. Like everything else, our mind is imputed upon a collection of many factors and therefore lacks inherent existence. A primary mind, or consciousness, for example, has five parts or "mental factors": feeling, discrimination, intention, contact and attention. Neither the individual mental factors nor the collection of these mental factors is the primary mind itself, because they are mental factors and therefore parts of the primary mind. However, there is no primary mind that is separate from these mental factors. A primary mind is merely imputed upon the mental factors that are its basis of imputation, and therefore it does not exist from its own side.

Having identified the nature of our primary mind, which is an empty like space that perceives or understands objects, we then search for it within its parts—feeling, discrimination, intention, contact and attention—until finally we realize its unfindability. This unfindability is its ultimate nature, or emptiness. We then think:

All phenomena that appear to my mind are the nature of my mind. My mind is the nature of emptiness.

In this way we feel that everything dissolves into emptiness. We perceive only the emptiness of all phenomena and we meditate on this emptiness. This way of meditating on emptiness is more profound than the meditation on the emptiness of our body. Gradually our experience of emptiness will become clearer and clearer until finally we gain an undefiled wisdom that directly realizes the emptiness of all phenomena.

THE EMPTINESS OF OUR I

The object we grasp at most strongly is our self or I. Due to the imprints of self-grasping ignorance accumulated over time without beginning, our I appears to us as inherently existent, and our self-grasping mind automatically grasps at it in this way. Although we grasp at an inherently existent I all the time, even during sleep, it is not easy to identify how it appears to our mind. To identify it clearly, we must begin by allowing it to manifest strongly by contemplating situations in which we have an exaggerated sense of I, such as when we are embarrassed, ashamed, afraid or indignant. We recall or imagine such a situation and then, without any comment or analysis, try to gain a clear mental image of how the I naturally appears at such times. We have to be patient at this stage because it may take many sessions before we gain a clear image. Eventually we will see that the I appears to be completely solid and real, existing from its own side without depending upon the body or the mind. This vividly appearing I is the inherently existent I that we cherish so strongly. It is the I that we defend when we are criticized and that we are so proud of when we are praised.

Once we have an image of how the I appears in these extreme circumstances, we should try to identify how it appears normally, in less extreme situations. For example, we can observe the I that is presently reading this book and try to discover how it appears to our mind. Eventually we will see that although in this case there is not such an inflated sense of I, nevertheless the I still appears to be inherently existent, existing from its own side without depending upon the body or the mind. Once we have an image of the inherently existent I, we focus on it for a while with single-pointed concentration. Then in meditation we proceed to the next stage, which is to contemplate valid reasons to prove that the inherently existent I we are grasping at does not in fact exist. The inherently existent I and our self that we normally see are the same; we should know that neither exists, both are objects negated by emptiness.

If the I exists in the way that it appears, it must exist in one of four ways: as the body, as the mind, as the collection of the body and mind, or as something separate from the body and mind; there is no other possibility. We contemplate this carefully until we become convinced that this is the case and then we proceed to examine each of the four possibilities:

1. If our I is our body, there is no sense in saying "my body," because the possessor and the possessed are identical.

    If our I is our body, there is no future rebirth because the I ceases when the body dies.

    If our I and our body are identical, then since we are capable of developing faith, dreaming, solving mathematical puzzles and so on, it follows that flesh, blood and bones can do the same.

    Since none of this is true, it follows that our I is not our body.

2. If our I is our mind, there is no sense in saying "my mind," because the possessor and the possessed are identical; but usually when we focus on our mind we say "my mind." This clearly indicates that our I is not our mind.

    If our I is our mind, then since we have many types of mind, such as the six consciousnesses, conceptual minds and non-conceptual minds, it follows that we have just as many I's. Since this is absurd, our I cannot be our mind.

3. Since our body is not our I and our mind is not our I, the collection of our body and mind cannot be our I. The collection of our body and mind is a collection of things that are not our I, so how can the collection itself be our I? For example, in a herd of cows none of the animals is a sheep, therefore the herd itself is not sheep. In the same way, in the collection of our body and mind, neither our body nor our mind is our I, therefore the collection itself is not our I.

4. If our I is not our body, not our mind, and not the collection of our body and mind, the only possibility that remains is that it is something separate from our body and mind. If this is the case, we must be able to apprehend our I without either our body or our mind appearing, but if we imagine that our body and our mind were completely to disappear there would be nothing remaining that could be called our I. Therefore it follows that our I is not separate from our body and mind.

We should imagine that our body gradually dissolves into thin air, and then our mind dissolves, our thoughts scatter with the wind, our feelings, wishes and awareness melt into nothingness. Is there anything left that is our I? There is nothing. Clearly, our I is not something separate from our body and mind.

We have now examined all four possibilities and have failed to find our I or self. Since we have already decided that there is no fifth possibility, we must conclude that our I that we normally grasp at and cherish does not exist at all. Where there previously appeared an inherently existent I, there now appears an absence of that I. This absence of an inherently existent I is emptiness, ultimate truth.

We contemplate in this way until there appears to us a generic, or mental, image of the absence of our self that we normally see. This image is our object of placement meditation. We try to become completely familiar with it by continually meditating on it single-pointedly for as long as possible.

Because we have grasped at our inherently existent I since beginningless time, and have cherished it more dearly than anything else, the experience of failing to find our self in meditation can be quite shocking at first. Some people develop fear, thinking, "I have become completely non-existent." Others feel great joy, as if the source of all their problems were vanishing. Both reactions are good signs and indicate correct meditation. After a while these initial reactions will subside and our mind will settle into a more balanced state. Then we will be able to meditate on the emptiness of our self in a calm, controlled manner.

We should allow our mind to become absorbed in space-like emptiness for as long as possible. It is important to remember that our object of meditation is emptiness, the mere absence of our self that we normally see, not mere nothingness. Occasionally we should check our meditation with alertness. If our mind has wandered to another object, or if we have lost the meaning of emptiness and are focusing on mere nothingness, we should return to the contemplations to bring the emptiness of our self clearly to mind once again.

We may wonder, "If my self that I normally see does not exist, then who is meditating? Who will get up from meditation, speak to others, and reply when my name is called?" Although our self that we normally see does not exist, this does not mean that our self does not exist at all. We exist as mere name. So long as we are satisfied with the mere name "ourself," there is no problem. We can think, "I exist," "I am going to town," and so on. The problem arises only when we look for our self other than the mere name "I," or "self." Our mind grasps at an I that ultimately exists, independently of conceptual imputation, as if there were a "real" I existing behind the label. If such an I existed, we would be able to find it, but we have seen that our I cannot be found upon investigation. The conclusion of our search was a definite non-finding of our self. This unfindability of our self is the emptiness of our self, the ultimate nature of our self. Our self that exists as mere name is our existent self. In the same way, phenomena that exist as mere name or mere imputation are existent phenomena. There are no self and other phenomena that exist other than mere imputation. In truth, our self and other phenomena existing as mere imputation is the ultimate nature of our self and other phenomena, not the conventional nature. At first these explanations are difficult to understand, but please be patient. We should apply effort to receive the powerful blessings of Wisdom Buddha Je Tsongkhapa through sincerely engaging in the practice of *Heart Jewel*.

When we first realize emptiness we do so conceptually, by means of a generic image. By continuing to meditate on emptiness over and over again, the generic image gradually becomes more and more transparent until it disappears entirely and we see emptiness directly. This direct realization of emptiness will be our first completely non-mistaken awareness, or undefiled mind. Until we realize emptiness directly, all our minds are mistaken awarenesses because, due to the imprints of self-grasping or true-grasping ignorance, their objects appear as inherently existent.

Most people veer toward the extreme of existence, thinking that if something exists it must exist inherently, thus exaggerating the way in which things exist without being satisfied with them as mere name. Others may veer toward the extreme of non-existence, thinking that if phenomena do not exist inherently they do not exist at all, thus exaggerating their lack of inherent existence. We need to realize that although phenomena lack any trace of existence from their own side, they do exist conventionally as mere appearances to a valid mind.

The conceptual minds grasping at our I and other phenomena as being truly existent are wrong awarenesses and should therefore be abandoned, but I am not saying that all conceptual thoughts are wrong awarenesses and should therefore be abandoned. There are many correct conceptual minds that are useful in our day-to-day lives, such as the conceptual mind remembering what we did yesterday or the conceptual mind understanding what we will do tomorrow. There are also many conceptual minds that need to be cultivated on the spiritual path. For example, conventional bodhichitta in the mental continuum of a Bodhisattva is a conceptual mind because it apprehends its object, great enlightenment, by means of a generic image. Moreover, before we can realize emptiness directly with a non-conceptual mind, we need to realize it by means of a subsequent valid cognizer, which is a conceptual mind. Through contemplating the reasons that refute inherent existence, there appears to our mind a generic image of the absence, or empty, of inherent existence. This is the only way that emptiness can initially appear to our mind. We then meditate on this image with stronger and stronger concentration until finally we perceive emptiness directly.

There are some people who say that the way to meditate on emptiness is simply to empty our mind of all conceptual thoughts, arguing that just as white clouds obscure the sun as much as black clouds, so positive conceptual thoughts obscure our mind as much as negative conceptual thoughts. This view is completely mistaken, for if we make no effort to gain a conceptual understanding of emptiness, but try instead to suppress all conceptual thoughts, actual emptiness will never appear to our mind. We may achieve a vivid experience of a space-like vacuity, but this is just the absence of conceptual thought—it is not emptiness, the true nature of phenomena. Meditation on this vacuity may temporarily calm our mind, but it will never destroy our delusions nor liberate us from samsara and its sufferings.

THE EMPTINESS OF PHENOMENA

All phenomena are included within eight, which are: production, disintegration, impermanence, permanence, going, coming, singularity and plurality. We should know that all these eight phenomena that we normally see do not actually exist because if we search for them with wisdom they will disappear. However, these phenomena appear clearly to us due to other causes and conditions. For example, if all the necessary atmospheric causes and conditions come together, clouds will appear. If these are absent, clouds cannot appear. The clouds appearing completely depend upon causes and conditions; without these they have no power to appear.

The same is true for the appearance of mountains, planets, bodies, minds and all other phenomena. Because their appearance depends upon factors outside themselves for their existence, they are empty of inherent, or independent, existence and are mere imputations of the mind.

Contemplating the teachings on karma—actions and their effects—can help us to understand this. Where do all our good and bad experiences come from? They are in truth the result of the positive and negative actions we created in the past. As a result of positive actions, attractive and agreeable people appear in our life, pleasant material conditions arise and we live in a beautiful environment; but as a result of negative actions, unpleasant people and things appear. This world is the effect of the collective actions created by the beings who inhabit it. Because actions originate in the mind—specifically in our mental actions—we can see that all worlds arise from the mind. This is similar to the way in which appearances arise in a dream. Everything we perceive when we are dreaming is the result of the ripening of karmic potentials in our mind and has no existence outside of our mind. When our mind is calm and pure, positive karmic imprints ripen and pleasant dream appearances arise; but when our mind is agitated and impure, negative karmic imprints ripen and unpleasant, nightmarish appearances arise. In a similar way, all the appearances of our waking world are simply the ripening of positive, negative or neutral karmic imprints in our mind.

Once we understand how things arise from their inner and outer causes and conditions and have no independent existence, then just seeing or thinking about the production of phenomena will remind us of their emptiness. Instead of reinforcing our sense of the solidity and objectivity of things, we will begin to see things as manifestations of their emptiness, with no more concrete existence than a rainbow arising out of an empty sky.

Just as the production of things depends upon causes and conditions, so too does the disintegration of things. Therefore, neither production nor disintegration can be truly existent. For example, if our new car were destroyed we would feel unhappy because we grasp at both the car and the disintegration of the car as truly existent; but if we understood that our car is merely an appearance to our mind, like a car in a dream, its destruction would not disturb us. This is true for all objects of our attachment: if we realize that both objects and their cessations lack true existence, there is no basis for becoming upset if we are separated from them.

All functioning things—our environments, enjoyments, body, mind and our self—change from moment to moment. They are impermanent in the sense that they do not last for a second moment. The book you are reading in this moment is not the same book that you were reading a moment ago, and it could only come into existence because the book of a moment ago ceased to exist. When we understand subtle impermanence—that our body, our mind, our self and so forth do not abide for a second moment—it is not difficult to understand that they are empty of inherent existence.

Even though we may agree that impermanent phenomena are empty of inherent existence, we might think that because permanent phenomena are unchanging and do not arise from causes and conditions, they must exist inherently. However, even permanent phenomena such as emptiness and unproduced space—the mere absence of physical obstruction—are dependent-related phenomena because they depend upon their parts, their bases and the minds that impute them; and therefore they are not inherently existent. Although emptiness is ultimate reality, it is not independent or inherently existent for it too depends upon its parts, its bases and the minds that impute it. Just as a gold coin does not exist separately from its gold, so the emptiness of our body does not exist separately from our body, because it is simply our body's lack of inherent existence.

Whenever we go anywhere we develop the thought, "I am going," and grasp at an inherently existent act of going. In a similar way, when someone comes to visit us we think, "They are coming," and we grasp at an inherently existent act of coming. Both these conceptions are self-grasping and wrong awarenesses. When someone goes away we feel that a truly existent person has truly left, and when they come back we feel that a truly existent person has truly returned.

However, the coming and going of people is like the appearance and disappearance of a rainbow in the sky. When the causes and conditions for a rainbow to appear are assembled, a rainbow appears, and when the causes and conditions for the continued appearance of the rainbow disperse, the rainbow disappears; but the rainbow does not come from anywhere, nor does it go anywhere.

When we observe one object, such as our I, we strongly feel that it is a single, indivisible entity, and that its singularity is inherently existent. In reality, however, our I has many parts, such as the parts that look, listen, walk and think, or the parts that are, for example, a teacher, a mother, a daughter and a wife. Our I is imputed upon the collection of all these parts. As with each individual phenomenon it is a singularity, but its singularity is merely imputed, like an army that is merely imputed upon a collection of soldiers, or a forest that is imputed upon a collection of trees.

When we see more than one object, we regard the multiplicity of these objects to be inherently existent. However, just as singularity is merely imputed, likewise plurality is just an imputation by mind and does not exist from the side of the object. For example, instead of looking at a collection of soldiers or trees from the point of view of the individual soldiers or trees, we could look at them as an army or a forest, that is, as a singular collection or whole, in which case we would be looking at a singularity rather than a plurality.

In summary, singularity does not exist from its own side because it is just imputed upon a plurality—its parts. In the same way, plurality does not exist from its own side because it is just imputed upon a singularity—the collection of its parts. Therefore singularity and plurality are mere imputations by conceptual mind and they lack true existence. If we realize this clearly, there is no basis for developing attachment and anger toward objects, either singular or plural. We tend to project the faults or qualities of the few onto the many, and then develop hatred or attachment on the basis of, for example, race, religion or country. Contemplating the emptiness of singularity and plurality can be helpful in reducing such hatred and attachment.

Although production, disintegration and so forth do exist, they do not exist inherently. It is our conceptual minds of self-grasping ignorance that grasp them as inherently existent. These conceptions grasp at the eight extremes: inherently existent production, inherently existent disintegration, inherently existent impermanence, inherently existent permanence, inherently existent going, inherently existent coming, inherently existent singularity and inherently existent plurality. These extremes are non-existent because they are extreme, something which is created and exaggerated by mistaken view. Our mind that believes and grasps at inherently existent production and so forth is extreme view. Since beginningless time, in life after life, because of following this extreme view we have experienced immense problems and suffering endlessly. Now is the time to stop all these problems and suffering permanently, by realizing directly that the production, disintegration, impermanence, permanence, going, coming, singularity and plurality that we normally perceive do not exist. Although these extremes do not exist, because of our ignorance we are always grasping them. The conceptions of these extremes lie at the root of all other delusions, and because delusions give rise to our performing contaminated actions that keep us trapped in the prison of samsara, these conceptions are the root of samsara, the cycle of impure life.

Inherently existent production is the same as the production that we normally see, and we should know that in reality neither of these exists. This is the same for the remaining seven extremes. For example, inherently existent disintegration and destruction and the disintegration and destruction that we normally see are the same, and we should know that neither of these exists. Our minds that grasp at these eight extremes are our self-grasping of phenomena. Because it is our self-grasping ignorance that causes us to experience endless suffering and problems, when this ignorance ceases permanently through meditation on the emptiness of all phenomena, all our suffering of this life and countless future lives will cease permanently and we will accomplish the real meaning of human life.

The subject of the eight extremes is profound and requires detailed explanation and lengthy study. Buddha explains them in detail in the *Perfection of Wisdom Sutras*; and in *Fundamental Wisdom*, a commentary to the *Perfection of Wisdom Sutras*, Nagarjuna also uses many profound and powerful reasons to prove that the eight extremes do not exist by showing how all phenomena are empty of inherent existence. Through analyzing conventional truths he establishes their ultimate nature, and shows why it is necessary to understand both the conventional and ultimate natures of an object in order to understand that object fully.

CONVENTIONAL AND ULTIMATE TRUTHS

In general, whatever exists is either a conventional truth or an ultimate truth, and since ultimate truth refers just to emptiness, everything except emptiness is a conventional truth. For example, things such as houses, cars and tables are all conventional truths.

All conventional truths are false objects because the way they appear and the way they exist do not correspond. If someone appears to be friendly and kind but his real intention is to gain our confidence in order to rob us, we would say that he is false or deceptive because there is a discrepancy between the way he appears and his real nature. Similarly, objects such as forms and sounds are false or deceptive because they appear to exist inherently, but in reality are completely devoid of inherent existence. Because the way they appear does not coincide with the way they exist, conventional truths are known as "deceptive phenomena." A cup, for instance, appears to exist independently of its parts, its causes and the mind that apprehends it, but in reality it totally depends upon these things. Because the way the cup appears to our mind and the way it exists do not correspond, the cup is a false object.

Although conventional truths are false objects, nevertheless they actually exist because a mind directly perceiving a conventional truth is a valid mind, a completely reliable mind. For instance, an eye consciousness directly perceiving a cup on the table is a valid mind because it will not deceive us—if we reach out to pick up the cup we will find it where our eye consciousness sees it. In this respect, an eye consciousness perceiving a cup on the table is different from an eye consciousness mistaking a cup reflected in a mirror for a real cup, or an eye consciousness seeing a mirage as water. Even though a cup is a false object, for practical purposes the eye consciousness that directly perceives it is a valid, reliable mind. However, although it is a valid mind it is nevertheless a mistaken awareness insofar as the cup appears to that mind to be truly existent. It is valid and non-deceptive with respect to the conventional characteristics of the cup—its position, size, color and so forth—but mistaken with respect to its appearance.

To summarize, conventional objects are false because although they appear to exist from their own side, in reality they are mere appearances to mind, like things seen in a dream. Within the context of a dream, however, dream objects have a relative validity, and this distinguishes them from things that do not exist at all. Suppose in a dream we steal a diamond and someone then asks us whether it was we who stole it. Even though the dream is merely a creation of our mind, if we answer "yes" we are telling the truth whereas if we answer "no" we are telling a lie. In the same way, even though in reality the whole universe is just an appearance to mind, within the context of the experience of ordinary beings we can distinguish between relative truths and relative falsities.

Conventional truths can be divided into gross conventional truths and subtle conventional truths. We can understand how all phenomena have these two levels of conventional truth by considering the example of a car. The car itself, the car depending on its causes, and the car depending on its parts are all gross conventional truths of the car. They are called "gross" because they are relatively easy to understand. The car depending on its basis of imputation is quite subtle and is not easy to understand, but it is still a gross conventional truth. The basis of imputation of the car is the parts of the car. To apprehend car, the parts of the car must appear to our mind; without the parts appearing, there is no way to develop the thought "car." For this reason, the parts are the basis of imputation of the car. We say, "I see a car," but strictly speaking all we ever see is parts of the car. However, when we develop the thought "car" by seeing its parts, we see the car. There is no car other than its parts, there is no body other than its parts, and so on. The car existing merely as an imputation by thought is the subtle conventional truth of the car. We have understood this when we realize that the car is nothing more than a mere imputation by a valid mind. We cannot understand subtle conventional truths unless we have understood emptiness. When we thoroughly realize subtle conventional truth we have realized both conventional truth and ultimate truth.

Strictly speaking, truth, ultimate truth and emptiness are synonymous because conventional truths are not real truths but false objects. They are true only for the minds of those who have not realized emptiness. Only emptiness is true because only emptiness exists in the way that it appears. When the mind of any sentient being directly perceives conventional truths, such as forms, they appear to exist from their own side. When the mind of a Superior being, a being who has realized emptiness directly, directly perceives emptiness, however, nothing appears other than emptiness; this mind is totally mixed with the mere absence of inherently existent phenomena. The way in which emptiness appears to the mind of a non-conceptual direct perceiver corresponds exactly to the way in which emptiness exists.

It should be noted that although emptiness is ultimate

truth it is not inherently existent. Emptiness is not a separate reality existing behind conventional appearances, but the real nature of those appearances. We cannot talk about emptiness in isolation, for emptiness is always the mere lack of inherent existence of something. For example, the emptiness of our body is the lack of inherent existence of our body, and without our body as its basis this emptiness cannot exist. Because emptiness necessarily depends upon a basis, it lacks inherent existence.

In *Guide to the Bodhisattva's Way of Life*, Shantideva defines ultimate truth as a phenomenon that is true for the uncontaminated mind of a Superior being. An uncontaminated mind is a mind that realizes emptiness directly. This mind is the only unmistaken awareness and is possessed exclusively by Superior beings. Because uncontaminated minds are completely unmistaken, anything directly perceived by them to be true is necessarily an ultimate truth. In contrast, anything that is directly perceived to be true by the mind of an ordinary being, a being who has not realized emptiness directly, is necessarily not an ultimate truth, because all minds of ordinary beings are mistaken, and mistaken minds can never directly perceive the truth.

Because of the imprints of conceptual thoughts that grasp at the eight extremes, everything that appears to the minds of ordinary beings appears to be inherently existent. Only the wisdom of meditative equipoise that directly realizes emptiness is undefiled by the imprints, or stains, of these conceptual thoughts. This is the only wisdom that has no mistaken appearance.

When a Superior Bodhisattva, a Bodhisattva who has realized emptiness directly, meditates on emptiness, his or her mind mixes with emptiness completely, with no appearance of inherent existence. He develops a completely pure, uncontaminated wisdom that is ultimate bodhichitta. When he rises from meditative equipoise, however, because of the imprints of true-grasping, conventional phenomena again appear to his mind as inherently existent, and his uncontaminated wisdom temporarily becomes non-manifest. Only a Buddha can manifest uncontaminated wisdom at the same time as directly perceiving conventional truths. An uncommon quality of a Buddha is that a single moment of a Buddha's mind realizes both conventional truth and ultimate truth directly and simultaneously. There are many levels of ultimate bodhichitta. For instance, the ultimate bodhichitta attained through Tantric practice is more profound than that developed through Sutra practice alone, and the supreme ultimate bodhichitta is that of a Buddha.

If through valid reasoning we realize the emptiness that is empty of the first extreme, the extreme of production, we will easily be able to realize the emptiness that is empty of the remaining seven extremes. Once we have realized the emptiness that is empty of the eight extremes we have realized the emptiness of all phenomena. Having gained this realization, we continue to contemplate and meditate on the emptiness of produced phenomena and so forth, and as our meditations deepen we will feel all phenomena dissolving into emptiness. We will then be able to maintain a single-pointed concentration on the emptiness of all phenomena.

To meditate on the emptiness of produced phenomena we can think:

My self, who was born through causes and conditions as a human being, is unfindable when I search for it with wisdom within my body and my mind, or separate from my body and mind. This proves that my self that I normally see does not exist at all.

Having contemplated in this way, we feel our self that we normally see disappears and we perceive a space-like emptiness that is the mere absence of our self that we normally see. We feel that our mind enters into this space-like emptiness and remains there single-pointedly. This meditation is called "space-like meditative equipoise on emptiness."

Just as eagles soar through the vast expanse of the sky without meeting any obstructions, needing only minimal effort to maintain their flight, so advanced meditators concentrating on emptiness can meditate on emptiness for a long time with little effort. Their minds soar through space-like emptiness, undistracted by any other phenomenon. When we meditate on emptiness we should try to emulate these meditators. Once we have found our object of meditation, the mere absence of our self that we normally see, we should refrain from further analysis and simply rest our mind in the experience of this emptiness. From time to time we should check to make sure that we have lost neither the clear appearance of emptiness nor the recognition of its meaning, but we should not check too forcefully as this will disturb our concentration. Our meditation should not be like the flight of a small bird, which never stops flapping its wings and is always changing direction, but like the flight of an eagle, which soars gently with only occasional adjustments to its wings. Through meditating in this way we will feel our mind dissolving into and becoming one with emptiness.

If we are successful in doing this, then during our meditation we are free from manifest self-grasping. If, on the other hand, we spend all our time checking and analyzing, never allowing our mind to relax into the space of emptiness, we will never gain this experience and our meditation will not serve to reduce our self-grasping.

In general we need to improve our understanding of emptiness through extensive study, approaching it from many angles and using many different lines of reasoning. It is also important to become thoroughly familiar with one complete meditation on emptiness through continuous contemplation, understanding exactly how to use the reasoning to lead to an experience of emptiness. We can then concentrate on emptiness single-pointedly and try to mix our mind with it, like water mixing with water.

THE UNION OF THE TWO TRUTHS

Strictly speaking, when we say the union of conventional truth and ultimate truth, in this context conventional truth refers only to subtle conventional truth, which is things existing as mere appearances. This subtle conventional truth and ultimate truth are in union, which means that they are non-dual, or one object. Thus, subtle conventional truth is not actual conventional truth but ultimate truth, a non-deceptive object. From the point of view of truth, conventional truths do not exist; they are false objects created by the ignorant mind of self-grasping. However, conventional truths exist for ordinary beings, who do not understand emptiness, but they do not exist for Superior beings, who realize emptiness directly. The instruction of the union of the two truths, the union of appearance and emptiness, is Buddha's ultimate view and intention. When we receive the fourth empowerment of Highest Yoga Tantra we receive the oral instructions of this union. When, through training continually in this union, we realize directly the union of the two truths, the union of appearance and emptiness, we become an enlightened Buddha who is completely free from subtle mistaken appearance, and who has the ability to benefit each and every living being every day through our countless emanations.

When something such as our body appears to us, both the body and the inherently existent body appear simultaneously. This is dualistic appearance, which is subtle mistaken appearance. Only Buddhas are free from such mistaken appearances. The main purpose of understanding and meditating on the union of the two truths is to prevent dualistic appearances—appearances of inherent existence to the mind that is meditating on emptiness—and thereby enable our mind to dissolve into emptiness. Once we can do this, our meditation on emptiness will be very powerful in eliminating our delusions. If we correctly identify and negate the inherently existent body, the body that we normally see, and meditate on the mere absence of such a body with strong concentration, we will feel our normal body dissolving into emptiness. We will understand that the real nature of our body is emptiness and that our body is merely a manifestation of emptiness.

Emptiness is like the sky and our body is like the blue of the sky. Just as the blue is a manifestation of the sky itself and cannot be separated from it, so our blue-like body is simply a manifestation of the sky of its emptiness and cannot be separated from it. If we realize this, when we focus on the emptiness of our body we feel that our body itself dissolves into its ultimate nature. In this way, we can easily overcome the conventional appearance of the body in our meditations, and our mind naturally mixes with emptiness.

In the *Heart Sutra*, Bodhisattva Avalokiteshvara says, "Form is not other than emptiness." This means that conventional phenomena, such as our body, do not exist separately from their emptiness. When we meditate on the emptiness of our body with this understanding, we know that the emptiness appearing to our mind is the very nature of our body, and that apart from this emptiness there is no body. Meditating in this way will greatly weaken our self-grasping mind. If we really believed that our body and its emptiness were the same nature, our self-grasping would definitely become weaker.

Although we can divide emptinesses from the point of view of their bases, and speak of the emptiness of the body, the emptiness of the I and so forth, in truth all emptinesses are the same nature. If we look at ten bottles, we can distinguish ten different spaces inside the bottles, but in reality these spaces are the same nature; and if we break the bottles, the spaces become indistinguishable. In the same way, although we can speak of the emptiness of the body, the mind, the I and so forth, in reality they are the same nature and indistinguishable. The only way in which they can be distinguished is by their conventional bases.

There are two principal benefits of understanding that all emptinesses are the same nature: in the meditation session our mind will mix with emptiness more easily, and in the meditation break we will be able to see all appearances as equal manifestations of their emptiness.

For as long as we feel that there is a gap between our mind and emptiness—that our mind is "here" and emptiness is "there"—our mind will not mix with emptiness. Knowing that all emptinesses are the same nature helps to close this gap. In ordinary life we experience many different objects—good, bad, attractive, unattractive—and our feelings toward them differ. Because we feel that the differences exist from the side of the objects, our mind is unbalanced and we develop attachment to attractive objects, aversion to unattractive objects and indifference to neutral objects. It is very difficult to mix such an uneven mind with emptiness. To mix our mind with emptiness we need to know that, although phenomena appear in many different aspects, in essence they are all empty. The differences we see are just appearances to mistaken minds; from the point of view of ultimate truth all phenomena are equal in emptiness. For a qualified meditator singlepointedly absorbed in emptiness, there is no difference between production and disintegration, impermanence and permanence, going and coming, singularity and plurality—everything is equal in emptiness and all problems of attachment, anger and self-grasping ignorance are solved. In this experience, everything becomes very peaceful and comfortable, balanced and harmonious, joyful and wonderful. There is no heat, no cold, no lower, no higher, no here, no there, no self, no other, no samsara—everything is equal in the peace of emptiness. This realization is called the "yoga of equalizing samsara and nirvana," and is explained in detail in both the Sutras and Tantras.

Since all emptinesses are the same nature, the ultimate nature of a mind that is meditating on emptiness is the same nature as the ultimate nature of its object. When we first meditate on emptiness our mind and emptiness appear to be two separate phenomena, but when we understand that all emptinesses are the same nature we will know that this feeling of separation is simply the experience of a mistaken mind. In reality our mind and emptiness are ultimately of one taste. If we apply this knowledge in our meditations, it will help to prevent the appearance of the conventional nature of our mind and allow our mind to dissolve into emptiness.

Having mixed our mind with emptiness, when we arise from meditation we will experience all phenomena equally as manifestations of their emptiness. Instead of feeling that the attractive, unattractive and neutral objects we see are inherently different, we will know that in essence they are the same nature. Just as both the gentlest and most violent waves in an ocean are equally water, likewise both attractive forms and repulsive forms are equally manifestations of emptiness. Realizing this, our mind will become balanced and peaceful. We will recognize all conventional appearances as the magical play of the mind, and we will not grasp strongly at their apparent differences.

When Milarepa once taught emptiness to a woman, he compared emptiness to the sky and conventional truths to clouds and told her to meditate on the sky. She followed his instructions with great success, but she had one problem—when she meditated on the sky of emptiness everything disappeared, and she could not understand how phenomena could exist conventionally. She said to Milarepa, "I find it easy to meditate on the sky but difficult to establish the clouds. Please teach me how to meditate on the clouds." Milarepa replied, "If your meditation on the sky is going well, the clouds will not be a problem. Clouds simply appear in the sky—they arise from the sky and dissolve back into the sky. As your experience of the sky improves, you will naturally come to understand the clouds."

In Tibetan, the word for both sky and space is "namkha," although space is different from sky. There are two types of space, produced space and unproduced space. Produced space is the visible space we can see inside a room or in the sky. This space may become dark at night and light during the day, and as it undergoes change in this way it is an impermanent phenomenon. The characteristic property of produced space is that it does not obstruct objects—if there is space in a room we can place objects there without obstruction. Similarly, birds are able to fly through the space of the sky because it lacks obstruction, whereas they cannot fly through a mountain! Therefore it is clear that produced space lacks, or is empty of, obstructive contact. This mere lack, or empty, of obstructive contact is unproduced space.

Because unproduced space is the mere absence of obstructive contact, it does not undergo momentary change and is therefore a permanent phenomenon. Whereas produced space is visible and quite easy to understand, unproduced space is a mere absence of obstructive contact and is much more subtle. However, once we understand unproduced space, we will find it easier to understand emptiness.

The only difference between emptiness and unproduced space is their object of negation. The object of negation of unproduced space is obstructive contact whereas the object of negation of emptiness is inherent existence. Because unproduced space is the best analogy for understanding emptiness, it is used in the Sutras and in many scriptures. Unproduced space is a non-affirming negative phenomenon—a phenomenon that is realized by a mind that merely eliminates its negated object without realizing another positive phenomenon. Produced space is an affirmative, or positive, phenomenon—a phenomenon that is realized without the mind explicitly eliminating a negated object. More details on these two types of phenomenon can be found in the books *The New Heart of Wisdom* and *Ocean of Nectar*.

THE PRACTICE OF EMPTINESS IN
OUR DAILY ACTIVITIES

In the Sutras Buddha said all phenomena are like illusions. In this context, all phenomena means all phenomena that we normally see or perceive. Thus the real meaning of the Sutra is that we should know that all phenomena that we normally see or perceive are like illusions. Although a magician's illusions appear clearly they do not actually exist. In the same way, although phenomena that we normally see or perceive appear clearly they do not actually exist. Although things appear to us as inherently existent we should remember that these appearances are deceptive and that in reality the things that we normally see do not exist. As mentioned earlier, in *King of Concentration Sutra*, Buddha says:

> A magician creates various things
> Such as horses, elephants and so forth.
> His creations do not actually exist;
> You should know all things in the same way.

The last two lines of this verse mean that just as we know that the horses and elephants created by the magician do not exist, in the same way we should know that all the things that we normally see do not actually exist. This chapter, *Ultimate Bodhichitta*, has extensively explained how all the things that we normally see do not exist.

When a magician creates an illusory horse, a horse appears very clearly to his mind but he knows that it is just an illusion. Indeed, the very appearance of the horse reminds him that there is no horse in front of him. In the same way, when we are very familiar with emptiness, the very fact that things appear to be inherently existent will remind us that they are not inherently existent. We should therefore recognize that whatever appears to us in our daily life is like an illusion and lacks inherent existence. In this way our wisdom will increase day by day, and our self-grasping ignorance and other delusions will naturally diminish.

Between meditation sessions we should be like an actor. When an actor plays the part of a king, he dresses, speaks and acts like a king, but he knows all the time that he is not a real king. In the same way we should live and function in the conventional world yet always remember that we ourself, our environment and the people around us that we normally see do not exist at all.

If we think like this we will be able to live in the conventional world without grasping at it. We will treat it lightly, and have the flexibility of mind to respond to every situation in a constructive way. Knowing that whatever appears to our mind is mere appearance, when attractive objects appear we will not grasp at them and develop attachment, and when unattractive objects appear we will not grasp at them and develop aversion or anger.

In *Training the Mind in Seven Points*, Geshe Chekhawa says, "Think that all phenomena are like dreams." Some of the things we see in our dreams are beautiful and some are ugly, but they are all mere appearances to our dreaming mind. They do not exist from their own side, and are empty of inherent existence. It is the same with the objects we perceive when we are awake—they too are mere appearances to mind and lack inherent existence.

All phenomena lack inherent existence. When we look at a rainbow it appears to occupy a particular location in space, and it seems that if we searched we would be able to find where the rainbow touches the ground. However, we know that no matter how hard we search we will never be able to find the end of the rainbow, for as soon as we arrive at the place where we saw the rainbow touch the ground, the rainbow will have disappeared. If we do not search for it, the rainbow appears clearly; but when we look for it, it is not there. All phenomena are like this. If we do not analyze them they appear clearly, but when we search for them analytically, trying to isolate them from everything else, they are not there.

If something did exist inherently, and we investigated it by separating it from all other phenomena, we would be able to find it. However, all phenomena are like rainbows—if we search for them we will never find them. At first we might find this view very uncomfortable and difficult to accept, but this is quite natural. With greater familiarity we will find this reasoning more acceptable, and eventually we will realize that it is true.

It is important to understand that emptiness does not mean nothingness. Although things do not exist from their own side, independent of the mind, they do exist in the sense that they are understood by a valid mind. The world we experience when we are awake is similar to the world we experience when we are dreaming. We cannot say that dream things do not exist, but if we believe that they exist as more than mere appearances to the mind, existing "out there," then we are mistaken, as we will discover when we wake up.

As mentioned before, there is no greater method for experiencing peace of mind and happiness than to understand and meditate on emptiness. Since it is our self-grasping that keeps us bound to the prison of samsara and is the source of all our suffering, meditation on emptiness is the universal solution to all our problems. It is the medicine that cures all mental and physical diseases, and the nectar that bestows the everlasting happiness of nirvana and enlightenment.

A SIMPLE TRAINING IN ULTIMATE BODHICHITTA

We begin by thinking:

I must attain enlightenment to benefit each and every living being every day. For this purpose I will attain a direct realization of the way things really are.

With this bodhichitta motivation, we contemplate:

Normally I see my body within its parts—the hands, back and so forth—but neither the individual parts nor the collection of the parts are my body because they are the parts of my body and not the body itself. However, there is no "my body" other than its parts. Through searching with wisdom for my body in this way, I realize that my body is unfindable. This is a valid reason to prove that my body that I normally see does not exist at all.

Through contemplating this point we try to perceive the mere absence of the body that we normally see. This mere absence of the body that we normally see is the emptiness of our body, and we meditate on this emptiness single-pointedly for as long as possible.

We should continually practice this contemplation and meditation, and then move to the next stage, meditation on the emptiness of our self. We should contemplate and think:

Normally I see my self within my body and mind, but neither my body, nor my mind, nor the collection of my body and mind is my self, because these are my possessions and my self is the possessor; and possessor and possessions cannot be the same. However, there is no "my self" other than my body and mind. Through searching with wisdom for my self in this way, I realize that my self is unfindable. This is a valid reason to prove that my self that I normally see does not exist at all.

Through contemplating this point we try to perceive the mere absence of our self that we normally see. This mere absence of our self that we normally see is the emptiness of our self, and we meditate on this emptiness single-pointedly for as long as possible.

We should continually practice this contemplation and meditation, and then move to the next stage, meditation on the emptiness of all phenomena. We should contemplate and think:

As with my body and my self, all other phenomena are unfindable when I search for them with wisdom. This is a valid reason to prove that all phenomena that I normally see or perceive do not exist at all.

Through contemplating this point we try to perceive the mere absence of all phenomena that we normally see or perceive. This mere absence of all phenomena that we normally see or perceive is the emptiness of all phenomena. We meditate continually on this emptiness of all phenomena with bodhichitta motivation until we are able to maintain our concentration clearly for one minute every time we meditate on it. Our concentration that has this ability is called the "concentration of placing the mind."

In the second stage, with the concentration of placing the mind, we meditate continually on the emptiness of all phenomena until we are able to maintain our concentration clearly for five minutes every time we meditate on it. Our concentration that has this ability is called "concentration of continual placement." In the third stage, with the concentration of continual placement, we meditate continually on the emptiness of all phenomena until we are able to immediately remember our object of meditation—the mere absence of all phenomena that we normally see or perceive—whenever we lose it during meditation. Our concentration that has this ability is called "concentration of replacement." In the fourth stage, with the concentration of replacement, we meditate continually on the emptiness of all phenomena until we are able to maintain our concentration clearly during the entire meditation session without forgetting the object of meditation. Our concentration that has this ability is called "concentration of close placement." At this stage we have very stable and clear concentration focused on the emptiness of all phenomena.

Then, with the concentration of close placement, we meditate continually on the emptiness of all phenomena until finally we attain the concentration of tranquil abiding focused on emptiness, which causes us to experience special physical and mental suppleness and bliss. With this concentration of tranquil abiding we will develop a special wisdom that realizes the emptiness of all phenomena very clearly. This wisdom is called "superior seeing." Through continually meditating on the concentration of tranquil abiding associated with superior seeing, our wisdom of superior seeing will transform into the wisdom that directly realizes the emptiness of all phenomena. This direct realization of emptiness is the actual ultimate bodhichitta. The moment we attain the wisdom of ultimate bodhichitta we become a Superior Bodhisattva. As mentioned before, conventional bodhichitta is the nature of compassion and ultimate bodhichitta is the nature of wisdom. These two bodhichittas are like the two wings of a bird with which we can fly and very quickly reach the enlightened world.

In *Advice from Atisha's Heart*, Atisha says:

> Friends, until you attain enlightenment, the Spiritual Teacher is indispensable; therefore rely upon the holy Spiritual Guide.

We need to rely upon our Spiritual Guide until we attain enlightenment. The reason for this is very simple. The ultimate goal of human life is to attain enlightenment, and this depends upon continually receiving the special blessings of Buddha through our Spiritual Guide. Buddha attained enlightenment with the sole intention of leading all living beings along the stages of the path to enlightenment through his emanations. Who is his emanation who is leading us along the stages of the path to enlightenment? It is clearly our present Spiritual Teacher who is sincerely and correctly leading us along the paths of renunciation, bodhichitta and the correct view of emptiness by giving these teachings and showing a practical example of someone who is sincerely practicing them. With this understanding we should strongly believe that our Spiritual Guide is an emanation of Buddha, and develop and maintain deep faith in him or her.

Atisha also says:

> Until you realize ultimate truth, listening is indispensable; therefore listen to the instructions of the Spiritual Guide.

Even if we were mistakenly to see two moons in the sky, this mistaken appearance would remind us that in fact there are not two moons, but only one. In a similar way, when the things that we normally see appear to us, just their appearance reminds us that they do not exist. Through understanding this we will stop grasping at them. If we are able to do this, it is a clear indication that our understanding of emptiness is qualified. Until our understanding of emptiness is qualified, and to prevent self-grasping from developing, we should listen to, read and practice the instructions of our Spiritual Guide.

If we sincerely practice with strong mindfulness and alertness the above instructions of how to stop grasping at the things that we normally see, our self-grasping will definitely reduce. As a result of this our daily problems will definitely reduce and finally our self-grasping will cease permanently. All our problems and suffering of this life and of our countless future lives will then permanently cease. While we have this precious human life we have the opportunity to accomplish this aim. We should never allow ourself to waste this precious opportunity.

All the contemplations and meditations presented in this book should be practiced in conjunction with the preliminary practices for meditation presented in Appendix I: *Liberating Prayer and Prayers for Meditation*. These preliminary practices will enable us to purify our mind, accumulate merit and receive the blessings of the enlightened beings, thus ensuring that our meditation practice is successful. A more detailed explanation of relying upon our Spiritual Guide can be found in the book *Joyful Path of Good Fortune*.

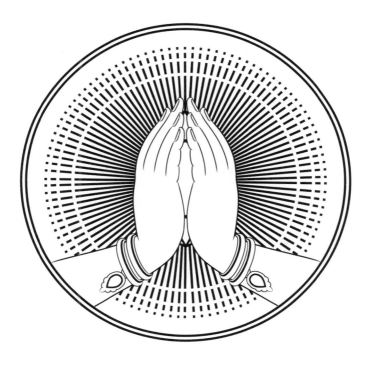

The hands in prayer holding a wishfulfilling jewel
symbolize that by following the spiritual path we
will eventually experience the completely pure
mind of enlightenment.

Dedication

Through the virtues I have collected by writing this book, may everyone be happy and free from misery. May all living beings find the opportunity to practice the instructions given in *How to Transform Your Life*, and may they attain the supreme inner peace of enlightenment.

Liberating Prayer

PRAISE TO BUDDHA SHAKYAMUNI

&

Prayers for Meditation

BRIEF PREPARATORY PRAYERS FOR MEDITATION

Liberating Prayer

PRAISE TO BUDDHA SHAKYAMUNI

O Blessed One, Shakyamuni Buddha,
Precious treasury of compassion,
Bestower of supreme inner peace,

You, who love all beings without exception,
Are the source of happiness and goodness;
And you guide us to the liberating path.

Your body is a wishfulfilling jewel,
Your speech is supreme, purifying nectar,
And your mind is refuge for all living beings.

With folded hands I turn to you,
Supreme unchanging friend,
I request from the depths of my heart:

Please give me the light of your wisdom
To dispel the darkness of my mind
And to heal my mental continuum.

Please nourish me with your goodness,
That I in turn may nourish all beings
With an unceasing banquet of delight.

Through your compassionate intention,
Your blessings and virtuous deeds,
And my strong wish to rely upon you,

May all suffering quickly cease
And all happiness and joy be fulfilled;
And may holy Dharma flourish for evermore.

Colophon: This prayer was composed by Venerable Geshe Kelsang Gyatso Rinpoche and is recited at the beginning of teachings, meditations and prayers in Kadampa Buddhist Centers throughout the world.

Prayers for Meditation

BRIEF PREPARATORY PRAYERS FOR MEDITATION

Going for refuge

I and all sentient beings, until we achieve enlightenment,
Go for refuge to Buddha, Dharma and Sangha.

(3x, 7x, 100x, etc.)

Generating bodhichitta

Through the virtues I collect by giving and other perfections,
May I become a Buddha for the benefit of all.   (3x)

Generating the four immeasurables

May everyone be happy,
May everyone be free from misery,
May no one ever be separated from their happiness,
May everyone have equanimity, free from hatred and
     attachment.

Visualizing the Field for Accumulating Merit

In the space before me is the living Buddha Shakyamuni surrounded by all the Buddhas and Bodhisattvas, like the full moon surrounded by stars.

Prayer of seven limbs

With my body, speech and mind, humbly I prostrate,
And make offerings both set out and imagined.
I confess my wrong deeds from all time,
And rejoice in the virtues of all.
Please stay until samsara ceases,
And turn the Wheel of Dharma for us.
I dedicate all virtues to great enlightenment.

Offering the mandala

The ground sprinkled with perfume and spread with flowers,
The Great Mountain, four lands, sun and moon,
Seen as a Buddha Land and offered thus,
May all beings enjoy such Pure Lands.

I offer without any sense of loss
The objects that give rise to my attachment, hatred and
    confusion,
My friends, enemies and strangers, our bodies and enjoyments;
Please accept these and bless me to be released directly from the
    three poisons.

IDAM GURU RATNA MANDALAKAM NIRYATAYAMI

Prayer of the Stages of the Path

The path begins with strong reliance
On my kind Teacher, source of all good;
O Bless me with this understanding
To follow him with great devotion.

This human life with all its freedoms,
Extremely rare, with so much meaning;
O Bless me with this understanding
All day and night to seize its essence.

My body, like a water bubble,
Decays and dies so very quickly;
After death come results of karma,
Just like the shadow of a body.

With this firm knowledge and remembrance
Bless me to be extremely cautious,
Always avoiding harmful actions
And gathering abundant virtue.

Samsara's pleasures are deceptive,
Give no contentment, only torment;
So please bless me to strive sincerely
To gain the bliss of perfect freedom.

O Bless me so that from this pure thought
Come mindfulness and greatest caution,
To keep as my essential practice
The doctrine's root, the Pratimoksha.

Just like myself all my kind mothers
Are drowning in samsara's ocean;
O So that I may soon release them,
Bless me to train in bodhichitta.

But I cannot become a Buddha
By this alone without three ethics;
So bless me with the strength to practice
The Bodhisattva's ordination.

By pacifying my distractions
And analyzing perfect meanings,
Bless me to quickly gain the union
Of special insight and quiescence.

When I become a pure container
Through common paths, bless me to enter
The essence practice of good fortune,
The supreme vehicle, Vajrayana.

The two attainments both depend on
My sacred vows and my commitments;
Bless me to understand this clearly
And keep them at the cost of my life.

By constant practice in four sessions,
The way explained by holy Teachers,
O Bless me to gain both the stages,
Which are the essence of the Tantras.

May those who guide me on the good path,
And my companions all have long lives;
Bless me to pacify completely
All obstacles, outer and inner.

May I always find perfect Teachers,
And take delight in holy Dharma,
Accomplish all grounds and paths swiftly,
And gain the state of Vajradhara.

Receiving blessings and purifying

From the hearts of all the holy beings, streams of light and
nectar flow down, granting blessings and purifying.

*At this point we begin the actual contemplation and
meditation. After the meditation we dedicate our merit while
reciting the following prayers:*

Dedication

Through the virtues I have collected
By practicing the stages of the path,
May all living beings find the opportunity
To practice in the same way.

May everyone experience
The happiness of humans and gods,
And quickly attain enlightenment,
So that samsara is finally extinguished.

Prayers for the Virtuous Tradition

So that the tradition of Je Tsongkhapa,
The King of the Dharma, may flourish,
May all obstacles be pacified
And may all favorable conditions abound.

Through the two collections of myself and others
Gathered throughout the three times,
May the doctrine of Conqueror Losang Dragpa
Flourish for evermore.

The nine-line *Migtsema* prayer

Tsongkhapa, crown ornament of the scholars
    of the Land of the Snows,
You are Buddha Shakyamuni and Vajradhara,
    the source of all attainments,
Avalokiteshvara, the treasury of unobservable
    compassion,
Manjushri, the supreme stainless wisdom,
And Vajrapani, the destroyer of the hosts of
    maras.
O Venerable Guru-Buddha, synthesis of all
    Three Jewels,
With my body, speech and mind, respectfully I
    make requests:
Please grant your blessings to ripen and
    liberate myself and others,
And bestow the common and supreme
    attainments.   (3x)

Colophon: These prayers were compiled from traditional
sources by Venerable Geshe Kelsang Gyatso Rinpoche.

APPENDIX II

What is Meditation?

What is Meditation?

*M*editation is a mind that is single-pointedly focused on a virtuous object, and whose function is to make the mind peaceful and calm. Whenever we meditate, we are performing a mental action that will cause us to experience inner peace in the future. Normally, throughout our life, we experience delusions day and night, and these are the opposite to mental peace. Sometimes, however, we naturally experience inner peace, and this is because in our previous lives we concentrated on virtuous objects. A virtuous object is one that causes us to develop a peaceful mind when we analyze and concentrate on it. If we concentrate on an object that causes us to develop an unpeaceful mind, such as anger or attachment, this indicates that for us the object is non-virtuous. There are also many neutral objects that are neither virtuous nor non-virtuous.

There are two types of meditation: analytical meditation and placement meditation. Analytical meditation involves contemplating the meaning of a spiritual instruction that we have heard or read. By contemplating such instructions deeply, eventually we reach a definite conclusion, or cause a specific virtuous state of mind to arise. This is the object of placement meditation. We then concentrate single-pointedly on this conclusion or virtuous state of mind for as long as possible to become deeply acquainted with it. This single-pointed concentration is placement meditation. Analytical meditation is often called "contemplation," and placement meditation is often called "meditation." Placement meditation depends upon analytical meditation, and analytical meditation depends upon listening to or reading spiritual instructions.

THE BENEFITS OF MEDITATION

The purpose of meditation is to make our mind calm and peaceful. As mentioned earlier, if our mind is peaceful we will be free from worries and mental discomfort, and so we will experience true happiness; but if our mind is not peaceful, we will find it very difficult to be happy, even if we are living in the very best conditions. If we train in meditation, our mind will gradually become more and more peaceful, and we will experience a purer and purer form of happiness. Eventually we will be able to stay happy all the time, even in the most difficult circumstances.

Usually we find it difficult to control our mind. It seems as if our mind is like a balloon in the wind—blown here and there by external circumstances. If things go well, our mind is happy, but if they go badly, it immediately becomes unhappy. For example, if we get what we want, such as a new possession, a new position or a new partner, we become excited and cling to them tightly. However, since we cannot have everything we want, and since we will inevitably be separated from the friends, position and possessions we currently enjoy, this mental stickiness, or attachment, serves only to cause us pain. On the other hand, if we do not get what we want, or if we lose something that we like, we become despondent or irritated. For example, if we are forced to work with a colleague whom we dislike, we will probably become irritated and feel aggrieved, with the result that we will be unable to work with him or her efficiently and our time at work will become stressful and unrewarding.

Such fluctuations of mood arise because we are too closely involved in the external situation. We are like a child making a sandcastle who is excited when it is first made, but who becomes upset when it is destroyed by the incoming tide. By training in meditation, we create an inner space and clarity that enables us to control our mind regardless of the external circumstances. Gradually we develop mental equilibrium, a balanced mind that is happy all the time, rather than an unbalanced mind that oscillates between the extremes of excitement and despondency.

If we train in meditation systematically, eventually we will be able to eradicate from our mind the delusions that are the causes of all our problems and suffering. In this way, we will come to experience the supreme permanent inner peace of nirvana. Then, day and night, in life after life, we will experience only peace and happiness.

At the beginning, even if our meditation does not seem to be going well, we should remember that simply by applying effort to training in meditation, we are creating the mental karma to experience inner peace in the future. The happiness of this life and of our future lives depends upon the experience of inner peace, which in turn depends upon the mental action of meditation. Since inner peace is the source of all happiness, we can see how important meditation is.

HOW TO BEGIN MEDITATION

The first stage of meditation is to stop distractions and make our mind clearer and more lucid. This can be accomplished by practicing a simple breathing meditation. We choose a quiet place to meditate and sit in a comfortable position. We can sit in the traditional cross-legged posture or in any other position that is comfortable. If we wish, we can sit in a chair. The most important thing is to keep our back straight to prevent our mind from becoming sluggish or sleepy.

We sit with our eyes partially closed and turn our attention to our breathing. We breathe naturally, preferably through the nostrils, without attempting to control our breath, and we try to become aware of the sensation of the breath as it enters and leaves the nostrils. This sensation is our object of meditation. We should try to concentrate on it to the exclusion of everything else.

At first our mind will be very busy, and we might even feel that the meditation is making our mind busier; but in reality we are just becoming more aware of how busy our mind actually is. There will be a great temptation to follow the different thoughts as they arise, but we should resist this and remain focused single-pointedly on the sensation of the breath. If we discover that our mind has wandered and is following our thoughts, we should immediately return it to the breath. We should repeat this as many times as necessary until the mind settles on the breath.

If we practice patiently in this way, gradually our distracting thoughts will subside and we will experience a sense of inner peace and relaxation. Our mind will feel lucid and spacious and we will feel refreshed. When the sea is rough, sediment is churned up and the water becomes murky, but when the wind dies down the mud gradually settles and the water becomes clear. In a similar way, when the otherwise incessant flow of our distracting thoughts is calmed through concentrating on the breath, our mind becomes unusually lucid and clear. We should stay with this state of mental calm for a while.

Even though breathing meditation is only a preliminary stage of meditation, it can be quite powerful. We can see from this practice that it is possible to experience inner peace and contentment just by controlling the mind, without having to depend at all upon external conditions. When the turbulence of distracting thoughts subsides and our mind becomes still, a deep happiness and contentment naturally arises from within. This feeling of contentment and well-being helps us to cope with the busyness and difficulties of daily life. So much of the stress and tension we normally experience comes from our mind, and many of the problems we experience, including ill health, are caused or aggravated by this stress. Just by doing breathing meditation for ten or fifteen minutes each day, we will be able to reduce this stress. We will experience a calm, spacious feeling in the mind, and many of our usual problems will fall away. Difficult situations will become easier to deal with, we will naturally feel warm and well disposed toward other people, and our relationships with others will gradually improve.

We should train in this preliminary meditation until we reduce our gross distractions, and then we can train in the actual meditations explained in this book. When we do these meditations, we should begin by calming the mind with breathing meditation, and then proceed to the stages of analytical and placement meditation according to the specific instructions for each meditation.

The Kadampa Way of Life

THE ESSENTIAL PRACTICE
OF KADAM LAMRIM

Introduction

This essential practice of Kadam Lamrim, known as *The Kadampa Way of Life*, contains two texts: *Advice from Atisha's Heart* and Je Tsongkhapa's *The Three Principal Aspects of the Path*. The first encapsulates the way of life of the early Kadampa practitioners, whose example of purity and sincerity we should all try to emulate. The second is a profound guide to meditation on the stages of the path, Lamrim, which Je Tsongkhapa composed based on the instructions he received directly from the Wisdom Buddha Manjushri.

If we try our best to put Atisha's advice into practice, and to meditate on Lamrim according to Je Tsongkhapa's instructions, we will develop a pure and happy mind and gradually progress toward the ultimate peace of full enlightenment. As Bodhisattva Shantideva says:

> By depending upon this boat-like human form,
> We can cross the great ocean of suffering.
> Since such a vessel will be hard to find again,
> This is no time to sleep, you fool!

Practicing in this way is the very essence of the Kadampa way of life.

Geshe Kelsang Gyatso
1994

Mindfulness Toolkit

Meditation Classes in Westminster

Each class consists of guided meditation and practical advice from the timeless wisdom of Buddha to help us solve daily problems and find happiness from within.

Wednesdays
7-8:30pm
$10 (members free, $7 students & seniors)

Starts April 12

Location: Front Range Community College
3645 West 112th Avenue
Westminster - 80031
Go to Entrance 2 in the front of building and on right side of flagpoles; then turn left at first hallway. Room C-0576

meditationincolorado.org/westminster

Advice from Atisha's Heart

When Venerable Atisha came to Tibet, he first went to Ngari, where he remained for two years giving many teachings to the disciples of Jangchub Ö. After two years had passed, he decided to return to India, and Jangchub Ö requested him to give one last teaching before he left. Atisha replied that he had already given them all the advice they needed, but Jangchub Ö persisted in his request and so Atisha accepted and gave the following advice.

How wonderful!

Friends, since you already have great knowledge and clear understanding, whereas I am of no importance and have little wisdom, it is not suitable for you to request advice from me. However because you dear friends, whom I cherish from my heart, have requested me, I will give you this essential advice from my inferior and childish mind.

Friends, until you attain enlightenment, the Spiritual Teacher is indispensable; therefore rely upon the holy Spiritual Guide.

Until you realize ultimate truth, listening is indispensable; therefore listen to the instructions of the Spiritual Guide.

Since you cannot become a Buddha merely by understanding Dharma, practice earnestly with understanding.

Avoid places that disturb your mind, and always remain where your virtues increase.

Until you attain stable realizations, worldly amusements are harmful; therefore abide in a place where there are no such distractions.

Avoid friends who cause you to increase delusions, and rely upon those who increase your virtue. This you should take to heart.

Since there is never a time when worldly activities come to an end, limit your activities.

Dedicate your virtues throughout the day and the night, and always watch your mind.

Because you have received advice, whenever you are not meditating, always practice in accordance with what your Spiritual Guide says.

If you practice with great devotion, results will arise immediately, without your having to wait for a long time.

If from your heart you practice in accordance with Dharma, both food and resources will come naturally to hand.

Friends, the things you desire give no more satisfaction than drinking sea water; therefore practice contentment.

Avoid all haughty, conceited, proud and arrogant minds, and remain peaceful and subdued.

Avoid activities that are said to be meritorious, but which in fact are obstacles to Dharma.

Profit and respect are nooses of the maras, so brush them aside like stones on the path.

Words of praise and fame serve only to beguile us; therefore blow them away as you would blow your nose.

Since the happiness, pleasure and friends you gather in this life last only for a moment, put them all behind you.

Since future lives last for a very long time, gather up riches to provide for the future.

You will have to depart leaving everything behind, so do not be attached to anything.

Generate compassion for lowly beings, and especially avoid despising or humiliating them.

Have no hatred for enemies, and no attachment for friends.

Do not be jealous of others' good qualities, but out of admiration adopt them yourself.

Do not look for faults in others, but look for faults in yourself, and purge them like bad blood.

Do not contemplate your own good qualities, but contemplate the good qualities of others, and respect everyone as a servant would.

See all living beings as your father or mother, and love them as if you were their child.

Always keep a smiling face and a loving mind, and speak truthfully without malice.

If you talk too much with little meaning, you will make mistakes; therefore speak in moderation, only when necessary.

If you engage in many meaningless activities, your virtuous activities will degenerate; therefore stop activities that are not spiritual.

It is completely meaningless to put effort into activities that have no essence.

If the things you desire do not come, it is due to karma created long ago; therefore keep a happy and relaxed mind.

Beware, offending a holy being is worse than dying; therefore be honest and straightforward.

Since all the happiness and suffering of this life arise from previous actions, do not blame others.

All happiness comes from the blessings of your Spiritual Guide; therefore always repay his kindness.

Since you cannot tame the minds of others until you have tamed your own, begin by taming your own mind.

Since you will definitely have to depart without the wealth you have accumulated, do not accumulate negativity for the sake of wealth.

Distracting enjoyments have no essence; therefore sincerely practice giving.

Always keep pure moral discipline for it leads to beauty in this life and happiness hereafter.

Since hatred is rife in these impure times, don the armor of patience, free from anger.

You remain in samsara through the power of laziness; therefore ignite the fire of the effort of application.

Since this human life is wasted by indulging in distractions, now is the time to practice concentration.

Being under the influence of wrong views, you do not realize the ultimate nature of things; therefore investigate correct meanings.

Friends, there is no happiness in this swamp of samsara, so move to the firm ground of liberation.

Meditate according to the advice of your Spiritual Guide and dry up the river of samsaric suffering.

You should consider this well because it is not just words from the mouth, but sincere advice from the heart.

If you practice like this, you will delight me, and you will bring happiness to yourself and others.

I who am ignorant request you to take this advice to heart.

This is the advice that the holy being Venerable Atisha gave to Venerable Jangchub Ö.

The Three Principal Aspects of the Path

Homage to the venerable Spiritual Guide.

I will explain to the best of my ability
The essential meaning of all the Conqueror's teachings,
The path praised by the holy Bodhisattvas,
And the gateway for fortunate ones seeking liberation.

You who are not attached to the joys of samsara,
But strive to make your freedom and endowment
    meaningful,
O Fortunate Ones who apply your minds to the path that
    pleases the Conquerors,
Please listen with a clear mind.

Without pure renunciation, there is no way to pacify
Attachment to the pleasures of samsara;
And since living beings are tightly bound by desire for
    samsara,
Begin by seeking renunciation.

Freedom and endowment are difficult to find, and
    there is no time to waste.
By acquainting your mind with this, overcome
    attachment to this life;
And by repeatedly contemplating actions and effects
And the sufferings of samsara, overcome attachment to
    future lives.

When, through contemplating in this way, the desire for
    the pleasures of samsara
Does not arise, even for a moment,
But a mind longing for liberation arises throughout
    the day and the night,
At that time, renunciation is generated.

However, if this renunciation is not maintained
By completely pure bodhichitta,
It will not be a cause of the perfect happiness of
    unsurpassed enlightenment;
Therefore, the wise generate a supreme bodhichitta.

Swept along by the currents of the four powerful
    rivers,
Tightly bound by the chains of karma, so hard to
    release,
Ensnared within the iron net of self-grasping,
Completely enveloped by the pitch-black darkness of
    ignorance,

Taking rebirth after rebirth in boundless samsara,
And unceasingly tormented by the three sufferings—
Through contemplating the state of your mothers in
    conditions such as these,
Generate a supreme mind [of bodhichitta].

But, even though you may be acquainted with
    renunciation and bodhichitta,
If you do not possess the wisdom realizing the way
    things are,
You will not be able to cut the root of samsara;
Therefore, strive in the means for realizing
    dependent relationship.

Whoever negates the conceived object of
    self-grasping
Yet sees the infallibility of cause and effect
Of all phenomena in samsara and nirvana,
Has entered the path that pleases the Buddhas.

Dependent-related appearance is infallible
And emptiness is inexpressible;
For as long as the meaning of these two appear to be
    separate,
You have not yet realized Buddha's intention.

When they arise as one, not alternating but simultaneous,
From merely seeing infallible dependent relationship
Comes certain knowledge that destroys all grasping
    at objects.
At that time, the analysis of view is complete.

Moreover, when the extreme of existence is dispelled
    by appearance,
And the extreme of non-existence is dispelled by
    emptiness,
And you know how emptiness is perceived as cause
    and effect,
You will not be captivated by extreme views.

When, in this way, you have correctly realized the
    essential points
Of the three principal aspects of the path,
Dear One, withdraw into solitude, generate strong effort,
And quickly accomplish the final goal.

Colophon: Both texts were translated under the compassionate
guidance of Venerable Geshe Kelsang Gyatso Rinpoche.

Glossary

Aggregate In general, all functioning things are aggregates because they are an aggregation of their parts. In particular, a person of the desire realm or form realm has five aggregates: the aggregates of form, feeling, discrimination, compositional factors and consciousness. A being of the formless realm lacks the aggregate of form but has the other four. A person's form aggregate is his or her body. The remaining four aggregates are aspects of his mind. See *The New Heart of Wisdom*.

Alertness A mental factor which is a type of wisdom that examines our activity of body, speech and mind and knows whether or not faults are developing. See *How to Understand the Mind*.

Aryadeva A third century AD Indian Buddhist scholar and meditation master, who was a disciple of Nagarjuna.

Asanga A great Indian Buddhist Yogi and scholar of the fifth century, author of *Compendium of Abhidharma*. See *Living Meaningfully, Dying Joyfully* and *The New Heart of Wisdom*.

Atisha (AD 982–1054) A famous Indian Buddhist scholar and meditation master. He was Abbot of the great Buddhist monastery of Vikramashila at a time when Mahayana Buddhism was flourishing in India. He was later invited to Tibet where he re-introduced pure Buddhism. He is the author of the first text on the stages of the path, *Lamp for the Path*. His tradition later became known as the "Kadampa Tradition." See *Modern Buddhism* and *Joyful Path of Good Fortune*. See also **Kadampa**, **Kadampa Buddhism** and **Kadampa Tradition**

Attachment A deluded mental factor that observes a contaminated object, regards it as a cause of happiness and wishes for it. See *How to Understand the Mind* and *Joyful Path of Good Fortune*.

Attention A mental factor that functions to focus the mind on a particular attribute of an object. See *How to Understand the Mind*.

Basis of imputation All phenomena are imputed upon their parts, therefore any of the individual parts, or the entire collection of the parts, of any phenomenon is its basis of imputation. A phenomenon is imputed by mind in dependence upon its basis of imputation appearing to that mind. See *The New Heart of Wisdom*.

Beginningless time According to the Buddhist world view, there is no beginning to mind, and so no beginning to time. Therefore, all living beings have taken countless previous rebirths.

Blessing The transformation of our mind from a negative state to a positive state, from an unhappy state to a happy state, or from a state of weakness to a state of strength, through the inspiration of holy beings such as our Spiritual Guide, Buddhas and Bodhisattvas.

Buddha's bodies A Buddha has four bodies—the Wisdom Truth Body, the Nature Body, the Enjoyment Body and the Emanation Body. The first is Buddha's omniscient mind. The second is the emptiness, or ultimate nature, of his or her mind. The third is his subtle Form Body. The fourth, of which each Buddha manifests a countless number, are gross Form Bodies that are visible to ordinary beings. The Wisdom Truth Body and the Nature Body are both included within the Truth Body, and the Enjoyment Body and the Emanation Body are both included within the Form Body. See *Joyful Path of Good Fortune* and *Ocean of Nectar*.

Channel wheel "Chakra" in Sanskrit. A focal center where secondary channels branch out from the central channel. Meditating on these points can cause the inner winds to enter the central channel. See *Modern Buddhism, Mahamudra Tantra* and *Clear Light of Bliss*.

Channels Subtle inner passageways of the body through which flow subtle drops moved by inner winds. See *Modern Buddhism, Mahamudra Tantra* and *Clear Light of Bliss*.

Clear light A manifest very subtle mind that perceives an appearance like clear, empty space. See *Modern Buddhism, Mahamudra Tantra* and *Clear Light of Bliss*.

Commitments Promises and pledges taken when engaging in certain spiritual practices.

Concentration A mental factor that makes its primary mind remain on its object single-pointedly. See *Joyful Path of Good Fortune* and *Meaningful to Behold*.

Conceptual thought/mind A thought that apprehends its object through a generic, or mental, image. See *How to Understand the Mind*.

Contact A mental factor that functions to perceive its object as pleasant, unpleasant or neutral. See *How to Understand the Mind*.

Contentment Being satisfied with one's inner and outer conditions, motivated by a virtuous intention.

Degenerate times A period when spiritual activity degenerates.

Deity "Yidam" in Tibetan. A Tantric enlightened being.

Desire realm The environment of hell beings, hungry ghosts, animals, human beings, demi-gods and the gods who enjoy the five objects of desire.

Dharma Buddha's teachings and the inner realizations that are attained in dependence upon practicing them. "Dharma" means "protection." By practicing Buddha's teachings, we protect ourself from suffering and problems.

Direct perceiver A cognizer that apprehends its object correctly and directly. See *How to Understand the Mind*.

Discrimination A mental factor that functions to apprehend the uncommon sign of an object. See *How to Understand the Mind*.

Elements, four Earth, water, fire and wind. These four elements are not the same as the earth of a field, the water of a river and so forth. Instead, the elements of earth, water, fire and wind in broad terms are the properties of solidity, liquidity, heat and movement respectively.

Emanation Animate or inanimate form manifested by Buddhas or high Bodhisattvas to benefit others.

Feeling A mental factor that functions to experience pleasant, unpleasant or neutral objects. See *How to Understand the Mind*.

Form Body The Enjoyment Body and the Emanation Body of a Buddha. See also *Buddha's bodies*.

Form realm The environment of the gods who possess form and who are superior to desire realm gods. So-called because the gods who inhabit it have subtle form. See *Ocean of Nectar*.

Formless realm The environment of the gods who do not possess form. See *Ocean of Nectar*.

Functioning thing A phenomenon that is produced and disintegrates within a moment. Synonymous with impermanent phenomenon, thing and product. See also *Impermanence*.

Generic image The appearing object of a conceptual mind. A generic image, or mental image, of an object is like a reflection of that object. Conceptual minds know their object through the appearance of a generic image of that object, not by seeing the object directly. See *How to Understand the Mind* and *The New Heart of Wisdom*.

Geshe A title given by Kadampa monasteries to accomplished Buddhist scholars. Contracted form of the Tibetan "ge wai she nyen," literally meaning "virtuous friend."

Geshe Chekhawa (AD 1102–1176) A great Kadampa Bodhisattva who composed the text *Training the Mind in Seven Points*, a commentary to Langri Tangpa's *Eight Verses of Training the Mind*. He spread the study and practice of training the mind throughout Tibet. See *Universal Compassion*.

Guide to the Bodhisattva's Way of Life A classic Mahayana Buddhist text composed by the great Indian Buddhist Yogi and scholar Shantideva, which presents all the practices of a Bodhisattva from the initial generation of bodhichitta through to the completion of the practice of the six perfections. For a translation, see *Guide to the Bodhisattva's Way of Life*; and for a full commentary, see *Meaningful to Behold*.

Gungtang Gungtang Konchog Tenpai Dronme (AD 1762–1823), a Gelug scholar and meditator famous for his spiritual poems and philosophical writings.

Guru Sanskrit word for "Spiritual Guide." See also **Spiritual Guide**.

Heart Sutra One of several *Perfection of Wisdom Sutras* by Buddha. Although much shorter than the other *Perfection of Wisdom Sutras*, it contains explicitly or implicitly their entire meaning. For a translation and full commentary, see *The New Heart of Wisdom*.

Heruka A principal Deity of Mother Tantra, who is the embodiment of indivisible bliss and emptiness. See *Essence of Vajrayana*.

Hinayana Sanskrit word for "Lesser Vehicle." The Hinayana goal is to attain merely one's own liberation from suffering by completely abandoning delusions. See *Joyful Path of Good Fortune*.

Holy being A being who is worthy of devotion.

Impermanence Phenomena are either permanent or impermanent. "Impermanent" means "momentary," thus an impermanent phenomenon is a phenomenon that is produced and disintegrates within a moment. Synonyms of impermanent phenomenon are functioning thing, thing and product. There are two types of impermanence: gross and subtle. Gross impermanence is any impermanence that can be seen by an ordinary sense awareness—for example the aging and death of a sentient being. Subtle impermanence is the momentary disintegration of a functioning thing. See *The New Heart of Wisdom*.

348

Inner winds Special subtle winds related to the mind that flow through the channels of our body. Our body and mind cannot function without these winds. See *Modern Buddhism, Mahamudra Tantra* and *Clear Light of Bliss.*

Intention A mental factor that functions to focus its primary mind on an object. Its principal function is to create karma. Of the three types of karma, or action—bodily, verbal and mental—intention itself is mental action. However, it is also the cause of bodily and verbal actions, because all bodily and verbal actions are preceded by mental actions. See *How to Understand the Mind.*

Je Tsongkhapa (AD 1357–1419) An emanation of the Wisdom Buddha Manjushri, whose appearance in fourteenth-century Tibet as a monk, and the holder of the lineage of pure view and pure deeds, was prophesied by Buddha. He spread a very pure Buddhadharma throughout Tibet, showing how to combine the practices of Sutra and Tantra, and how to practice pure Dharma during degenerate times. His tradition later became known as the "Gelug," or "Ganden Tradition." See *Heart Jewel* and *Great Treasury of Merit.*

Kadampa A Tibetan word in which "Ka" means "word" and refers to all Buddha's teachings, "dam" refers to Atisha's special Lamrim instructions known as the "stages of the path to enlightenment," and "pa" refers to a follower of Kadampa Buddhism who integrates all the teachings of Buddha that they know into their Lamrim practice.

Kadampa Buddhism A Mahayana Buddhist school founded by the great Indian Buddhist Master Atisha (AD 982–1054).

Kadampa Geshe See **Geshe.**

Kadampa Tradition The pure tradition of Buddhism established by Atisha. Followers of this tradition up to the time of Je Tsongkhapa are known as "Old Kadampas," and those after the time of Je Tsongkhapa are known as "New Kadampas."

Lama See *Spiritual Guide.*

Lamrim A Tibetan term, literally meaning "stages of the path." A special arrangement of all Buddha's teachings that is easy to understand and put into practice. It reveals all the stages of the path to enlightenment. For a full commentary, see *Joyful Path of Good Fortune.*

Langri Tangpa (AD 1054–1123) A great Kadampa Geshe and Bodhisattva who was famous for his realization of exchanging self with others. He composed *Eight Verses of Training the Mind.* See *The New Eight Steps to Happiness.*

Lineage A line of instruction that has been passed down from Spiritual Guide to disciple, with each Spiritual Guide in the line having gained personal experience of the instruction before passing it on to others.

Living being Synonymous with sentient being. Any being who possesses a mind that is contaminated by delusions or their imprints. Both "living being" and "sentient being" are terms used to distinguish beings whose minds are contaminated by either of these two obstructions from Buddhas, whose minds are completely free from these obstructions.

Lojong See *Training the mind.*

Lord of Death Although the mara of uncontrolled death is not a living being, it is personified as the Lord of Death, or "Yama."

It is depicted in the diagram of the Wheel of Life clutching the wheel between its claws and teeth. See *Joyful Path of Good Fortune*.

Mahamudra A Sanskrit word, literally meaning "great seal." According to Sutra, this refers to the profound view of emptiness. Since emptiness is the nature of all phenomena, it is called a "seal," and since a direct realization of emptiness enables us to accomplish the great purpose—complete liberation from the sufferings of samsara—it is also called "great." According to Secret Mantra, great seal is the union of spontaneous great bliss and emptiness. See *Mahamudra Tantra*, *The Oral Instructions of Mahamudra* and *Clear Light of Bliss*.

Mahayana Sanskrit word for "Great Vehicle," the spiritual path to great enlightenment. The Mahayana goal is to attain Buddhahood for the benefit of all sentient beings by completely abandoning delusions and their imprints. See *Joyful Path of Good Fortune*.

Maitreya The embodiment of the loving kindness of all the Buddhas. At the time of Buddha Shakyamuni, he manifested as a Bodhisattva disciple in order to show Buddha's disciples how to be perfect Mahayana disciples. In the future, he will manifest as the fifth founding Buddha.

Mala A rosary used to count recitations of prayers or mantras, usually with one hundred and eight beads.

Manjushri The embodiment of the wisdom of all the Buddhas. See *Great Treasury of Merit* and *Heart Jewel*.

Mantra A Sanskrit word, literally meaning "mind protection." Mantra protects the mind from ordinary appearances and conceptions. See *Tantric Grounds and Paths*.

Mara Sanskrit for "demon," and refers to anything that obstructs the attainment of liberation or enlightenment. There are four principal types of mara: the mara of the delusions, the mara of contaminated aggregates, the mara of uncontrolled death and the Devaputra maras. Of these, only the last are actual living beings. See *The New Heart of Wisdom*.

Mental continuum The continuum of a mind that has no beginning and no end.

Mental factor A cognizer that principally apprehends a particular attribute of an object. There are fifty-one specific mental factors. Each moment of mind comprises a primary mind and various mental factors. See *How to Understand the Mind*.

Mere appearance All phenomena are mere appearance because they are imputed by mind in dependence upon a suitable basis of imputation appearing to mind. The word "mere" excludes any possibility of inherent existence. See *Ocean of Nectar*.

Merit The good fortune created by virtuous actions. It is the potential power to increase our good qualities and produce happiness.

Milarepa (AD 1040–1123) A great Tibetan Buddhist meditator and disciple of Marpa, celebrated for his beautiful songs of realization.

Mindfulness A mental factor that functions not to forget the object realized by the primary mind. See *How to Understand the Mind* and *Meaningful to Behold*.

Nagarjuna A great Indian Buddhist scholar and meditation master who revived the Mahayana in the first century AD by bringing to light the teachings on the *Perfection of Wisdom Sutras*. See *Ocean of Nectar* and *The New Heart of Wisdom*.

Object of negation An object explicitly negated by a mind realizing a negative phenomenon. In meditation on emptiness, or lack of inherent existence, it refers to inherent existence. Also known as "negated object."

Observed object Any object upon which the mind is focused. See *How to Understand the Mind*.

Obstructions to liberation Obstructions that prevent the attainment of liberation. All delusions, such as ignorance, attachment and anger, together with their seeds, are obstructions to liberation. Also called "delusion-obstructions."

Obstructions to omniscience The imprints of delusions, which prevent simultaneous and direct realization of all phenomena. Only Buddhas have overcome these obstructions.

Ordinary being Anyone who has not realized emptiness directly.

Perfection of Wisdom Sutras Sutras of the second turning of the Wheel of Dharma, in which Buddha revealed his final view of the ultimate nature of all phenomena—emptiness of inherent existence. See *The New Heart of Wisdom* and *Ocean of Nectar*.

Primary mind A cognizer that principally apprehends the mere entity of an object. Synonymous with consciousness. There are six primary minds: eye consciousness, ear consciousness, nose consciousness, tongue consciousness, body consciousness and mental consciousness. Each moment of mind comprises a primary mind and various mental factors. A primary mind and its accompanying mental factors are the same entity but have different functions. See *How to Understand the Mind*.

Pure Land A pure environment in which there are no true sufferings. There are many Pure Lands. For example, Tushita is the Pure Land of Buddha Maitreya, Sukhavati is the Pure Land of Buddha Amitabha, and Dakini Land, or Keajra, is the Pure Land of Buddha Vajrayogini and Buddha Heruka. See *Living Meaningfully, Dying Joyfully*.

Purification Generally, any practice that leads to the attainment of a pure body, speech or mind. More specifically, a practice for purifying negative karma by means of the four opponent powers. See *Joyful Path of Good Fortune* and *The Bodhisattva Vow*.

Realization A stable and non-mistaken experience of a virtuous object that directly protects us from suffering.

Refuge Actual protection. To go for refuge to Buddha, Dharma and Sangha means to have faith in these Three Jewels and to rely upon them for protection from all fears and suffering. See *Modern Buddhism, Joyful Path of Good Fortune* and *Meaningful to Behold*.

Root mind The very subtle mind located at the center of the heart channel wheel. It is known as the "root mind" because all other minds arise from it and dissolve back into it. See *Mahamudra Tantra*.

Secret Mantra Synonymous with Tantra. Secret Mantra teachings are distinguished from Sutra teachings in that they reveal methods for training the mind by bringing the future result, or Buddhahood, into the present path. Secret Mantra is the supreme path to full enlightenment. The term "Mantra" indicates that it is Buddha's special instruction for protecting our mind from ordinary appearances and conceptions. Practitioners of Secret Mantra overcome ordinary appearances and conceptions by visualizing their body, environment, enjoyments and deeds as those of a Buddha. The term "Secret" indicates that the practices are to be done in private, and that they can be practiced only by those who have received a Tantric empowerment. See *Clear Light of Bliss, Mahamudra Tantra, Modern Buddhism* and *Tantric Grounds and Paths*.

Sentient being See **Living being**.

Shantideva (AD 687–763) A great Indian Buddhist scholar and meditation master. He composed *Guide to the Bodhisattva's Way of Life*. See *Meaningful to Behold* and *Guide to the Bodhisattva's Way of Life*.

Spiritual Guide "Guru" in Sanskrit, "Lama" in Tibetan. A Teacher who guides us along the spiritual path. See *Joyful Path of Good Fortune* and *Great Treasury of Merit*.

Stages of the path See **Lamrim**.

Subsequent cognizer A completely reliable cognizer whose object is realized in direct dependence upon a conclusive reason. See *How to Understand the Mind*.

Subtle impermanence See **Impermanence**.

Superior being "Arya" in Sanskrit. A being who has a direct realization of emptiness. There are Hinayana Superiors and Mahayana Superiors.

Superior seeing A special wisdom that sees its object clearly, and that is maintained by tranquil abiding and the special suppleness that is induced by investigation. See *Joyful Path of Good Fortune*.

Sutra The teachings of Buddha that are open to everyone to practice without the need for an empowerment. These include Buddha's teachings of the three turnings of the Wheel of Dharma.

Tantra See *Secret Mantra*.

Training the mind "Lojong" in Tibetan. A special lineage of instructions that came from Buddha Shakyamuni through Manjushri and Shantideva to Atisha and the Kadampa Geshes, which emphasizes the generation of bodhichitta through the practices of equalizing and exchanging self with others combined with taking and giving. See *Universal Compassion* and *The New Eight Steps to Happiness*.

Training the Mind in Seven Points A commentary to *Eight Verses of Training the Mind*, composed by Geshe Chekhawa. For a full translation and commentary, see *Universal Compassion*.

True suffering A contaminated object produced by delusions and karma. See *Joyful Path of Good Fortune* and *How to Solve Our Human Problems*.

Truth Body "Dharmakaya" in Sanskrit. The Nature Body and the Wisdom Truth Body of a Buddha. See also *Buddha's bodies*.

Vajrayogini A female Highest Yoga Tantra Deity who is the embodiment of indivisible bliss and emptiness. She is the same nature as Heruka. See *The New Guide to Dakini Land*.

Valid cognizer/mind A cognizer that is non-deceptive with respect to its engaged object. There are two types: subsequent valid cognizers and direct valid cognizers. See *How to Understand the Mind*.

Very subtle mind There are different levels of mind: gross, subtle and very subtle. Subtle minds manifest when the inner winds gather and dissolve within the central channel. See *Mahamudra*

Tantra and *Clear Light of Bliss.*

Vinaya Sutras Sutras in which Buddha principally explains the practice of moral discipline, and in particular the Pratimoksha moral discipline.

Vow A virtuous determination to abandon particular faults that is generated in conjunction with a traditional ritual. The three sets of vows are the Pratimoksha vows of individual liberation, the Bodhisattva vows and the Secret Mantra vows. See *The Bodhisattva Vow* and *Tantric Grounds and Paths.*

Wisdom A virtuous, intelligent mind that makes its primary mind realize a meaningful object. A wisdom is a spiritual path that functions to release our mind from delusions or their imprints. An example of wisdom is the correct view of emptiness.

Worldly concerns, eight The objects of the eight worldly concerns are happiness and suffering, wealth and poverty, praise and criticism and good reputation and bad reputation. These are called "worldly concerns" because worldly people are constantly concerned with them, wanting some and trying to avoid others. See *Universal Compassion* and *Joyful Path of Good Fortune.*

Yogi/Yogini Sanskrit words usually referring to a male or a female meditator who has attained the union of tranquil abiding and superior seeing.

Bibliography

*V*enerable Geshe Kelsang Gyatso Rinpoche is a highly respected meditation master and scholar of the Mahayana Buddhist tradition founded by Je Tsongkhapa. Since arriving in the West in 1977, Venerable Geshe Kelsang has worked tirelessly to establish pure Buddhadharma throughout the world. Over this period he has given extensive teachings on the major scriptures of the Mahayana. These teachings provide a comprehensive presentation of the essential Sutra and Tantra practices of Mahayana Buddhism.

Books

The following books by Venerable Geshe Kelsang Gyatso Rinpoche are all published by Tharpa Publications.

The Bodhisattva Vow. A practical guide to helping others.
    (2nd ed., 1995)
Clear Light of Bliss. A Tantric meditation manual.(3rd ed., 2014)
Essence of Vajrayana. The Highest Yoga Tantra practice of
    Heruka body mandala. (1997)
Great Treasury of Merit. How to rely upon a Spiritual Guide.
    (1992)

Guide to the Bodhisattva's Way of Life. How to enjoy a life of great meaning and altruism. (A translation of Shantideva's famous verse masterpiece.) (2002)

Heart Jewel. The essential practices of Kadampa Buddhism. (2nd ed., 1997)

How to Solve Our Human Problems. The four noble truths. (1st American ed., 2007)

How to Transform Your Life. A blissful journey. (3rd American ed., 2017)

How to Understand the Mind. The nature and power of the mind. (4th ed., 2013)

Introduction to Buddhism. An explanation of the Buddhist way of life. (1st American ed., 2008)

Joyful Path of Good Fortune. The complete Buddhist path to enlightenment. (2nd ed., 1995)

Living Meaningfully, Dying Joyfully. The profound practice of transference of consciousness. (1999)

Mahamudra Tantra. The supreme Heart Jewel nectar. (2005)

Meaningful to Behold. Becoming a friend of the world. (5th ed., 2007)

Modern Buddhism. The Path of Compassion and Wisdom. (2nd ed., 2015)

The New Eight Steps to Happiness. The Buddhist way of loving kindness. (3rd American ed., 2016)

The New Guide to Dakini Land. The Highest Yoga Tantra practice of Buddha Vajrayogini. (3rd ed., 2012)

The New Heart of Wisdom. Profound teachings from Buddha's heart. (An explanation of the *Heart Sutra*.) (5th ed., 2013)

The New Meditation Handbook. Meditations to make our life happy and meaningful. (2nd American ed., 2013)

Ocean of Nectar. The true nature of all things. (1995)
The Oral Instructions of Mahamudra. The very essence of
    Buddha's teachings of Sutra and Tantra. (2nd. edn., 2016)
Tantric Grounds and Paths. How to enter, progress on and
    complete the Vajrayana path. (1994)
Universal Compassion. Inspiring solutions for difficult times.
    (4th ed., 2002)

Sadhanas and Other Booklets

Venerable Geshe Kelsang Gyatso Rinpoche has also supervised the
translation of a collection of essential sadhanas, or ritual prayers
for spiritual attainments, available in booklet or audio formats.

Avalokiteshvara Sadhana. Prayers and requests to the Buddha of
    Compassion.
The Blissful Path. The condensed self-generation sadhana of
    Vajrayogini.
The Bodhisattva's Confession of Moral Downfalls. The purification
    practice of the *Mahayana Sutra of the Three Superior Heaps.*
Condensed Essence of Vajrayana. Condensed Heruka body
    mandala self-generation sadhana.
Condensed Long Life Practice of Buddha Amitayus.
Dakini Yoga. The middling self-generation sadhana of
    Vajrayogini.
Drop of Essential Nectar. A special fasting and purification
    practice in conjunction with Eleven-faced Avalokiteshvara.
Essence of Good Fortune. Prayers for the six preparatory practices
    for meditation on the stages of the path to enlightenment.
Essence of Vajrayana. Heruka body mandala self-generation
    sadhana according to the system of Mahasiddha Ghantapa.
Feast of Great Bliss. Vajrayogini self-initiation sadhana.

Great Liberation of the Father. Preliminary prayers for Mahamudra meditation in conjunction with Heruka practice.

Great Liberation of the Mother. Preliminary prayers for Mahamudra meditation in conjunction with Vajrayogini practice.

The Great Mother. A method to overcome hindrances and obstacles by reciting the *Essence of Wisdom Sutra* (the *Heart Sutra*).

A Handbook for the Daily Practice of Bodhisattva and Tantric Vows.

Heart Jewel. The Guru yoga of Je Tsongkhapa combined with the condensed sadhana of his Dharma Protector.

Heartfelt Prayers. Funeral service for cremations and burials.

The Hundreds of Deities of the Joyful Land According to Highest Yoga Tantra. The Guru yoga of Je Tsongkhapa as a Preliminary Practice for Mahamudra

The Kadampa Way of Life. The essential practice of Kadam Lamrim.

Keajra Heaven. The essential commentary to the practice of *The Uncommon Yoga of Inconceivability.*

Lay Pratimoksha Vow Ceremony.

Liberating Prayer. Praise to Buddha Shakyamuni.

Liberation from Sorrow. Praises and requests to the Twenty-one Taras.

Mahayana Refuge Ceremony and Bodhisattva Vow Ceremony.

Medicine Buddha Prayer. A method for benefiting others.

Medicine Buddha Sadhana. A method for accomplishing the attainments of Medicine Buddha.

Meditation and Recitation of Solitary Vajrasattva.

Melodious Drum Victorious in all Directions. The extensive fulfilling and restoring ritual of the Dharma Protector, the

great king Dorje Shugden, in conjunction with Mahakala,
Kalarupa, Kalindewi and other Dharma Protectors.

The New Essence of Vajrayana. Heruka body mandala self-generation practice, an instruction of the Ganden Oral Lineage

Offering to the Spiritual Guide (Lama Chopa). A special way of relying upon a Spiritual Guide.

Path of Compassion for the Deceased. Powa sadhana for the benefit of the deceased

Pathway to the Pure Land. Training in powa—the transference of consciousness.

Powa Ceremony. Transference of consciousness for the deceased.

Prayers for Meditation. Brief preparatory prayers for meditation.

Prayers for World Peace.

A Pure Life. The practice of taking and keeping the eight Mahayana precepts.

Quick Path to Great Bliss. The extensive self-generation sadhana of Vajrayogini.

Requests to the Holy Spiritual Guide Venerable Geshe Kelsang Gyatso from his Faithful Disciples.

The Root Tantra of Heruka and Vajrayogini. Chapters One and Fifty-one of the *Condensed Heruka Root Tantra.*

The Root Text: Eight Verses of Training the Mind.

Treasury of Wisdom. The sadhana of Venerable Manjushri.

The Uncommon Yoga of Inconceivability. The special instruction of how to reach the Pure Land of Keajra with this human body.

Union of No More Learning. Heruka body mandala self-initiation sadhana.

The Vows and Commitments of Kadampa Buddhism.

Wishfulfilling Jewel. The Guru yoga of Je Tsongkhapa combined with the sadhana of his Dharma Protector.

The Yoga of Buddha Amitayus. A special method for increasing lifespan, wisdom and merit.

The Yoga of Buddha Heruka. The essential self-generation sadhana of Heruka body mandala & Condensed six-session yoga.

The Yoga of Buddha Maitreya. Self-generation sadhana.

The Yoga of Buddha Vajrapani. Self-generation sadhana.

The Yoga of Enlightened Mother Arya Tara. Self-generation sadhana.

The Yoga of Great Mother Prajnaparamita. Self-generation sadhana.

The Yoga of Thousand-armed Avalokiteshvara. Self-generation sadhana.

The Yoga of White Tara, Buddha of Long Life.

To order any of our publications, or to order a catalog, please visit www.tharpa.com/us or contact your nearest Tharpa Office (see page 365).

T͟harpa Publications W͟orldwide

*B*ooks from T͟harpa Publications are currently published in English (American and British), Chinese, French, German, Italian, Japanese, Portuguese and Spanish. Most languages are available from any T͟harpa Publications office listed below.

Visit us at www.T͟harpa.com or contact your local office for more information.

United States

T͟harpa Publications US
47 Sweeney Road
Glen Spey, NY 12737
Phone: 845-856-5102
Fax: 845-856-2110
E-mail: info.us@tharpa.com
www.tharpa.com/us
www.tharpa.com/us-es

Asia

T͟harpa Asia
1/F, Causeway Tower,
16-22 Causeway Road,
Causeway Bay, Hong Kong
Tel: (852) 2507 2237
Fax: (852) 2507 2208
Email: info.asia@tharpa.com
www.tharpa.com/hk-en

Australia

T͟harpa Publications Australia
25 McCarthy Road
Monbulk VIC 3793
Phone: +61 (0)3 9756 7203
E-mail: info.au@tharpa.com
www.tharpa.com/au

United Kingdom

T͟harpa Publications UK
Conishead Priory
Ulverston, Cumbria,
LA12 9QQ
Phone: +44 (0)1229-588599
E-mail: info.uk@tharpa.com
www.tharpa.com/uk

Brazil

Editoria T͟harpa Brasil
Rua Fradique Coutinho, 701
Pinheiros, 05416-011
São Paulo - SP, Brazil
Phone: +55 (11) 3476-2330
E-mail: contato.br@tharpa.com
www.tharpa.com/br

Canada

T͟harpa Publications Canada
631 Crawford St.
Toronto, ON, M6G 3K1
Phone: 416-762-8710
Toll Free: 866-523-2672
Fax: 416-762-2267
E-mail: info.ca@tharpa.com
www.tharpa.com/ca (English)
www.tharpa.com/ca-fr (French)

France
Editions Tharpa
Château de Segrais
72220 Saint-Mars-d'Outillé
Phone: +33 (0)2 43 87 71 02
E-mail: info.fr@tharpa.com
www.tharpa.com/fr

Germany
Tharpa-Verlag Deutschland
Mehringdamm 33, Aufgang 2
10961 Berlin
Phone: +49 (030) 430 55 666
E-mail: info.de@tharpa.com
www.tharpa.com/de

Japan
Tharpa Japan
E-mail: info@kadampa.jp
www.kadampa.jp

Mexico
Tharpa Mexico
Enrique Rébsamen No. 406
Col. Narvate Poniente
C.P. 03020, México, D.F.
Phone: +01 (55) 56396186
Phone/Fax: +01 (55) 56396180
E-mail: info.mx@tharpa.com
www.tharpa.com/mx

Portugal
Publicações Tharpa Portugal
Rua Moinho do Gato, 5
Várzea de Sintra
2710-661 Sintra
Phone: +351 219231064
E-mail: info.pt@tharpa.com
www.tharpa.pt

Republic of South Africa
c/o Mahasiddha KMC
24 Shongweni Heights
5 Angus Drive, Hillcrest
Durban, 3610
Phone: +27 (0)31 551 3429
Fax: +27(0)31 266 0096
E-mail: info.za@tharpa.com
www.tharpa.com/za

Spain
Editorial Tharpa España
Calle Manuela Malasaña No 26
28004 Madrid
Phone: +34 917 55 75 35
E-mail: info.es@tharpa.com
www.tharpa.com/es

Switzerland
Tharpa Verlag Schwiez
Mirabellenstrasse 1
CH-8048 Zürich
Phone: +41 44 401 02 20
Fax: +41 44 461 36 88
E-mail: info.ch@tharpa.com
www.tharpa.com/ch

Index

The letter "g" indicates an entry in the glossary

A

actions and effects 45–59. *See also* karma; non-virtuous actions; virtuous actions
  impure/contaminated 46, 56–58, 164, 282
  pure/uncontaminated 47, 50, 233
  types 52, 56–59
actions, mental 104, 277
Advice from Atisha's Heart 138, 305, 331, 333–338
affectionate love 91, 211
  eight benefits of 216–217
affirmative phenomenon 297
aging 34, 67–71, 90
alertness 184, 273, 306
analogies
  actor 299

bird tied down by stones 89
blue sky and clouds 149, 296
deep ocean 215
dream 25, 171, 207
eagles soaring 289
great earth 105
magic crystal 128
magician's illusion 255, 264, 298–299
muddy water 12, 140
ocean of suffering 215
poisonous tree 101, 107
rainbow and sky 278, 280
salt water 169, 213
saw a tree 106
seeing two moons 306
shopping 183–184
sky and blue of sky 292

"this" and "that" mountain
189
two moons 306
two wings of a bird 250,
305
anger 98, 148, 162
abandoning 14, 92, 134,
146
against delusions 180
cause of 137, 166, 168
faults of 9, 51
object of 204
overcoming through
meditating on emptiness
266, 294
animal rebirth 30, 54, 57,
87–88
limitations of 4
animals 89, 106, 114, 235,
236
kindness of 123, 195
suffering of 78, 199, 202
appearance 277, 306. *See
also* inherent existence,
appearance of; mere
appearance
deceptive 253, 256, 283,
298
dream 11, 277
dualistic 292
mistaken 113, 288, 292,
306

of waking world 277
to mind 254, 285
appearance and emptiness,
union of 291
Aryadeva 212
Asanga 158, 206, 209
Atisha 82, 186, 223, 244,
331
quotes by 223, 305, 306
Atisha's assistant 145, 146
attachment 9, 93, 97, 162,
200, 256
abandoning 89–91, 146,
179, 233
and love 91, 134, 170,
204, 217
cause of 166
object of 9
overcoming through medi-
tating on emptiness 266,
278, 281, 294, 299
to friends 72, 127–128,
168, 196, 204, 325
to fulfilling wishes 98
to own views 98
to possessions, etc. 71, 325
to religious views 98
to reputation, etc. 168
to wealth 169
attention 267
Avalokiteshvara 28, 239, 293

B

basis of imputation
  for car 285
  for I 148, 190, 193
  for mind 267
beginningless time 55, 115,
    135, 164, 272
belief 229, 231–232
benefiting others 14–15, 175,
    185, 187–188
Ben Gungyal 142, 177
birth 63–65, 119
blame 77, 136
  delusions 151
  self-cherishing 181–182
blessings 13, 159, 222, 237,
    305
  purpose of 184, 186, 221
bliss 53, 175
bodhichitta 114, 227,
    243–250. See also ulti-
    mate bodhichitta
  artificial/spontaneous 247
  benefits of 244
  cause of 134, 144, 219,
    249
  conditions for 249
  conventional 305
  developing 246–250
  from viewing all living
    beings as supreme 143,
    186, 243

meaning of 243
nature of 250
obstacle to 172
superior 219
Bodhisattva 114, 132, 241,
    244, 275
  good qualities 237
  powers of 221, 227
  Superior 288, 305
  way of looking 138, 237
Bodhisattva path. See spiritual path, to enlightenment
Bodhisattva vow 174
Bodhi Tree 217
body 119, 124, 173, 189,
    240
  and I 148
  and mind 18–19, 23–24
  continuously residing 234
  conventionally existent 265
  deceptive nature of 263
  divine 190
  impermanent 42, 72
  impure/contaminated 61,
    74
  inherently existent 265,
    292
  manifestation of emptiness
    292–293
  parts of 259
  pure/uncontaminated 47,
    79

true/ultimate nature of 263–265

unfindable 302

breathing meditation 238–239, 326–328

bringing the result into the path 230

Buddha 112–113, 157–158, 173, 175, 220, 221, 247, 291
  equanimity of 237
  example of 101–102
  existing by convention 266
  qualities of 146, 192, 246
  quotes by
    all phenomena are like dreams 255
    all phenomena are like illusions 298
    magician's creations 298
    searching for body with wisdom 258
  Tantric 190
  ultimate view and intention of 291
  uncommon quality of 288
  way of looking 147, 149, 163

Buddhadharma 252

Buddhahood 187. See also enlightenment

Buddha Jewel 82, 196

Buddha Land 217

Buddha nature/seed 114, 152–153, 195–196, 219, 234

very subtle body 234

C

cancer 148, 198, 226

car 8, 116, 278, 285
  emptiness of 258

cause and effect. See actions and effects; karma

changing suffering 216

channels 238

cherishing love 92, 133, 211, 243. See also cherishing others
  spontaneous 193

cherishing others 114–117. See also cherishing love
  benefits of 117, 127–132, 139, 176, 191–192
  obstacle to 150, 172

clairvoyance 34

clear light 24
  of death 22
  of sleep 21

coming and going 276
  extremes of 279

commitments 87
  of training the mind 174–175

compassion 148, 149, 167, 195–209, 243. *See also* great compassion; universal compassion
benefits of 196
cause of 114, 134, 138, 144
how to develop 197–203
of Buddha 131, 149, 175, 196
root of Three Jewels 196
supreme wealth of 203–209
what is 196
completing actions 58
concentration 70, 94, 105, 144, 229, 248
of close placement 304
of continual placement 304
of placing the mind 303
of replacement 304
conceptual thought 140, 149, 231, 275–276, 281
imprints of 287
Condensed Perfection of Wisdom Sutra 258
Conqueror Buddha, Son or Daughter of 244
consciousness 267
consideration for others 85–89, 129–130, 194
contact 267
contaminated rebirth 61, 62, 91, 202
contentment 328
controlling the mind 4, 11–12, 19, 324–325. *See also* transforming the mind
conventional bodhichitta. *See* bodhichitta
conventional nature 274, 295
conventional search 257
conventional truth 265
and ultimate truth 283–290
deceptive phenomena 283–284
gross and subtle 285
subtle 291
conventional world 299
convention, existing by way of 266
correct belief 81, 229, 231
correct imagination 231
countless living beings 111, 180
criticism 146, 163, 170–171
cycle of impure life. *See* samsara

D

daily life, integrating spiritual practice in 248–249
death 23, 74, 198, 222

causes of 40
    meditation on 31–43
    process 24
    realization of 32–33
    sufferings of 71–73, 90
    time of 51, 58
    untimely 41
death, intermediate state, and
        rebirth 23, 24–25, 51
deceptive phenomena 284
declaration of truth 227
dedication 51, 237, 309
Deity 191
delusions 4, 9–10, 19, 43,
        97, 99, 123, 151–152,
        208, 256, 276, 323
    abandoning 14, 81, 100,
        162–163, 176, 325
    faults of 31, 147–151, 181,
        201
    meditate on emptiness to
        overcome 266, 294
    not intrinsic 12, 139–140,
        149
    permanent cessation of 113
    principal 100
    recognizing 162, 177
    reducing 229, 299
    root of 57, 167
        conceptions of eight
            extremes 282
demi-gods 52, 89, 235
depression 98, 168

desire realm 53, 103
desires 75–77, 86, 162, 169,
        200
Dharma 39, 99, 214, 245.
    See also Dharma Jewel
    mirror of 134–135, 141,
        142
    teachings 37–38, 46,
        84–85, 114–115
    as medicine 143, 182,
        221–222
Dharma book 84, 143
Dharma Jewel 82, 196
direct perceiver 286
discouragement 168
discrimination 161, 267
disintegration 276
dissatisfaction 75, 77, 115,
        234
distractions 53, 106
    dispelling 94, 169, 238,
        326–328
divine eye(s) 85, 106
dog 88–89, 157, 195
    stories 158–159, 206, 220
door to liberation 32, 55
doubt 84
dream(s) 12, 24, 278
    analogy 171, 207
    appearances 11, 277
    elephant 254
    mere appearance to mind
        300, 301

mind 11
phenomena as like 255
relative validity of 285
significance of 25–29
world 254
dualistic appearance 292

E

effort 83, 93–95, 144
armor-like 184
eight extremes 281, 287, 294
emptiness that is empty of
288–289
elements, four 40–41
emanations 104, 157–158,
206, 209, 305
of Buddha 246, 292
of Geshe Chekhawa 207
empathy 193, 202
emptiness 55, 92, 103, 106,
176, 253–254, 265
all same nature 293–295
application in meditation
break 294
basis for training in ultimate bodhichitta 251
conventional bases of 293
difference from empty 251
direct realization of 250,
252, 265, 274, 287, 305
existing by convention 266

generic image of 272, 274
manifestations of 278, 294,
295
non-mistaken awareness of
274
object of negation of 270,
297
of body 256–266, 268,
279, 292, 303
of book 266
of car 258
of coming and going 276,
279
of emptiness 279, 286
of I 268–275, 289, 303

of impermanent phenom-
ena 276, 278
of mind 267–268
of obstructive contact 297
of permanent phenomena
276, 278
of phenomena 149, 254,
268, 276–282, 289
of produced phenomena
276
how to meditate on 289
of singularity and plurality
276, 280–281
phenomena not other than
258
practice of, in our daily
activities 298–301

signs of correct meditation on 273
solution to problems 301
space-like 264, 273, 289
space-like meditative equipoise on 289
studying 290
synonyms of 286
yoga of equalizing samsara and nirvana 295
enemies 122, 133, 157
inner 148, 180
enlightened beings 81, 112. *See also* Buddha
sentient beings as 149
enlightenment 112–115, 215, 219, 235
attaining 134, 143, 253
cause of 125–126, 231
depending on receiving blessings 305
faith in 83
happiness of 175, 247, 253
meaning and goal of human life 305
obstacle to 172, 230
quick path to 230
what is 112
equalizing self and others 117, 155, 179–180
equanimity 92, 237
exchanging self with others 120, 161–194

actual practice 191–194
how possible? 188–191
existence from its own side/side of the object 259, 269, 275, 284, 286, 294, 300, 301
existent self and phenomena 274
external conditions 13, 77, 325
and happiness 7, 19, 203–204, 328
depend on mind 168, 208
external object 11
extremes, eight 281
extremes of existence/non-existence 274
extremes of materialism and spirituality 13
extreme view 281

F

faith 81–87, 186, 222, 229, 306
three types of 81
false objects 283–284, 286
familiarity 179, 191, 239, 247
with self-cherishing 135, 153, 163
family 8, 115, 133, 195
faults 84, 134, 136, 174, 181

of delusions 150
of others 137–139,
    147–152
of self-cherishing 165–176
fear 255, 272
feelings 267
unpleasant 11, 97
food 7, 41
formless realm 53, 103
form realm 53, 103
fortunate realms 53
Four Hundred Verses 212
Friendly Letter 188
friends 8, 115, 116
compassion for 133, 195
depend on mind 122, 157,
    204–205
impermanent 72
frustration 10, 74, 172
functioning thing 278
Fundamental Wisdom 283
future lives 22, 30, 37–38,
    326
countless 90
suffering of 100
cessation of 282
liberation from 79

G

Gampopa 222–223
generic image 231, 272, 274,
    275

Geshe 142, 185, 223, 226
Geshe Chekhawa 174, 178,
    180, 206–207, 267, 300
giving 144
by means of love 233–235
meaning of 233
meditation on 234–237
results of 88
gods 53, 78, 89
long-life 93
Gonpo Dorje 99
good heart 3, 92, 131, 233,
    244
supreme 243–250
great compassion 172,
    195–209, 203, 249
Guide to the Bodhisattva's
    Way of Life 137, 147,
    189, 193, 223, 234, 256,
    258, 287, 331
guilt 151, 181
Gungtang 38, 68, g
Guru g

H

habit 12
hallucinations 61, 149
happiness 111, 208, 324
cause of 4, 7–15, 19–21,
    46
from cherishing 165,
    175–176, 184

in samsara, no real 234
levels of pure 215
of enlightenment 175
of future lives 30, 326
pure and everlasting 79,
    187
pure/true 47, 112, 114,
    204, 214, 235
searching for 3–4
what is 17, 212
hatred 9, 93
overcoming through medi-
    tating on emptiness 281
health 13
Heart Jewel 274
Heart Sutra 293
hell beings 54–55, 58, 78,
    89, 200, 207, 235
suffering of 202
hell realm 52, 54–55, 207
hero/heroine 227
Heruka 240
higher rebirth 57, 88–89,
    138. *See also* fortunate
    realms
cause of 57
meaning of 89
Highest Yoga Tantra
fourth empowerment of
    291
Hinayana 165
holy beings 158
How to Understand the Mind
    22

human beings 3, 89, 102,
    235
human life
precious, rare and meaning-
    ful 4
ultimate goal and meaning
    of 107, 131, 209, 305
human rebirth 52, 58, 62,
    138, 202. *See also* pre-
    cious human life
sufferings of 61–79
humility 155–159
hungry ghosts 54, 58, 78, 89,
    200, 235
suffering of 202

J

ignorance 61, 92, 93, 122,
    207, 252, 261. *See
    also* self-grasping
illusions 55
imagination 230–231
immeasurable love 216
impermanence 214, 276
subtle 278
impermanent phenomena
    296
emptiness of 279
imprints
karmic 277
of actions 46, 72
of conceptual thoughts 287

of delusions 113
of self-grasping 164, 165,
 255, 268, 274, 288
imputation 266, 285–286
indifference 166
inherent existence 259, 266,
 299, 300
 appearance of 113, 164,
 283, 298
 eight extremes of 281
 object of negation of 270,
 297
 of body 259, 265, 292
 of body we normally see
 292
 of I 57, 126, 164–165, 272
 identifying 268–269
 of self we normally see
 156, 269
 synonyms of 253
inherently existent I and mine
 appearance of 113
inner peace 7–14
inner winds 24–25, 238
insects, not killing 236
intelligence 106, 175
intention 83, 188, 229, 267,
 283
intermediate state 24–25, 51.
 See also death, intermediate state, and rebirth
intermediate state being 118
I/self 148, 193

and others 189–190, 194
basis of imputation of 280
identifying as mere appearance 253
mistaken way of identifying
 61, 252
self that we normally see
 176, 252, 269, 273
ultimate nature of 273

J

Jampaling Monastery 227
jealousy 72, 91, 127, 162,
 235, 256
 overcoming 92, 146
Jesus 221
Je Tsongkhapa 186, 274, 331
 quotes by 252
Joyful Path of Good Fortune
 245, 307

K

Kadampa 223, 331
 Geshe 142, 185, 223, 226
Kadampa Way of Life, The
 329–342
karma 37, 45–59, 106, 144,
 277. *See also* actions;
 actions, mental
 for this life 34, 41

general characteristics of 47–51
results of 51
teachings on 142
karmic connection 21, 22, 154–156, 220, 237
karmic imprints 277
Kharak Gomchen 239
killing 86
kindness 118–126, 144, 151, 209, 217
of animals 123, 195
of Buddha 147–148
of living beings 147–148
of mother 118–123, 151, 193, 197
King Chandra 141
King of Concentration Sutra 298

L

Lamrim 183, 223, 331
Langri Tangpa, Geshe 143, 155, 156, 194
laziness 38, 94–95
of attachment 32, 94
leprosy 240
Liberating Prayer 313–314
liberation 20, 55, 79, 104, 221, 228, 231. *See also* nirvana
how to attain 12

permanent 233
seeking 31, 62, 222
liberation, path to 79, 104
five levels of 104
lifespan 35, 36, 41
lifestyle 115, 116
lineage 186
listening to Dharma instructions 306
living beings
basic wish of 3
countless 111, 180
loneliness 127, 198
Lord of Death 34
love 92, 153, 154–155
and attachment 91–92, 134, 170, 204–205, 217–218
benefits of 216
cause of 138, 144–145
for self 174–175
of Buddha 149, 217
pure 170, 187, 217
three types of 211
loving kindness 127, 157
lower realms 53, 88
lower rebirth 57, 137, 143, 171
meaning of 89

M

Mahamudra 223

Mahayana
  path 172
Maitreya 159, 206, 209
Maitripa 252
Maitriyogi 220
mala 227
Manjushri 186, 227, 331
mantra 28, 84
mara/demon 204, 217
Marpa Lotsawa, quote by
  252
meaningful objects 97–108,
  215
Meaningful to Behold 194,
  245
meditation 94, 182, 323–328
  analytical & placement
    323–324
  benefits of 324–325
  breathing 238, 326–328
  object of 215, 324
  obstacle to 70
meditation break 203,
  248–249
meditation session 153,
  248–249
meditative equipoise 288
mental awareness 231
mental continuum 22, 23,
  122, 149. *See also* mind
mental factors 22
mere absence 266, 279, 286,
  292, 297

of all phenomena we nor-
  mally see 303
of the body we normally see
  262, 264, 302
of the self we normally see
  272, 289, 303
mere appearance 257, 262,
  291
  existing conventionally as
    265, 275
  like dream 11–12, 25, 207
  part of conventional truth
    285
  to waking/dreaming mind
    254, 300
  using to solve problems
    278, 299
mere imputation 274, 277
  of singularity/plurality 280
mere name 12, 262, 265,
  273, 274
merit 41, 156
  accumulating 156, 184
  result of 130, 186, 227,
    245
middle way 13
Milarepa 99, 207, 223, 252
  life stories 220
  quotations 38, 67–68
  teaching on emptiness 296
mind 148, 207, 277, 295
  and body 18, 23–24, 25
  and brain 18

and its object same nature 207

and object 11, 207

appearances to 254, 265, 266, 285

basis of imputation of 267

beginningless 90, 122

conceptual/non-conceptual 231, 275

creator of all 230–231

creator of world 277–278

depending on 254

dreaming/waking 11–12

examining 177

existing by convention 266

impure/contaminated 55, 158, 207, 277

imputed by 266

levels of 21–22

mirror of 98

mistaken/unmistaken 163

primary 22

projections of 254, 259, 266

pure/uncontaminated 79, 140, 208

  definition of 287

root 140, 162

valid 275

very subtle 22, 24

mindfulness 42, 94, 306

mind of enlightenment. *See* bodhichitta

miracle powers 34

mirage 10, 255, 256, 265, 284

mirror of Dharma 84–85, 134–142

mistaken appearance 12, 61, 122, 149, 252, 284

  Buddhas free from 288

  subtle 292

  two moons reminding us of 306

mistaken awareness 284

  due to imprints of self-grasping 274

mistaken conception 122

mistaken view 281

Modern Buddhism 191

moral discipline 86, 94, 105, 130, 144

  contaminated virtue 56

  nature of 105

mother 63–64, 155, 157

  kindness of 118–123, 151, 193, 197

  of author 26–29, 240

motivation 124, 191, 237, 249

Mount Kailash 240

mouse 172, 199, 236

N

Nagarjuna 42, 88, 188, 216, 283
neutral actions 47–48, 56
New Guide to Dakini Land, The 191
New Heart of Wisdom, The 261, 297
nirvana 9, 14, 15, 48, 49, 55, 79, 103, 189, 301. *See also* liberation
non-affirming negative phenomenon 297
non-attachment 89–91, 93
non-conceptual direct perceiver 286
non-conceptual mind 275
non-hatred 91–92, 93
non-ignorance 92–93
non-virtuous actions 46, 56, 81, 85–86, 150
    cause of 46, 113, 117, 130, 166, 171
    effects of 47, 117, 130, 137, 165
    purification of 226
    ten 56
nothingness 272, 273, 301

O

object 207
    external 11
    imagined/real 230
    observed 163
    of meditation 324
    virtuous/non-virtuous 323
object of negation 270, 297
Ocean of Nectar 261, 297
ocean of suffering 215. *See also* samsara
opponents to delusions 141, 179
ordinary being 23, 135, 144, 158–160, 164–165, 258, 285, 287
    appearances to 287
out of body experiences 24

P

pain 11, 99, 163
    manifest 198–200, 221
Palden, Geshe 227
past lives 118. *See also* rebirth
    countless 122
path, inner and external 104
paths, five 104
path to enlightenment 244, 251

path to liberation, main 105
patience 144–145, 169
  of voluntarily accepting
    suffering 224
  with ourself 151
  with practice 181
peaceful mind
  how to develop and main-
    tain 17
peace of mind 8, 208, 221
  cause of 172, 323
  destroying 256
  method to experience 301
  permanent 19, 79, 113–
    114, 326
Perfection of Wisdom Sutras
  283
permanence 276
permanent phenomena 279,
  297
  emptiness of 279
phenomena
  existing conventionally
    266, 274–275
  like dreams 255, 300
  like illusions 255, 298
  like rainbows 300
  not other than emptiness
    258
phenomena, eight 276–282
plurality 276
plurality, extreme of 280–281
possessions 71, 77, 111–112,

157, 325
potential 5, 57, 114–115,
  140, 152, 195, 229. *See
  also* Buddha nature/seed
  for taking rebirth in a Pure
    Land 233
  to benefit living beings
    219, 226, 229
poverty 48, 54, 170
prayer 225, 227
Prayers for Meditation
  315–320
precious human life 4–5, 62,
  102, 246, 307, 331
  meaning 9, 19, 33, 146
  ultimate goal 94, 111–115
  wasting 22, 24, 38, 99
preciousness 135, 143–144
  of Buddha 146
  of others 133, 136, 144–
    146, 155–156, 209
  of sentient beings 146, 156
pride 83, 135, 137, 159, 162
  abandoning 138
primary mind 267–268
problems 31, 328
  cause of 57, 77, 170
  in the mind 10, 20
  solving 5, 8, 20, 127, 143,
    184, 232
  universal solution to 301
produced phenomena
  emptiness of 289

produced space 296
production 276
projection 10
protection 37, 72, 82, 91,
    128, 217
Pure Land 103, 104, 206,
    240, 250
  rebirth in 233–234
purification 50, 226
  results of 140, 158, 184
  signs of 229
  through compassion 205
  through taking 224–225,
    232, 239–240

Q

qualities 135, 138, 159, 244
  of others 136, 138
quick path to enlightenment
    229

R

rainbow 255, 278, 280, 300
realization of emptiness 79
  eradicating self-grasping
    179
realizations 5, 15, 145–146,
    155–157, 186, 194, 226
  cause of 87, 115, 146, 156,
    231

Tantric 230
realized being 157–158
rebirth 23–30, 51–56, 90
  beginningless 62–63, 240
  contaminated 52, 59, 62,
    81
  in a Pure Land 233
  uncontrolled 37, 74, 171
refuge 82, 113
reincarnation 23–30
rejoicing 81, 87, 128
relationships 136–137, 213
  improving 87, 127, 328
relative truths and relative
    falsities 285
religion 128
renunciation 62, 79, 89–91,
    101, 103, 104, 105, 305
  developing 179, 182–183
  realization of 79
  training in 79
reputation 83, 156
robber and horse, story of
    123

S

samsara 61–79, 91, 202, 216,
    222, 263, 276, 295. *See
    also* ocean of suffering
  beginningless 55, 90
  endless 59, 62
  nature of 214

root of 162, 164, 282
Sangha Jewel 82, 196
scopes, three 43
Secret Mantra 190, 230
seeds of actions 51
seeds of delusions 179
self-cherishing 115–118,
    151, 224, 256
  abandoning 116–118, 154,
    161, 244
  and self-grasping 135, 165
  destroying 228, 232
  faults of 117, 128, 139,
    165–175, 180–182,
    191–192
  how to stop developing
    176–188
  identifying 162–165,
    177–178
  object of 135, 156, 163–
    164, 188–189
  of Hinayana practitioners
    165
  opponent to 146
self-confidence 139, 173–174
self-generation 190
self-grasping 93, 97, 98,
    100, 228, 232, 273. See
    also ignorance
  and self-cherishing 135,
    164–165
  imprints of 268, 274, 288
  nine types of 103

of body 189
of own self 57–58, 65,
    113, 135
of Peak of Samsara 103
of phenomena 282
permanent cessation of
    103, 106, 306
reducing 293, 306
results of 46
self-respect 173–174
sense awareness 231
sense of shame 85–89
Serlingpa 244
Shakyamuni, Buddha 186,
    225
  life stories 217
  quotations 95, 138, 152,
    214
Shantideva 137, 165, 186,
    193, 223, 234, 258, 262,
    263, 265, 331
sickness 34, 65–67, 74, 90,
    229, 232–233
  cause of 7, 47, 167
  curing 35, 239–240
  of Spiritual Guide 221
singularity 276
singularity, extreme of
    280–281
six perfections 144, 250
six realms 51–56, 171, 235
sleeping, dreaming and wak-
    ing 21, 23, 24–25, 51

spirits 217
Spiritual Guide 129, 186,
    221, 223
  as emanation of Buddha
    306
  Dharma book as 85
  function of 142
  inner 247
  reliance upon 305–307
spiritual path 31–32, 55, 95,
    102, 208, 248–249
  to enlightenment 115, 173
spiritual practice 36–38,
    181–182, 214
  and daily life 248–249
  engaging in, pure 43, 89
  essence of 19, 196
  levels of, pure 43
  obstacle to 32, 70, 89, 204
  purpose of 9, 13, 19
spiritual progress 89,
    125–126
Spiritual Teacher 305
stages of the path 183, g
  prayer 317–319
state beyond sorrow 189
stealing 48, 285
strangers 116, 122, 133
stress 328
subsequent valid cognizer
    275
suffering 11, 90, 101, 111,
    221–222, 228
  accepting 193

  as hallucinations 149, 252
  basis for experiencing 168
  causes of 19, 46, 130, 213
  changing 186, 212–213
  conceptions of eight
    extremes, root of 282
  good qualities of 222, 223
  liberation from 100, 102
  manifest 198–200
  meditation on 182–183
  of animals 78, 199
  of humans 61–79
  of separation 73, 90
  permanent cessation of
    103, 106
  root of 113
  true 62
  what is 17
  wish to avoid 100
suicide 23, 168, 169
Superior being 196, 286–
    287, 291
superior seeing 304
suppleness 94

$\mathcal{T}$

taking 222–231, 237
  actual meditation 227–233
  meaning of 220
  own suffering 224–226
taking and giving 219–241,
    243

benefits of 220, 226–227,
239–240
on breath 237–238
Tantra 190–191, 230
Tantric Grounds and Paths
191
teapot story 29–30
things that we normally see
12, 252, 298, 299, 306
three higher trainings 104
Three Jewels 82, 196
Three Principal Aspects of the
Path, The 331, 339–341
throwing actions 58–59
tolerance 180, 194
training the mind 188, 194
main point of 154
practitioners 241
Training the Mind in Seven
Points 174, 178, 267,
300
tranquil abiding 304
transference of consciousness
24
transforming adverse conditions 175
transforming the mind 19
true existence 254, 256, 262,
266, 278, 284
true nature
of body 262
of phenomena 265, 276
truth 265

synonyms of 286
Tsunda 84

U

ultimate bodhichitta 250,
288, 305
definition of 251
levels of 288
simple training in 301–306
ultimate nature 79, 93, 265,
283, 292
of I 273
of mind 268
of self and other phenom-
ena 274
ultimate search 257, 258
ultimate truth 250, 251, 291
conventional truth and
283–290
definition of 287
synonyms of 286
uncontaminated mind,
definition of 287
uncontrolled desire 4, 43, 89
unfindability 265, 300
of body 262
of I 272, 273
of mind 268
unhappiness 11, 127,
168–171, 178–179,
324–325
cause of 4

union of the two truths
    291–297
universal compassion 131,
    202, 229. *See also* com-
    passion, great compassion
unmistaken awareness 287
unproduced space 279,
    296–297
Upala 48–49

V

Vajrayogini 190–191
valid cognizer/mind 122,
    231, 284, 286, 301
very subtle body 234
very subtle mind 255
Vinaya Sutras 214
virtuous actions 51, 56, 57,
    81
    cause of 130–131, 176
    effects of 46, 47
vows 87
    Bodhisattva 174

W

war 167, 170, 198
wealth 75, 157
    as obstacle 8, 169, 204
    inner 145, 204
wisdom 4, 85, 106–107,

144, 179, 186, 187, 209,
    214, 223, 229
    increasing 299
    lineage 186
    nature and functions of
        208
    of meditative equipoise
        287
    omniscient 112
    realizing emptiness 92
    uncontaminated 288
wishfulfilling jewel 234, 247
wish-granting jewel 112,
    131, 144
wishing love 92, 211–218
world 36, 42, 161
    cause of 46
    conventional 299
    created by mind 277
    dream 255, 301
    dream/waking 24
    mere appearance 207
    pure/impure 47, 207
    waking 255, 277, 300, 301
worldly
    concerns, eight 205
    people 265
worldly attainments 112,
    156–157, 231
worldly people 265
worldly pleasures/enjoyments
    41, 66, 71, 212
    attachment to 32

causes of 88
deceptive 75, 90, 114
impermanent 36, 73
world peace 15
world view 117, 139
worry 11
wrong awarenesses 100, 163,
    275, 279

yoga of equalizing samsara
    and nirvana 295
Yogi/Yogini 30, 141, 220

Recommendations

If you enjoyed *How to Transform Your Life*, the following books and meditation CD will help deepen your understanding and practical experience of Buddhism and meditation.

Ask your favorite bookseller for these products or order online at **www.tharpa.com/us**

Books

MODERN BUDDHISM
The Path of Compassion and Wisdom

By developing and maintaining compassion and wisdom in daily life, we can transform our lives, improve our relationships with others and look behind appearances to see the way things actually exist. In this way we can solve all our daily problems and accomplish the real meaning of our human life. With compassion and wisdom, like the two wings of a bird, we can quickly reach the enlightened world of a Buddha.

The free eBook and PDF are available at
www.emodernbuddhism.com

HOW TO SOLVE OUR HUMAN PROBLEMS
The Four Noble Truths

This inspiring book shows how Buddha's popular teaching on the Four Noble Truths can help us solve basic human problems such as dissatisfaction and anger, and provides a profound illumination of our human experience and our potential for deep inner freedom.

INTRODUCTION TO BUDDHISM
An Explanation of the Buddhist Way of Life

An ideal guide for everyone interested in Buddhism and meditation. This book presents the central principles behind the Buddhist way of life, such as meditation and karma, as tools for developing qualities such as inner peace, love and patience.

THE NEW MEDITATION HANDBOOK
Meditations to Make our Life Happy and Meaningful

Discover the inner peace and lightness of mind that comes from meditation. Twenty-one meditations explain step-by-step how to develop increasingly beneficial states of mind, that together form the entire Buddhist path to enlightenment.

Meditation CD

MEDITATIONS FOR A KIND HEART
The Healing Power of Cherishing Others

These three guided audio meditations help listeners put the teachings from *How to Transform Your Life* into practice. Meditations on Cherishing Others, Taking Away Suffering and Giving Happiness are each 10–13 minutes. The CD includes a full-color, 16-page booklet that explains the five stages of meditation. Also in this series are *Meditations for Relaxation* and *Meditations for a Clear Mind*.

VISIT OUR WEBSITE
tharpa.com/us

See our complete selection of books, ebooks,
guided meditations, mp3s and artwork

LEARN MORE ABOUT BUDDHISM
AND MEDITATION
www.kadampa.org

Find a meditation class near you
(there are over 250 Kadampa centers and branches
across the US, and 1,200 around the world)

FOLLOW US ONLINE
facebook.com/tharpaus · twitter.com/tharpaus

For inspiring quotes, images, video and
information on new products and special offers.

THARPA PUBLICATIONS
47 Sweeney Road
Glen Spey, NY 12737
info.us@tharpa.com
(845) 856-5102 or (888) 741-3475